Teaching Outside the Box

Teaching Outside the Box

HOW TO GRAB YOUR STUDENTS
BY THEIR BRAINS

LouAnne Johnson

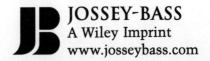
JOSSEY-BASS
A Wiley Imprint
www.josseybass.com

Published by Jossey-Bass
A Wiley Imprint
989 Market Street, San Francisco, CA 94103-1741   www.josseybass.com

Library of Congress Cataloging-in-Publication Data

Johnson, LouAnne.
  Teaching outside the box : how to grab your students by their brains / LouAnne Johnson.
      p. cm.
  Includes bibliographical references and index.
  ISBN-13 978-0-7879-7471-8 (alk. paper)
  ISBN-10 0-7879-7471-4 (alk. paper)
  1. Teaching. I. Title.
  LB1025.3.J676 2005
  371.102—dc22   2005003696

Printed in the United States of America
FIRST EDITION

PB Printing   10 9 8 7 6 5

The Jossey-Bass Education Series

CONTENTS

ACKNOWLEDGMENTS

This book would not have been possible without the teachers who taught me to believe in myself and follow my heart: Evelyn Hodak, Eleanora Sandblade, Caroline DeSalvo, Jerry Novelli, James Miller, Mary Ann Greggan, Mary Ellen Boyling, Jane Allen, and Kenneth Brodeur.

A shout out to my "posse"—the unforgettable, lovable, "unteachable" Carlmont Academy students who taught me how to teach.

And special thanks to Shelley Todd for testing so many theories and techniques in her own classroom, to Deanne Mogon for forging through my rough drafts, and to Alfredo Santana for his steadfast moral support and incorrigible optimism.

THE AUTHOR

LouAnne Johnson, author of the *New York Times* best-seller *Dangerous Minds,* is a former U.S. Navy journalist, Marine Corps officer, and high school teacher. Johnson is the author of seven nonfiction books, including *The Queen of Education* and *The Girls in the Back of the Class.* At present, she is a community college instructor.

A native of rural northwestern Pennsylvania, Johnson served nine years on active military duty, achieving the rank of Journalist First Class in the Navy and 2nd Lieutenant in the Marine Corps. She holds a B.S. in psychology and a master's degree in teaching English.

In 1989, Johnson began teaching as an intern at a northern California high school. Two years later, she was appointed department chair of a special program for at-risk teens. During the government evaluation of ten similar pilot programs, Johnson's group was rated first in academic achievement, increased self-esteem, and student retention. Her memoir about that experience, *My Posse Don't Do Homework,* was adapted for the 1995 hit movie *Dangerous Minds,* starring Michele Pfeiffer. *My Posse Don't Do Homework* also was condensed in *Reader's Digest* magazine, and, under the title *Dangerous Minds,* has been published in eight languages, including Italian, German, Japanese, and French.

Johnson has continued to teach English at the high school and college levels, and has designed and presented workshops in classroom management and motivation for teachers across the country. A staunch advocate of school reform, she has presented keynote addresses to over one hundred organizations, including the National School Boards Association, the National Council on Curriculum Development, and the European Council of International Schools. She has appeared on several television shows, including *Oprah, CBS Eye to Eye, NBC Weekend Today, Maury Povich,* and *CNN Talkback Live.*

INTRODUCTION

Whenever I finish writing a book and face the task of writing an introduction, my childhood comes back to haunt me. "Don't toot your own horn," Grandma Johnson used to warn me. "People will think you have a big head."

I honestly don't believe my head is exceptionally big. I know that I'm not the best teacher in the world, but I also know that my philosophy works. My philosophy, briefly, is this:

> When students believe that success is possible, they will try.
> So my first priority in any class is to help my students
> believe in themselves and their ability to learn.

During the past several years, I have presented keynote speeches and workshops for thousands of teachers from around the world. And their feedback proves that my philosophy works as well for them as it does for me. I have spent the past year taking notes, gathering information, reading the latest research on brain-based learning, corresponding with student teachers by e-mail, observing veteran teachers in action, advising teachers with classroom management problems, and trying to articulate in clear detail every aspect of my approach to teaching. My goal is to help make teaching enjoyable for both teachers and students. It breaks my heart to see so many frustrated teachers who truly care about their students but seem unable to reach them, just as it breaks my heart to see so many children who truly hate school.

On the other hand, my heart sings when I receive a letter such as this one from Laura Hauser, who sent me an e-mail asking for advice about taking over another teacher's class of "difficult" students:

31 August 2004

Ms. Johnson,

This is the end of my third week of teaching. I was given 125 "remedial" students. The other teachers told me they wouldn't show up to class. If they did, they would either sleep or disrupt the class; they wouldn't do homework and they didn't care if they passed or failed and I'd have to throw most of them out at some point or another.

I took a lot of your advice to heart. I went in on day one and told them all I could guarantee they would have the best year in school they had ever had. I asked if that interested any of them, and they all admitted it did. I told them I only asked for three things and I would do the rest. They had to show up every day; they had to come in with the attitude that they could and would learn something; and they had to try. I told them the story of Edison taking ten thousand tries to invent the lightbulb and told them that I was only asking that they try three or four times. I asked how many had been told they were stupid or couldn't do math. Every hand went up. I told them it wasn't true; they just hadn't been taught math in a way they could understand it. I told them there were two words I would not tolerate in my class—"I can't"—because they all could and there wasn't a stupid one in the bunch.

Three weeks later my classes show up on time. The few who skipped in the beginning don't skip anymore, and no one skips on Friday because it's cookie day. They do logic problems every day that require them to think, and now they ask for more. They do their homework; and if they get a low grade, they ask to fix it and turn it back in. I've told them I only care that they learn it and that if they're willing to do their homework or tests again, I am certainly willing to grade them again. I cut them some slack in the discipline department, but when I speak they stop and listen; and when I take someone outside and ask them to settle down, they do. I'm having a blast, and so are my students. Students tell me it's the first time a math teacher has actually cared about them and made them feel like they could succeed. Students that have on-the-job training in the afternoon come and hang out in math instead of leaving—some show up three periods a day—and participate in each class.

I can't thank you enough. If I had listened to those other teachers and not to you, I would be having a miserable year. But it's more rewarding than I could have imagined!

I know you're very busy finishing up your book, but thought you would like to know how much fun I'm having!

Laura Hauser

My fondest hope is that this book will help many more teachers define their own teaching philosophies, develop their own positive discipline policies, and experience the joy of teaching, just as Laura has.

I truly believe that teaching children is the noblest profession. Yes, the pay is insultingly low, and the working conditions are sometimes appallingly shabby. But we don't teach for the money, we do it for the love.

Teaching Outside the Box

Are You Teacher Material?

How can I tell if I'm really teacher material?" a teacher candidate asked me in an e-mail. "Can I learn to be a good teacher? Or is it something you have to be born with?" She went on to explain that she had recently abandoned a well-paid position in advertising in order to pursue her dream of becoming a teacher.

"I know I will make a lot less money as a teacher," she wrote, "and I have accepted that reality, but now I'm wondering what will happen if I get my degree and get a job, and then I hate teaching. What if I find out that I just can't do it? I have a feeling that teaching is going to be very different from being a student teacher or observing experienced teachers. I guess what I'm asking is: do you have any advice that might help me make the right decision about becoming a teacher?"

"To teach or not to teach?" is a question that stumps many people. Far too many of us know bright, energetic people who spent five or more years earning a bachelor's degree and teaching credential only to quit after one or two years in the classroom. New teachers give up for a long laundry list of reasons, but the most common complaints include disrespectful and disruptive students, apathetic or ineffective administrators, overwhelming stacks of paperwork, lunchroom politics, parental pressure and pestering, and mental or emotional exhaustion.

Those complaints are valid. Teaching is very demanding and difficult work. Children today suffer from a host of emotional, mental, and physical challenges that affect their behavior and ability to learn. And unfortunately, many of their role models encourage them to treat themselves and others with extreme disrespect. Dealing with children requires abundant reserves of patience and tact. An indestructible sense of humor also helps. Government regulations have created a testing and accountability monster that consumes mountains of money, paperwork, time, and energy—and teachers have the task of feeding the monster. The monster is fickle too, so if last-minute changes upset you, teaching will tax you to the limits of your flexibility. If you don't bend, you will definitely break. Of course, you already know that the pay is atrocious, primarily because people outside of education view teaching as baby-sitting with books. Subsequently, if wealth and prestige are important to you, teaching will be a disappointment. And teaching can be physically painful: hours of standing on your feet, bending over to read small print on small desks, and lugging boxes of books and papers to and fro can send you home with tired feet, an aching back, and a headache.

And then there are the students. It might seem facetious to say that you should like children if you plan to teach school, but apparently many people overlook this obvious fact. Every staff lunchroom has at least a few (and most have a large handful) complainers and groaners who spend their breaks and lunch hours plotting against "the enemy," sharing their strategies for revenge, nursing their wounds, and displaying their battle scars. These are not necessarily bad people, but they are people who grew up and immediately forgot their own childhoods. Like people who fall in love with the idea of owning a dog, dreaming of the unconditional love a dog will offer, forgetting that puppies pee on the carpet, vomit on the bath mat, chew your slippers, and poop on the lawn, some would-be teachers envision themselves standing in front of a quiet, orderly classroom, facing a sea of silent, adoring, obedient, angelic little faces. When those angelic faces turn out to belong to noisy, messy, occasionally ill-mannered, selfish, and obstinate little stinkers, those teachers go into shock. Some fail to recover. They become bitter, humorless, and overly strict; and they spend the rest of their years in the classroom making themselves and their students miserable by trying to make reality fit their impossible fantasies.

All right, that's the downside of teaching. If you're still reading, still thinking you might like to be a teacher, then you are persistent and optimistic—two very helpful attributes for would-be teachers. And you are right to be hopeful, because the upside of teaching is so much bigger and so much more important than the downside.

Teaching is the most wonderful profession in the world. As a teacher, you make a direct, tangible contribution to the future of our country and the world by helping young people acquire knowledge and skills. You know that you are spending your life in an honorable pursuit and that your life has a purpose. Teaching provides endless challenges and opportunities for growth. Every day, teaching tests your interpersonal communications skills, your academic knowledge, or your leadership ability. On a good day, you'll be tested in all three areas, and you'll pass all three tests. You have the opportunity as a teacher to share your passion for learning with young people. If you are a good teacher, you will also inspire, motivate, and challenge those youngsters to develop their individual strengths and talents; and you will feel the incomparable joy when one of them (usually far more than one) realizes how much you have given and makes his or her way back to your classroom to give you a hug and a teary thank-you. And you will cry your own tears. And when you go home, you will share that student's thank-you with your family and friends, and they will all cry a few tears. When you go to bed that night, the last thing you will think before you go to sleep is, *I did a fine thing. I helped a child become a successful adult.* And that night, you will dream the sweetest dreams.

SUPER, EXCELLENT, OR GOOD?

Teachers come in three basic flavors—super, excellent, and good. Which flavor of teacher you decide to become depends on your personal strengths, intimate relationships, professional goals, and individual priorities. Before you begin teaching, seriously consider how much time and emotional energy you can afford to spend on your work outside the home. Take a long look at your life, your relationships, your financial and emotional obligations, your personal and career goals. If you find it hard to view your own life objectively, discussing your situation with a friend or close relative may improve your perspective. If your sister points out that you like expensive clothes and your husband reminds you that you become impatient and overly critical under stress, for example, you will need to decide whether you are willing to trim your wardrobe and do the hard work required to develop more patience.

Decide what is important to you and which aspects of your life should take priority. Will your children, parents, spouse, or partner feel neglected if you spend some of your free time creating lesson plans or counseling students? How much emotional energy will you need to conserve during the day in order to have enough left over for your family at night? Will you feel comfortable counseling students about their personal problems, or would you rather leave such things up to their own parents or guardians?

There is no right or wrong answer to these questions, but if you know the answers before you begin teaching, you will be a happier, more successful instructor. Not everybody can or should be a super teacher. It is perfectly acceptable to be a excellent or good teacher. (Poor teaching, however, is never acceptable.)

Super teaching requires the highest amounts of physical, emotional, and mental energy. Super teachers usually arrive at school early and stay late. They also attend seminars and continuing education classes, volunteer for student activities, and make themselves available to students who need extra help, both in and out of the classroom. Because super teachers enjoy a solid rapport with their students, they don't have to focus as much time or energy on discipline in their classrooms. Instead, there is a give-and-take, an ebb and flow, the teaching equivalent of the runner's high that so many athletes find addictive. Unfortunately, unless they are extraordinary people with impressive reserves of natural energy or unless they make an effort to rejuvenate themselves regularly, super teachers may find themselves in danger of burning out.

Super teaching demands huge amounts of physical and mental effort; depending on your budget, it may absorb some money as well. If you are single, childless, and unattached, you may choose to devote the bulk of your energies to teaching for some period of time. However, if you are a single mother with three young children and have a close friend or intimate partner, you may not be willing or able to devote the amount of emotional energy that being a super teacher requires. Having children doesn't disqualify you from becoming a super teacher, it simply means that you will need to make sure that your family understands and supports your teaching. If your children are well-adjusted, self-motivated, and respectful of you and your partner; if your partner supports your career goals; and if you have a high level of energy, then you may be able to handle the stresses involved in super teaching. But don't beat yourself up if you can't be extraordinary. Being an excellent or good teacher is a true achievement.

Excellent teachers enjoy their work, but they limit the amount of time and energy they devote to teaching. They care about their students and do their best to help them—but not at the expense of their own families. Excellent teachers do work overtime because teaching well requires a certain amount of unpaid overtime (grading papers, making lesson plans, and supervising field trips), but excellent teachers put a limit on the amount of overtime they are willing to work.

Excellent teaching requires less energy expenditure than super teaching, but excellent teaching may still wear you out if you aren't careful; make time to nurture yourself and your family. And you may have to explain more than once to your friends and family that your job is a high priority and that you need to spend some time in the evenings and on weekends developing your lessons and skills. Again, don't be too hard on yourself if you find that you can't juggle as many teaching balls as you thought you could, especially during your first few years. Mastering just the basics of sound teaching is a major accomplishment, and students still thrive in the classrooms of good old everyday teachers.

Good teachers do their jobs well but know their own limits. They make a very clear distinction between professional and personal time. They treat their students with respect and do their best to make sure that all students learn the material required for the next level of education, but they don't feel obligated to save every single student. Good teachers arrive at school early enough to be prepared, but they don't hold open house before school or during lunch hour. And they don't spend hours in their classroom after school for informal chats or counseling sessions. They lock the doors to their classrooms at night and focus on their own lives, their own educations, their hobbies, their friends, and their families. By creating a distinct division between their personal and professional lives, good teachers conserve their emotional and mental energy. As a result, they often enjoy long and successful teaching careers; they are the ones who sadly wave good-bye to those excellent and super teachers who overestimated their personal resources and burst into flames after a few years of mach-speed teaching.

Regardless of whether you choose to be a super, excellent, or good teacher, you will still be contributing to society, performing honorable and necessary work, and helping to shape the future of our country. Aside from yourself, your students, and a few supervisors, nobody will know how much energy you devote to your job. But we don't become teachers out of a need for public recognition or reward. We don't teach out of a desire for prestige; we teach because we believe it's important. Teaching superbly is like running a marathon by yourself in the dark. Few people even notice what you're doing, and those who notice don't pay much attention—but their oblivion doesn't slow you down. You still enjoy the thrill and satisfaction of finishing the race, and you are definitely a winner.

EARN SOME EXTRA CREDIT BEFORE YOU BEGIN

Let us assume that you have a strong desire to help young people, a passion for your subject, a solid education, and a license from an accredited teacher-training institution. Are passion, motivation, education, and training enough? My answer is a very loud "No." Those attributes can create an excellent foundation, but teaching requires much more than knowledge and the desire to teach. Teaching requires a solid grasp of motivational techniques, leadership and conflict resolution skills, human psychology (child, adolescent, and adult), computer literacy, the ability to whittle an impossibly huge pile of paperwork into a succinct and teachable curriculum, and the ability to think on your feet (a pair of extremely comfortable shoes for those feet will help).

Some teacher-training programs include excellent components in some of those areas, but based on the e-mails and letters I have received and the conversations I have had with teachers throughout the country, far too many teacher-training programs are heavy on theory and light on practical skills and techniques that teachers must have in order to teach effectively. Knowing how to design worksheets, lessons plans, and exams is an important skill. Creating intriguing bulletin boards, art projects, and group activities can make the difference between a stuffy classroom filled with bored underachievers and an exciting classroom buzzing with the electricity that motivated little learners can generate. But even the most enthusiastic, creative, accomplished, and intelligent new teacher will struggle if he or she doesn't have a firm grasp on the basic concepts of human psychology and behavior: what motivates people to act the way they act, how to convince people to change their behavior voluntarily, how to challenge and inspire people to attempt difficult tasks, how to develop a solid rapport with people from diverse economic and cultural backgrounds, and how to quickly and effectively convince people to follow your lead.

Look for teacher-training programs that focus on successful leadership techniques instead of ineffective punitive disciplinary approaches. If possible, opt for a program in which teacher candidates do their student teaching during the first part of their education program instead of the last. Some people realize after just a few days in the classroom that they weren't meant to be teachers; it's a shame when those would-be teachers have to face the choice of continuing in a teacher program in which they don't belong or changing to a new major and spending thousands of dollars preparing for a different career. And heaven help both the students and the teachers when those teachers who know that they have chosen the wrong field decide to teach until they can afford to go back to school or find another job. Everybody loses in that situation.

If you have the choice, opt for a full year of student teaching (I would recommend two years), preferably at a number of different schools where you will have the opportunity to work with students at different age levels and from different backgrounds. (An Internet search for schools of education will allow you to review and compare different programs across the country.) You may find that although you thought you would enjoy teaching kindergarten, high school is where you belong. Or you may find that the squirrelly sophomores that everybody complains about are the ones you enjoy the most.

Make sure that your student teaching experience actually provides teaching experience. If you are assigned to a single master teacher for your entire student teaching time frame and that teacher does not allow you to interact with students beyond distributing papers (or worse yet, expects you to sit in the back of the room and observe for weeks on end), then ask your college advisor to change your assignment. Don't complain about the master teacher, just say that you believe you need a more hands-on approach in order to make sure that teaching really suits you. Your advisor may try to discourage you from insisting on a change, but be firm. You are the customer. You are paying for your education, and you deserve to be taught how to teach. Your instructors may label you difficult, but I promise you that a little flak from your professors is nothing compared to the flak you will take from students if they sense that you are ill prepared to teach.

If your teacher education program allows you the opportunity to take elective courses, psychology, leadership, conflict resolution, and time management are good choices. The more you can learn about what makes people tick (and how to wind and unwind them), the easier it will be for you to establish a controlled learning environment in your classroom. Community colleges often offer a variety of continuing education courses, as well as courses designed to improve the quality of life for local residents. If you don't have access to classroom instruction, countless courses are available online—although some are little more than advertising bait to sell books and other products. Some of the products may be worthwhile, but unless the Web sites offer you a generous sample of their materials and a money-back guarantee for instruction, you would be wise to check with librarians, teachers, or other people who might be able to point you in the direction of quality instruction.

Fortunately, thanks to the Internet, you can learn quite a bit about a number of subjects on your home or public library computer. The Web site www.teachers.net, for example, allows you to read the logs of conversations between teachers on topics ranging from classroom discipline to motivational lesson plans. If you enter "classroom discipline" or "motivational techniques" into a search engine, you will find a host of provocative articles, Web sites, and pointers for future reading.

THOSE WHO CAN'T TEACH CAN STILL DO

Don't despair if you find that, in spite of your desire to nurture and guide young people, teaching children isn't your bag of books. Nonteaching jobs in education still enable you to provide instruction, guidance, and counseling: teacher aides, security officers, bus drivers, coaches, counselors, curriculum designers, independent consultants, test proctors, and career planners all make important contributions. You might consider working as an adjunct, adult education, or English as a Second Language instructor at a community college, library, or detention facility. Teaching adults requires many of the same skills as teaching youngsters, but adult students are much more likely to be motivated, well-behaved, and receptive to instruction. In addition, there are opportunities to teach in day care centers, after-school programs, church-sponsored community service programs, mentor programs, and school-to-work programs that match students with adults who help them prepare to enter the workplace.

If you have a burning desire to teach a subject you love, you may have to do some searching of your soul, your situation, and your options; but there are students who want to learn as passionately as you want to teach.

Do Your Homework

Why do so many teacher candidates ace their education courses, read all the latest journals, carefully observe good teachers, shine like stars during their student teaching, and then crash and burn during their first year in the classroom?

Because education, desire, intelligence, passion, and talent do not automatically enable you to communicate complex ideas to other people.

Because in teacher training programs, the instructors are on your side, and they have a vested interest in your success; whereas your students (and sadly, even some fellow teachers) couldn't care less if you fail. In fact, some of them find it entertaining to watch you flounder.

Because unlike your college classmates, who admired your pretty lesson plans and praised the cleverness of your lectures and worksheets, your students may not be at all interested in learning.

Because effective teaching is more a matter of psychology than pedagogy. As one young man wisely explained to me, "You teachers can make me sit here and hold these stupid books all day long, but you can't make me read them."

Fortunately, psychology is interesting to read and think about, relatively simple to understand, and eminently applicable to teaching. Perhaps you have detailed instructions about what you are expected to teach, with curriculum guidelines that list specific reading selections and activities that your class must complete during a given time. Or perhaps you have the freedom and responsibility of creating your own curriculum. In either case, if you grab your students by their brains quickly, during the first days of class, they won't have the time or inclination to resist your instruction. In Chapter Four, "Make the First Week of Class a First-Class Week," I will suggest specific activities for grabbing your students during the first days of school; but right now I would like to focus on developing and articulating your own philosophy of teaching.

When I first began teaching, I could not have stated my philosophy in one simple sentence. I was too busy trying to organize paperwork, plan lessons, referee arguments, convince students to cooperate, find a disciplinary approach that worked, and extinguish those thousand little fires that threaten to burn down every teacher's classroom every day. A struggling student helped me focus my thinking. When I was assigned to teach a class of sophomores whose regular teacher suddenly decided to retire, I entered the classroom with high hopes and boundless energy and found myself facing a group of students with zero hope and subzero motivation.

"It don't matter what we do," one girl explained. "Before she left, our teacher done flunked us all. Wrote a red F in the grade book beside everybody's name."

At the mention of the grade book filled with Fs, I saw those students' shoulders slump and their heads droop. As they issued a giant group sigh, I could feel their hopelessness. So I hurried to assure them that I didn't have their previous teacher's grade book and that I intended to start everybody in my new grade book with an A—in red ink. It may sound melodramatic, but I swear I could hear the hope fluttering in those students' hearts. Every single face turned toward me, even the faces of students who insisted that they didn't care one fig about school.

From the back of the room, I heard a boy whisper, "She's lyin'."

A second later another boy whispered, "Shut up! What if she ain't lyin'? I ain't never had an A before."

In that moment my philosophy of teaching was born, and it has served me well. My teaching philosophy is based on one simple belief:

> *When students believe success is possible, they will try. If they don't believe they can succeed, it doesn't matter how easy the material or how smart the students, they will fail.*

Therefore, my primary job is to convince my students that success is possible and to help them succeed. I communicate that philosophy to my students frequently, to remind them that whenever I ask them to do something, my goal is to help them be successful—not simply to issue orders. Once I solidified my philosophy, teaching became much simpler and more enjoyable, and my students stopped fighting with me and started learning.

During the following years, using student behavior and achievement as my guides, I developed secondary philosophies about discipline, grades, and exams, which I will share with you in the coming chapters. Right now, however, I would like to ask you to consider the ideas and issues in this chapter before you step into the classroom, so that you will be better able to articulate your own teaching philosophy. I believe this consideration will help you become a much more dynamic and effective teacher.

CHOOSE YOUR PERSONA

Your classroom is a miniature theater: it holds a small, captive audience and an even smaller cast—you. You are the star of the show, and when you first stand on that stage, your small audience can seem overwhelmingly large. The brighter your spotlight, the faster you'll capture your audience. Later on, you may choose to share the stage with your students, but until your students have learned their roles, you will need to take center stage. I don't mean that you should posture grandly and strut about your room. You do have a show to run, however, and specific goals to accomplish. Your responsibility is to lead your cast toward those goals; their role is to follow, although it is perfectly acceptable for them to politely suggest changes in the script.

Because your students will take their cues from you, it's very important that you decide before you step onstage how you will portray your character. What kind of image do you want to project to your students? How do you want them to see you: as the scientific expert, the hip dude who knows algebra inside out, the cool nerd, the toughest but best chemistry teacher on earth, the drill-sergeant grammarian, the stand-up comic who happens to know all about history, the serious student of literature or science, the hard-boiled journalist, the tough but tender coach?

Pretending to be somebody you are not is a terrible idea and one that is bound to fail because students are very adept at quickly assessing their teachers' characters.

They will decide during the first few moments they see you what kind of person you are. They will look at your clothes, your hair, your skin color (not to judge you, but to assess how you may judge them). They will note your most subtle body language, your gestures, your posture, the length of your stride, the tone of your voice, your expression as you observe other students, and most especially they will notice the look in your eyes when you make eye contact with them. They will decide whether you seem crabby or nice or tough or easy or scared or confident or boring. All of this will happen within the first few minutes of your first class meeting—long before you begin to teach. And once your students decide who you are, you'll have a hard time convincing them to change their perceptions. You can change their minds, but it demands so much time and energy that if you goof and get started on the wrong foot (as I have done more than once), you may be inclined to simply cope with the status quo and hope things will improve over time. Coping and hoping, however, are poor substitutes for self-confidence and leadership.

Whatever persona you choose should be one that is natural for you, one that you can maintain for the entire school year. I am not advising you to put on a mask or try to change your personality but to consider how to make best use, as a teacher, of your unique characteristics, traits, and talents. Here's how I think of myself as a teacher: I am strict but flexible, inclined to use humor instead of threats, intolerant of rude or disrespectful behavior, passionate about my subject, and willing to meet students halfway.

It took me a while to perfect my drill-sergeant–stand-up comic–counselor persona, and I made many changes along the way. My first year I tried too hard to be cool, and it caused discipline problems. I joked around a lot because I wanted the kids to like me, to think of me as an older friend. What I didn't realize at that time was that they didn't need more friends. They have plenty of friends—friends who offer them dope and cigarettes and plagiarized research papers; friends who think that heavy metal is great music and that Ripple is fine wine. What my students needed was for me to be a teacher, an adult who would accept my responsibility as their guide and a leader who sometimes had to be the bad guy in order to help them. During my second teaching year, I took the advice of a veteran teacher who said, "Don't smile until after Christmas." I decided to be the drill sergeant who could stare a student to death. I couldn't do it. I'm a smiling kind of woman, so my message was inconsistent; my students responded by misbehaving half the time.

Finally, I sat down and figured out what my biggest strengths and weaknesses were. Then I combined my three strongest assets and came up with a combination that worked for me. Now I make a few important rules that cannot be broken under any circumstances; I take the time to know each student personally; and I use humor whenever possible to make my point without making students lose face.

DRESS THE PART

In the search for my most effective persona, I discovered an interesting student response to my clothing: they perceive some outfits as more serious than others, and they behave accordingly. If the lesson for the day requires creativity, spontaneity, and lots of student input, I wear more informal clothing: corduroy jeans and a sweater, perhaps. On days when I want to limit the amount of spontaneity, during an important exam or a lesson that will serve as an important building block for future lessons, I wear a suit.

Using clothes to project an image is basic psychology, and we see it all around us. The makers of TV commercials, especially commercials for pharmaceuticals or health products, often dress their announcers in white lab coats that give the impression of medical authority, so that viewers will be more inclined to believe them when they tell us that we'll have fewer gastrointestinal disturbances or sinus headaches. "Difficult" students often use clothing—leather jackets and ripped jeans, for instance, or turquoise hair—to advertise their contempt for authority and send a clear challenge to adults, a warning to keep our distance. Corporate executives are often very adept at power dressing. Young teachers or people who tend to be shy and introverted may take some tips from the fashion experts who advise young executives how to give the impression of authority: wear black pants and a white shirt, for example.

When you select your teaching wardrobe, keep in mind the persona you wish to convey. Make sure that your clothes don't send a conflicting message. If your goal is to create a very authoritative persona, for example, you may not be as successful if you dress very informally, especially if you wear the same clothes your students wear. They may tend to treat you as a peer instead of a teacher, in spite of your verbal instructions.

While we're on the subject of clothing, I'd like to suggest that you pay special attention to your feet. Many new teachers, myself included, are sorely surprised to find out how much their feet can hurt after just one day of teaching. Even if you are in good physical condition and are used to spending long periods of time on your feet, teaching will still take its toll on your soles. I most strongly recommend investing in a pair of well-made, comfortable shoes such as those made specifically for comfort by companies such as Born, Birkenstock, Clarks, Dansko, Mephisto, and Naot.

TRAIN THOSE LITTLE PUPPIES

How do you want students to feel and act in your classroom? Do you want them to sit quietly and raise their hands before responding to your questions, or do you want them to speak freely, even if it means interrupting each other or you? Do you want them to feel free to come into your classroom early and chat with you or with other students, or do you want them to keep their socializing outside the classroom and focus solely on academic activities inside your room? Do you want students to engage in enthusiastic discussions in which they freely voice their personal opinions (which may lead to interesting arguments), or do you prefer to control any discussion to avoid conflict and keep the conversation on topic?

Consider your students' age, the difficulty of your subject matter, and the number of students in each group you teach. How do you envision them behaving during a given class period? Perhaps you picture them sitting at their desks, politely raising their hands for you to call on them. Or perhaps your vision involves a more energetic, less controlled environment, where students wave their hands wildly or feel inspired to shout out their ideas. After you have developed a good rapport with your students, you will be able to change the pace and procedures to fit different kinds of lessons, but you are likely to develop a better rapport and experience fewer discipline problems if you stick to one method for at least the first few weeks of classes.

Here's just one example. If you want students to raise their hands before speaking, you need to state your expectations and act accordingly. If you have stated a preference for hand raising and then acknowledge students who speak out of turn during your lessons, you will have just demonstrated that you don't mean what you say. If you persist in acknowledging your shout-out talkers, you may soon find that you have a lot of talkers and a lot of other students who have lost respect for your authority. On the other hand, if you don't mind the movement and noise that accompany student spontaneity, and you allow students to speak out during lessons, you may find it very difficult to get those students to sit quietly and raise their hands during a given activity if you decide later on that you need a more orderly classroom in order to teach a specific skill. Until you are sure that your students will follow your direction, it's best to stick to the one method that you would prefer them to use most of the time. I think of it as setting my students' default behavior. Unless I give specific instructions, how do I want them to behave?

If you aren't certain what kind of classroom environment you want to create, think about your own school days. Which classes did you enjoy most? Which did you dread attending? What kind of environment did those teachers create? How did they communicate their attitudes to you? Chances are good that you will teach the way your favorite teachers taught you—or the way your worst teachers taught you. Far too often, teachers whose own teachers humiliated them will turn around and use those same techniques on their students, without even realizing what they are doing. In my opinion, humiliating children is cowardly, and I believe that persistently embarrassing or humiliating children is psychologically and emotionally abusive. You can be strict without being cruel, and students will accept a strict but fair teacher as well as they will accept a laid-back, tolerant teacher. But if you start the year using one approach and then try to change midterm, you may confuse some students; and they may not cooperate when you try to retrain them. Many people are resistant to change, especially children who may feel insecure about many aspects of their personal lives.

Of course, you may choose to change your approach to one that you believe will improve your teaching, but be wary of changing your teaching style as a reaction to student behavior. If you begin the year as a soft-spoken, even-tempered teacher and then become a shouter or develop a short fuse that ignites at the smallest disruption, students will realize that they can control your behavior. Some students will then do their best to push your buttons because watching a teacher fume can be highly entertaining.

Training students is very similar to training puppies. If you let a puppy sleep on the bed every night for a week, she won't understand why you are punishing her by making her sleep on the floor the next week. She will wait until you are asleep and hop up onto the bed. And if you wake up and boot her off, her tender feelings will be hurt, and you will feel like a big bully. Likewise, if you train your little canine companion to sleep on the floor, and then one night you decide you'd like a foot warmer, she may be hesitant to jump up onto the bed. She may agree to warm your feet for a while before jumping back down to her proper place on the floor. Or she may enjoy the change of pace so much that she refuses to sleep on the floor the following night. Either way, you have one confused puppy on your hands.

CONTROL YOUR CLASSROOM, NOT YOUR STUDENTS

In Chapter Five I will discuss discipline plans in detail, but right now I'd like to share with you one of the most important lessons I have ever learned about teaching. When I began teaching, after nine years on active military duty and seven in the corporate sector, I thought I had a good grasp of the basics of discipline. When my master teacher left me in charge of his sophomore honors English class, I was determined not to take any flak from my students. Unfortunately, my students didn't care one whit about my determination. The harder I tried to control them, the harder they resisted. They all threw their books on the floor at the same time when my back was turned, so I made a seating chart that separated friends from each other. They coughed loudly if anybody tried to answer a question that I had asked, so I gave them harder assignments. They crossed their arms and refused to look at me when I talked to them, so I sent the ringleaders to the office, where they sat for a while before returning to my classroom with a note asking me to be more specific about what infractions they had committed, because refusing to look at the teacher wasn't a punishable offense under the student code of conduct. So I sent them to lunch detention or after-school detention or in-school suspension. And when they returned, they acted exactly as they had before they left my room— except now they were determined to exact revenge.

One day I lost my temper and started screaming. I threw books and papers on the floor and pitched a proper childish tantrum. Those college-bound students looked at me, but they were more amused than impressed. Finally, I realized what they had been trying to teach me: I cannot control my students' behavior, but I can control myself and my classroom. As soon as I understood that simple concept, I stopped responding to their behavior and started making them respond to mine. Once that became my standard practice, I had few discipline problems in any class, even when I taught at-risk and remedial students.

This may seem like a simple concept, but it makes a tremendous difference in the way teachers and students relate to each other. Let's take a disruptive talker as an example. You are in the midst of giving instruction, and a student intentionally interrupts by talking out of turn, ignoring your attempts to make her be quiet. You now have the choice of trying to control the student or controlling your classroom.

You may say, "Tiffany, I want you to be quiet this instant, or you are going to get demerits (or detention, parent phone call, referral to the office, or what have you)." Tiffany already knows the consequences of talking out. She is just curious about what happens when she breaks one of your rules. The rest of the students are also very interested in learning this important information. If she is a considerate child, Tiffany may settle down and be quiet—for a while. Or she may choose to step the argument up another level by counterchallenging your challenge to her. She now is in control of the situation. She knows that you are going to react to whatever she does. Even if you end up sending her to the office or suspending her, the other students all know that they can control your behavior. You may win the battles, but they can make you fight whenever they are bored or uninterested in doing whatever activity you intend to assign. They already know that you can't control them, and they will amuse themselves by putting you through your paces—irritation, frustration, anger, threats, punishments. If they can make your face turn red, they earn extra points. And if they can make you cry, they score a touchdown.

Let's back up to the point at which Tiffany disrupts your instruction. If you stop immediately and glare at Tiffany silently for a few seconds, she may decide to back down without entering into a confrontation that she knows she will lose. She is very likely to choose this option if you not only glare but take a few slow, deliberate steps in her direction without taking your eyes from her face. If she is determined to find out what happens if she pushes a little harder, Tiffany may continue talking. Now you say, "Tiffany, I would like you to step outside for a moment, please." Don't wait for her to move. Walk to the door and open it. Turn and look at her with full expectation that she will join you. (We'll discuss students who refuse to step outside in Chapter Five, but for now let's focus on the majority who will agree.)

When Tiffany joins you in the hall, you can explain that disrespectful behavior is not acceptable in your classroom and that she may remain in the hallway for a few seconds to decide whether or not she chooses to cooperate with you. Explain that if she chooses to cooperate, she may return to her seat. If she chooses not to cooperate, you will have no choice but to send her to the office. Tell her you hope she chooses to return but that the choice is hers because she is responsible for her own behavior. Leave Tiffany there in the hallway for a short while to consider her options. Return to your room and resume teaching.

Either Tiffany will decide to behave and will return to her seat, or she will decide she wants to go to the office. You have made her responsible for her behavior, and you have taught her—and all of your students—that they may not disrupt your teaching. If you have a very difficult class, you may have to repeat the step outside and choose your behavior process three, four, even a dozen times; but each time you step outside with a student, those students still in the room will be thinking about what they will do if you call them outside. Thinking is exactly what you want them to do. Eventually they will realize that they can't make you dance and that you aren't going to cooperate with their efforts to manipulate you.

Oh, yes, one more important suggestion. When you reach the end of your list of disruptive students, thank your entire class for their cooperation. Tell them you appreciate their mature behavior and are impressed with the amount of self-respect they have demonstrated. Some of them will smile immediately. Others will try to act like they don't care, but even the ones who believe they are too cool for school will secretly appreciate being appreciated.

YOUR OPTIONAL AGENDA

What are you really teaching in your classroom? During my first year in the classroom, I confessed to my master teacher, Al Black, that I was afraid I wasn't teaching my students enough. I explained that I believed students should reach a minimum standard to achieve a passing grade, but I wasn't sure where to set the minimum standard for my different English classes.

"Minimum standard of what?" Al asked me. "Commas, spelling, vocabulary? Should a kid know four ways to use a comma and the correct spelling of four hundred words? Should he know what *defenestrating* means? What if he doesn't know that particular word, but he knows a thousand other ones? What is the standard? I'm not talking about the district's objectives. I'm talking about your own standards. What is it you expect those kids to know when they leave your class?"

"I don't know," I admitted, "but I worry about whether I'm really teaching them anything."

"All teachers wonder whether they're really teaching anything," Al told me. He continued:

> I used to wonder it myself, hundreds of years ago when I was your age. But then I learned something important. You aren't teaching English. "What are you teaching?" you may ask. You're teaching kids how to analyze information, relate it to other information they know, put it together, take it apart, and give it back to you in the form that you re-

quest it. It doesn't matter what the class is; we all teach the same things. We just use different terms. You use commas and adjectives; biology teachers use chromosomes and chlorophyll; math teachers use imaginary numbers and triangles. And you're also teaching an optional agenda: you're teaching your kids to believe in themselves. So don't worry about whether you're teaching them grammar. You're teaching those kids. Trust me, you're teaching them.

After I had a chance to think about Al's comments, I realized that what he called the "optional agenda" is the most important factor in teaching, more important than school district objectives, because it is your optional agenda that answers the all-important question: What do you want your students to know when they leave your class?

What do you want your students to know? Naturally, as an English teacher, I want my students to have improved reading and writing skills, bigger vocabularies, increased comprehension of abstract ideas, better thinking skills, and an appreciation for literature. So I design specific lessons for vocabulary building and literary analysis and composing logical arguments—hundreds of different lessons over the years, tailored for different levels of ability. After my discussion with Al, when I spread out my various lesson plans and looked for common areas among them, my own optional agenda became very clear. Time and again I'd framed my lessons within larger lessons. One composition assignment, for example, urged students to write about a time they had faced and overcome a problem. A supplementary short story unit that I put together from a variety of sources included fictional accounts of people dealing with challenges such as divorce, the death of a loved one, peer pressure, and prejudice. The poetry I selected for special attention involved pursuing your dreams, standing up for your principles, admitting your errors.

My answer to Al's question is the same today as it was then: I want my students to have better academic skills, but I also want them to have a strong sense of their own ethical standards, an unquenchable thirst for knowledge, a desire to succeed according to their own definitions of success, and the strength of character to treat all people with basic human dignity and respect.

What is your optional agenda?

Your values and ethics will shape your agenda. Even if you don't intentionally try to include your beliefs and attitudes in your lessons, they will be there, hidden within the context of the reading assignments you select, in the methods you use to determine who passes and who fails, in the tone of your voice when you address certain students, and in a thousand other subtle clues. Every day you will be teaching your students what you believe is important. You will be conveying your own ethics, attitudes, beliefs, and moral values to your students. If you can articulate your optional agenda, you can use that knowledge to enhance your teaching. Knowing your optional agenda will also help you avoid unintentionally teaching your students things you don't want to teach them—which brings us to the next area of consideration.

FACE YOUR OWN PREJUDICES

Although most of us try very hard to rid ourselves of prejudices, I have yet to meet a person who is completely free of prejudice. Our cultural and religious backgrounds, our families and friends, and our experiences combine to make us prejudge people who are blond or brunette, tall or short, fat or thin, ugly or beautiful, extroverted or introverted, brilliant or dim, nerdy or popular, Catholic or Jewish or Protestant or Muslim, black or brown or white or yellow or red.

I believe it is important that we, as teachers, try harder than most people to eliminate our prejudices and minimize the effects of the ones we just can't seem to defeat, because so many of our students will remember the things we say and do for the rest of their lives. We spend more waking hours with most children, especially the youngest and most tender children, than their own parents do. Unless they have reason not to, most children love and respect their teachers (yes, even many of those defiant adolescents who claim that they hate school and everything associated with it). Many, many students learn to love and respect themselves—or despise and disrespect themselves—based on the way their teachers treat them. Think about your own childhood. If any teacher ever called you lazy, stupid, hopeless, ugly, clumsy, or worthless, I'm sure you remember the moment quite clearly. Just as I am sure you remember if a teacher ever called you intelligent, special, sharp, brilliant, charming, talented, or wonderful.

Skin color and ethnic origin are still the primary sources of prejudice in our nation. Many people believe that because of our civil rights laws, affirmative action programs, and the many organizations devoted to promoting equality and justice, skin-color prejudice no longer exists in our country. We have made remarkable progress toward eradicating that prejudice, but we still have a long way to go. During the past decade, I have visited more than half of the states in our nation; in every state I met teachers who were dismayed and appalled at the racial and ethnic prejudices they witness on a recurring basis in their schools and communities. In fact, the only people I have met who truly believe racial prejudice is not a problem in our schools are white people. Brown people maintain that prejudice is still a big problem, and I believe they are in a position to assess the situation most accurately.

Here's why I continue to harp on the subject of racial prejudice: some years ago my sophomore class included a young man who happened to have extremely dark skin. He also had an extremely gentle and loving personality, an enthusiastic attitude toward school, and an extraordinary talent for football. The teachers on our team all liked Dante, and we agreed that his was the shiniest of stars in our class. One afternoon near the end of that school year, Dante stayed after school to talk to me.

"I just wanted to thank you," he said, "because you were the only teacher who wasn't afraid to make me do my homework. All the other teachers are afraid of me because I'm a big black man. They act like they think if they make me mad, I'll hurt them." As he spoke, Dante's eyes filled with tears, and his voice was choked with emotion. Watching him, I felt my own tears rising.

"So what do you do when those teachers act like that?" I asked.

"I act like I'm going to hurt them." Dante tried to laugh, but his chuckle turned into a cough that stopped just short of a sob.

For a split second, I nearly laughed myself, because it sounded funny. But I quickly realized that Dante's remark was not funny at all. Those teachers were prompting Dante to act as though he intended to hurt them. Whether intentionally or not, they were manipulating him into fulfilling their stereotype of black men as angry and violent. To fear a child simply because of his or her skin color is the same as saying, "I know that you are inherently violent simply because of who you are. It is only a matter of time before your true nature is revealed."

We all know how indignant we feel when someone accuses us of lying even though we are telling the truth and how outraged we feel when someone accuses us of doing something we haven't done. Adults are sometimes capable of rationalizing, justifying, or ignoring false accusations and insinuations. But children and adolescents are not experienced enough in human nature to justify or ignore adult behavior, and they don't know how to avoid being manipulated by adults. Most certainly, they are unequipped to cope with the overwhelming feelings of frustration, disbelief, indignation, and anger that arise when adults insinuate that they are violent (or stupid or worthless) because of their skin color or ethnic background. I believe that repeatedly exposing children to such subtle but serious prejudice is psychologically abusive and surely will have long-term effects on their self-esteem, their attitudes toward school, and their outlook on humanity.

I said earlier that I have yet to meet a person who is free from prejudice, and I include myself in that sweeping statement. After talking to Dante, I sat down and forced myself to face my own prejudices. I had read the journal articles and the psychology textbooks. I knew that studies have proved that most white (and many black) Americans' anxiety levels rise when they see brown or black men approaching them in public. And I had to admit that my own anxiety level would rise higher if a black or brown man approached me than if a white man did. Yet I had never in my life been attacked by a brown or black male. I had, on more than one occasion, had an unpleasant social encounter with a white male. Therefore, it made no sense for me to fear black and brown men more than white. Because I had been raised in an all-white town in the North where I had no contact with anybody of any color other than white, I had no experiences to shape my attitudes. Other than Bill Cosby and Muhammad Ali, I don't remember another positive black male role model from my childhood through my thirties, at which point I stopped watching TV completely. During nine years of active military service before I became a teacher, I had had only one slightly antagonistic experience with a black man but dozens of severely antagonistic episodes involving male Caucasian soldiers and sailors who didn't welcome women in their ranks. I could only conclude that I had formed my prejudice from hearing news reports of young black and Hispanic males waging wars on big-city streets and from watching movies and TV programs that consistently portrayed minority males as pimps, drug dealers, shiftless alcoholics, crack addicts, gangbangers, wife beaters, cop killers, and convicts.

My solution to purging my prejudice was to meet and talk to as many successful and educated black and brown men as I could. I sought them as mentors for my students. I befriended them in the school lunchroom and during community activities—not simply as research subjects but as human beings. After several weeks I knew I had made some significant progress in minimizing my racial prejudices when I met a black man I didn't like at all. Disliking that man was pivotal in my rehabilitation. Prior to that meeting, I would have felt compelled to like him or to act as though I did, in order not to appear to be prejudiced.

After nearly twenty years of ongoing self-treatment, I feel free to like or dislike anybody I meet, of any skin color or ethnic background, based on the way that person treats me—and especially the way that person treats children and dogs. I don't pretend there is no violence in the world. I try to keep my distance from anybody of any color who appears to be drunk, stoned, sociopathic, or potentially dangerous. But I don't expect any particular person to be violent simply because of his or her ethnic origin. And I have learned to cope with students who have prejudices toward me, such as the young man who strutted into my sophomore English class one day and announced as he passed by, without making eye contact, that he didn't like white people.

"I can't help it if I glow in the dark," I told him. "I was born that way, and I can't do anything about it. If you're going to dislike me for something, please dislike me for something that I am directly responsible for, something I can control, such as my attitude, my politics, or my behavior. Why don't you cut me some slack until you get to know me? And I will do the same for you. I will decide whether or not I like you based on the way you act, not on your skin color."

My prejudiced pal just shrugged and pretended to ignore me, but he must have listened—although he rarely spoke to me and clearly did not feel any affection toward me. At the end of his second year as my student, he wrote in his journal that the most important thing he had learned in school that year was that "not all white people are bad." I considered that a high compliment from him. But even more important, I knew that he could no longer be 100 percent prejudiced because he had met at least one exception to his rule. He inspired me to try to introduce other students to their own exceptions.

We all know that students tend to meet their teachers' expectations—high or low. So unless we have good reason to believe that a particular student is prone to violent behavior, we must expect the best from all of our students. And we must eradicate our irrational fears because we can't successfully teach children when we are afraid of them.

One final note: after my talk with Dante, I suggested that he read an essay by Brent Staples called "Night Walker," in which Staples describes how he has learned to control the rage he feels when people obviously fear him simply for his skin color alone. To defuse potential confrontations, Staples whistles well-known classical tunes to let people know he isn't a mugger—his "equivalent of the cowbell that hikers wear when they are in bear country." (This essay was originally published in *Ms.* magazine as "Just Walk on By," and was reprinted elsewhere under different titles. It can be found in a number of essay anthologies.) Although reading an essay doesn't solve the problem, it does provide an articulate, intelligent response that may help young minority males (and females) cope with a difficult world.

RESPECT YOURSELF

New teachers often ask, "How do I make students respect me, when they walk into the room determined to disrespect me before they even meet me?" Clearly, you cannot *make* anybody respect you. You can demand respect all you want, but you can't force it. Children already understand this concept, so they aren't simply being stubborn when they resist your demands for respect. They are insulted by your demands because you clearly don't think they are intelligent enough to understand the dynamics of your interactions with them. Thus, the harder you try to force them to respect you, the more insulted they will be, and the more they will disrespect you.

Sometimes we find ourselves with an entire room full of disrespectful students. And some teachers draw the battle lines. They become more strict, establishing rigid rules and inflexible procedures. They allow students to draw them into the teacher-versus-student battle that so many young people enjoy because it is entertaining, easier than doing lessons, and most important, because they already know how to act disrespectful. They are very good at it, and they will get even better if you disrespect them in return. I know from experience how frustrating it is to try to continue modeling respectful behavior when students greet your efforts with disdain, defiance, disrespect, or complete disregard. And I know how tempting it is to let the children manipulate you into responding as they expect you to. But if you can resist, if you can continue to respect them as human beings, separating the child from the childish behavior, eventually most of them will realize that you are sincere, that you do respect them as people—and it is extremely difficult to go on hating somebody who truly respects and cares for you.

Here's how I approach the issue of respect. I explain to my students on the first day in class that the one thing I value more than any other behavior is self-respect. I explain that I believe lack of respect for others stems from a lack of self-respect, so I will be working to help them develop self-respect, self-discipline, self-esteem, and self-confidence. Then I do my utmost to live up to my own high expectations. When a student disrespects me, I call the student out in the hallway to talk to me, but I still speak respectfully to that student. (On those infrequent occasions when the student has managed to push enough buttons to make me so angry that I can't speak respectfully, I either leave the student standing outside the room until I can gain control, call for security to escort the student to the office, or ask a fellow teacher or counselor to take my class for a few minutes while I take a walk to calm down.)

Some students may not know how to respond to genuine respect because they have never encountered it before. You may have to continue being respectful for a very long time (sometimes an entire year) until they realize that you aren't pretending. They may be suspicious of your good intentions. One boy told me that when he acted belligerent and I continued to address him respectfully, he assumed my plan was to trick him somehow.

"I figured something was up, you know," he told me later. "I'm like, she's slick, but what's she got up her sleeve? Ain't nobody gonna be that nice unless they want something from you. I finally figured out you was trying to show me how to act right. Do the right thing, man."

You don't have to like a student in order to treat him or her with respect. I'm sure you work with adults you don't particularly like, but you don't actively disrespect them, especially in front of your peers. Also, I think it's important to accept that not all students may like you. That is fine. Students don't have to like you, just as they don't have to like each other. They can still learn the information you teach. And they need to learn to conduct themselves with self-respect so that they can learn to be successful students who enjoy positive relationships with other people in their personal and professional lives.

After observing both successful and struggling teachers, I have a theory about why some adults have trouble eliciting respect from students, even when those adults honestly believe they respect their students. When a teacher approaches from a standpoint of wanting to reform, shape up, or save students, those students sense that the teacher is condescending. They know that the teacher feels superior to them, and they resent the teacher's attitude, even though the teacher truly wants to help them. Imagine that another adult approached you and said, "You are such a mess. You make stupid choices; you waste your time and talents; and your values and ethics are inferior to mine. But I can show you how to be more like me so that you can be a better person. I can help you, if you will only listen to me."

How would you feel if somebody said those things to you, even if the person were more accomplished and successful than you are? I don't think you would be receptive, because you would be thinking, *What right does this person have to speak to me this way?* Your emotions would block your intellect, and no real communication of information could occur. Instead, your attention would be focused on trying to assert your own strength, control your anger, express your anger, or return the insult.

If we want students to respect us, we must respect them as human beings deserving of basic human dignity. We must accept that they may have different values and lifestyles and that they may have made choices that we would never have made. But they are young, uneducated, and inexperienced (even if they are streetwise). We can't expect them to make logical, mature, and intelligent decisions unless adults have taught them how to think and provided them with role models who exhibit mature and intelligent behavior. Here's your chance to provide that role model. Instead of wasting their time by criticizing and belittling students for joining gangs, taking drugs, having rampant unsafe sex, and cheating on assignments, you will be much more likely to earn their respect if you ask them why they have made the choices they have made—and listen to their answers. If they ask for your advice, feel free to give it. Otherwise, keep asking questions until they learn to question their own choices and behaviors. You can't save your students from themselves. But teach them to think, to solve problems, to analyze choices, to be successful people, and they will save themselves.

As you consider how you are going to demonstrate your respect for your students as human beings, please take a moment to recall your own childhood teachers. I would bet my gigantic teacher's salary that you are not thinking of algebraic formulas or prepositional phrases. More likely, you remember a compliment that sent your spirits soaring or a humiliation that still makes your cheeks burn. I remember my own second-grade teacher using masking tape to attach my glasses to my face because I kept taking them off when other kids teased me about wearing them. The teacher said she meant to teach me to keep my glasses on my face and stop acting silly, but what she taught me was how embarrassing and infuriating it is to be helpless under the control of an authority figure who misuses her power. After that day I left my glasses at home and refused to wear them to school ever again. I squinted in school every year until my high school graduation. I still remember that second-grade teacher, but I also remember **my fifth-grade** teacher, Mrs. Hodak, who encouraged me to write and appointed me to the glorious position of class newspaper editor. When I acted silly, Mrs. Hodak would look at me over the top of her glasses and wait for me to come to my senses and settle down. Then she would hug me. Mrs. Hodak taught me to think about my behavior. She taught me to challenge myself and follow my dreams. She taught me the true meaning of respect, and I will love her until the day I die.

GRADES: PERCENTAGE? CURVE? COIN TOSS?

How will you use grades in your classroom: to provide incentives, to record progress, to evaluate your teaching, to punish daydreamers and procrastinators—or all four? I opt to use only the first three because when teachers use bad grades or deduct points as punishment, they contribute to the cycle of misbehavior and failure that undermines our school system. I believe grades should measure how well students have learned the material and skills, and their grades indicate how well I have presented the lessons and motivated my students. A grade book filled with Ds and Fs is a warning flag that I am not doing my job well.

Every teacher must create a grading policy that reflects his or her own standards and ethics, but the most effective teachers maintain high standards, a flexible attitude, and a constant focus on fairness. Effective teachers keep students informed of their progress at frequent intervals, to avoid surprises and complaints. Your school may use a pass/fail option, straight percentages, or a letter-grade system. Your department may add its own criteria, 95 percent required for an A, for example. But it will be up to you to assign the grades. Even a subject such as math, which is more objective than most, leaves room for subjectivity in grading. Will you give credit only for correct answers on homework, or will you allow credit for student papers that have incorrect answers but indicate considerable effort or basic understanding of important concepts? If a student has perfect attendance, completes her homework faithfully, cooperates during class but suffers from test anxiety that makes her fail every major exam, what grade will you assign her? Will you go strictly by percentage, even though it doesn't accurately represent her ability? Will you assign less weight to her exam scores? Perhaps you'll arrange an alternative testing program for her, allowing her to take her exams after school or with a trusted counselor in attendance.

What about your underachiever? If a student is clearly capable of earning an A without studying, but he decides to read comic books in the back of your classroom whenever he can and rarely bothers to complete a homework assignment, will you give him an A when he aces the midterm and final exams? Will your grade reflect his academic ability and natural intelligence, or will you consider his poor work ethic and laziness?

Will you grade every single assignment, or will you give full credit on some assignments for students who make a sincere effort to learn a new skill, even if they make a lot of mistakes? Will you allow students who work diligently on every task to earn extra credit that may raise their grade a notch to reflect their hard work, enthusiasm, and persistence? Will you start all students at ground zero and then make it as difficult as you can for them to work their way up to an A? Will you just start assigning work and figure out how to grade students after you see what they can do? Will you start all students with an A and work hard to help them keep it?

Because they believe we need to raise the bar, some teachers blast their classes with impossible workloads from the second the school year begins. And some teachers boast that "Nobody earns an A in my class because I'm too darned tough." My question to such teachers is: What would motivate a student to try hard if he or she knows in advance that an A is impossible to achieve in your class?

The real question every teacher must answer is not so much "What grade does a student deserve?" as it is "What do you want your students to learn?" Of course, you must grade major exams according to your district policy. But although grading every assignment strictly by percentage teaches students that they must achieve whatever standards are set for them in a particular situation, it also may teach them that academic ability is more important than social skills, respect for other people, enthusiasm, a willingness to tackle challenges, and the ability to learn from mistakes.

At the end of the school year, you may wonder whether your grades accurately reflect and reward your students' efforts. You won't be the only teacher wondering. That's why so many teachers ask students to grade themselves or to write a paragraph or an essay arguing for their grades. I've used a variation of that assignment with great success. My students enjoy it, and I learn as much about my teaching as I do about their learning. I call my self-grading assignment "A Different Perspective."

I first read aloud to my students from the book, *The True Story of the 3 Little Pigs by A. Wolf (as told to Jon Scieszka).* The illustrated book, which takes about five minutes to read, tells the story from the wolf's point of view: suffering from a bad cold, he accidentally sneezed down the pigs' houses while trying to borrow a cup of sugar so that he could bake a birthday cake for his grandmother.

Next I assign the students the task of writing letters to themselves—from me. In their letters they must imagine that they are seeing themselves from my perspective as they describe their behavior and evaluate their performance in my classroom. They must assign themselves the grade that they believe I would assign, and they must justify that grade.

Sometimes students find the assignment confusing and need help getting started. I write a few example beginnings on the board: "Dear Joey, It's been a distinct pleasure having you as a student. You are too wonderful for words"; "Dear Patrice: Wake up and smell your tennis shoes before it's too late!" and so on.

One or two jokers usually write silly letters, but most students take the assignment to heart. They are honest and more critical than I would be. Sometimes a student who has an A in my book assigns himself a lower grade because he really didn't try his hardest. Other times I realize that a student spent an extraordinary amount of time and effort at home as well as in my classroom. I rarely lower a grade after reading the letters, but I sometimes raise one. In addition to letting me see whether my grades are on target, the letters give me insight into my own performance in the classroom. They let me know that I spend too much time on one area and not enough on another or that I divided my attention unfairly between boys and girls. Those student letters remind me that I must work to earn my own A.

One final note about grading. If you teach subjects that involve abstract principles or concepts, such as ethics, economics, or algebra (especially algebra), be aware that some students may have problems because of their individual rates of development. There is a point in every child's development when the brain makes the switch from concrete to abstract thinking. This switch has nothing to do with intelligence. Conscientious, industrious students who are used to succeeding in school often become frustrated when they cannot grasp new concepts; and you may think they aren't trying, because they usually earn high grades. For example, when we study symbolism in literature, many bright students understand the definition of symbolism and the examples I give them to illustrate the technique, but they cannot create their own examples for an exam. Instead of deducting points from those students' papers, I give them credit if they can define the concept and remember some of my examples. My hope is that later on, when they are able to understand, they will recall those examples and use them as a model for creating their own.

COVERING CURRICULUM IS NOT TEACHING

If you are a master organizer with a creative flair and the ability to teach advanced, regular, and remedial students, undeterred by myriad distractions and interruptions, then you probably have no trouble covering all of the curriculum required for your subject or course. If you don't spend a minute worrying about how you're going to fit everything you want to teach into one school year, then you're an uncommonly talented teacher who should skip this section. The rest of us worry, because it's common for teachers, especially new teachers, to fear that they can't teach everything they need to teach because there is too much material, too much paper shuffling, too many energy-consuming administrative tasks, and not enough time. Instead of sharing this fear and discussing ways to become more effective teachers, most of us worry privately and fear that our colleagues will think we're ineffective or unqualified if we admit that we sometimes feel inadequate to the task of teaching all the required skills and information for our courses.

The question every teacher must face is this: Given a conflict, where does my priority lie—in covering the curriculum material and preparing for tests or in meeting my students' needs? It's easy to err in either direction. Some teachers take the district guidelines to heart and race their way through the required textbooks and activities, leaving those students who can't learn fast enough trailing behind the pack. Unfortunately, sometimes an entire class ends up falling behind, and the teacher is the only one who really understands the material when it's time for final exams. Other teachers bend to the pressure from above and spend all their class time teaching a specific test. Their students may learn how to take that specific test, and the school district may look good on paper; but I believe those students could be better served if they learned how to think and read and write well, which would prepare them to succeed in college or at work, in addition to preparing them to pass any exam. Still other teachers turn giddy from the pressure to perform or pay the price (not being offered a contract or granted tenure, for example), so they toss aside the textbooks and spend their entire class periods chatting with students about current events or designing fun projects that take weeks to complete, leaving their students unprepared for the following year's requirements.

It is possible, although not easy, to find a middle ground. My district supervisor gave me a big boost in the right direction when she explained her viewpoint at a meeting of our teaching team. Working together, we four teachers had the task of teaching fifty at-risk teens, students who had severe attendance problems, substandard reading ability, and apathetic attitudes toward education.

"Covering curriculum is not teaching," our supervisor explained. "Nobody expects you to address the problems these kids have, bring them up to grade level, and cover your entire textbooks in one year. I advise you to select the key elements in your texts and teach those elements well. Don't worry about covering every single thing; just teach the most important concepts and skills, and teach your students how to learn so they can pick up the slack." We took her advice and were amazed at how well it worked. Instead of dividing our textbooks into segments and arbitrarily deciding how long each new skill should take to master, we made a list of what we wanted to teach and started with the most important and basic skills. For example, our math teacher had to back up and reteach the number line and negative and positive numbers. We were a little nervous at first, but when our students realized that we would slow down as they needed in order to spend time on areas of special interest, they repaid us by working harder at the mundane tasks in between. Our students performed as well as the "regular" students in English, history, and computer courses; and our math students zoomed right past the regular geometry classes, earning higher grades and completing more of the same textbook!

Those students reminded us of a lesson we sometimes forget: children are capable of learning much more than we require during a given school year. If we slow down or back up to fill in the gaps in their knowledge base and if they are confident that we have their best interests at heart, they will accelerate their learning and accomplish goals far beyond any we set for them.

THERE IS NO SUCH THING AS A CASUAL REMARK TO A CHILD

Sometimes I think we forget how impressionable children are (even older children). We forget how excruciating the smallest pain can be, how exhilarating the tiniest victory, and how lasting the effect of a comment from an adult they admire. One day before class started, a group of football players were boasting about their latest gridiron glories. I noticed another boy, Sean Campbell, blush and fidget as he watched the athletes trade playful insults in front of a group of admiring girls and boys. A skinny youngster, all elbows and knees, Sean often dropped things or tripped over his shoelaces. When one of the ball players complimented himself on a sixty-five yard touchdown, Sean sighed and looked out the window. I walked around the room until I stood near Sean's desk.

"I'm very proud of you, Paul," I told the touchdown scorer. "But I hope you go on to achieve great things after school too. I'd hate for you to be one of those people who peak at age sixteen, whose lives are all downhill after high school."

"I'm cool," Paul responded with a grin. "You know the scouts are already looking at me."

I was looking at Sean, who was looking at Paul.

"You're going to be one of those men who peak much later in life," I said softly to Sean.

"Yeah, I was thinking that," Sean said. His cheeks flushed bright red, but he sat up straighter and stopped staring wistfully at Paul and his entourage. Pleased that I had boosted Sean's self-esteem, I took the scenic route as I strolled back to my desk.

In the far corner of the room, as I passed by the desk of an extremely shy girl named Marcy Bryant, I stopped and smiled at her. "You too," I said. "I think you're going to be a late bloomer, but you're going to be a big, beautiful flower."

Marcy folded into herself and hid her face as she did whenever anybody looked at her. Not wanting to embarrass her further, I quickly made some chitchat with other students and returned to the front of the room.

I forgot all about the incident until a few months later, at open house. Toward the end of the event, Sean's mother walked into my room and introduced herself. As I reached out to shake hands with her, she took my right hand with both her hands. She squeezed my hand and held on.

"I wanted to thank you for what you said to Sean," she said. "He said you told him you knew he was going to peak late in life and he shouldn't worry about not being the best athlete or the most popular right now. You should have seen him smile when he told me. And he has been a different person ever since. You changed his life. I can't thank you enough."

I was so stunned at Mrs. Campbell's remarks that I just stood there, grinning stupidly at her until she left the room. I had completely forgotten about that day, but Sean had remembered. I floated through the rest of the evening on a little cloud of happiness. One incident like that can keep a teacher motivated for months. But just as I was ready to turn out the lights and lock the door, Marcy's mother peeked around the door frame.

"Am I too late to say hello?" she asked. Some children work hard to be different from their parents, but Marcy was definitely her mother's daughter. I welcomed Mrs. Bryant into my room and motioned for her to sit down in one of the student desks for a chat.

"Oh, I don't want to take up your time," Mrs. Bryant said. She held her purse tightly with both hands, and I had the impression that she was resisting the temptation to hold the purse up in front of her face to hide behind it.

"I just wanted to thank you," she said. "Marcy told me you said she was a late bloomer but that she is going to be a beautiful flower someday. She cried when she told me. We both did. She used to be worried about what would happen to her when she grew up, but she doesn't worry any more. Now she's a happy child."

I didn't say anything because I knew I would cry if I opened my mouth. I just nodded and smiled at Mrs. Bryant as she ducked her head and slipped out the door.

After Sean's mother had talked to me, I admit I was feeling a little proud of myself. But after Marcy's mother left, I felt a little frightened. Two students believed that one ten-second forgotten conversation had changed their lives. If that was true, then what about all the other conversations I couldn't remember? Had I said anything that negatively affected children as strongly as those positive comments had? I tried to remember whether I had said anything harsh the last time I had run out of patience or had been frustrated by too much talking or pencil sharpening or giggling or note writing during class. I couldn't think of any negative comments I may have made, but then I had forgotten the late-bloomer comments too.

Before I turned off the lights and locked the door to my classroom that night, I wrote a note on an index card and taped it to the top of my desk as a reminder. My note read:

Be careful. Everything you say, every single day, may be recorded in your students' hearts forever.

The Big Three: Preparation, Preparation, Preparation

A ward-winning realtors often list their top three criteria for success: "Location, location, location." And effective teachers often list the top three criteria for their success as preparation, preparation, preparation. If you don't get your ducks all in a row well ahead of time, you may find yourself dealing with stray quackers all year long, because once the school year begins, even experienced, effective teachers find themselves running at top speed on the teaching treadmill. In addition to saving time and energy later on, you will find that spending a couple of weeks getting organized before school starts will allow you to focus on the most challenging and interesting aspect of your delightful job—your students.

You will need some equipment and supplies in order to get yourself organized. Because many schools operate on limited or shrinking budgets, supplies may be scarce. As soon as you sign your contract to teach, ask a friend or relative to host a teacher-to-be shower. Provide a suggestion list for gifts: file folders, storage crates and bins, portable bookshelves, colored markers and art supplies, poster board, construction paper, scissors, tape, staplers, pencils, pens, paper clips, three-ring binders, subscriptions to educational publications designed for children, children's books, young adult books, dictionaries, notebook paper, pastel printer paper, and so on. If your friends and relatives are employed and generous, you might add bigger items such as a room-sized air cleaner, a radio with a CD player, or a digital camera. Don't be shy. You aren't asking for gifts for yourself; you are asking for donations to help you educate the future of our country. People will be happy to contribute and even happier if you periodically provide them with an e-mail or printed newsletter highlighting your students' achievements. An especially nice touch and one that may bring tears to your donors' eyes is to have your grateful students send handwritten thank-you notes.

Once you have some supplies, where do you start? I'd suggest making some lists. I come from a long line of list-making women, so I made dozens of important little lists during my first years as a classroom teacher. Every time I observed a really good teacher, attended a training session, read an interesting theory, or woke up in the middle of the night with a brilliant idea, I made a list of things I could do to improve my classroom environment or my teaching methods. Sometimes I could actually find a list when I needed it, but usually those helpful little lists got stuck in my grade book, lost among student homework papers, or forgotten on the front of my refrigerator under one of those cute little apple-shaped magnets. Eventually I gathered all my lists and analyzed them to see whether I could combine them into one workable list. I couldn't. But I did manage to distill them into three lists, sorted into the categories of my classroom, my paperwork, and myself. In this chapter I'll share my lists with you, first as a detailed discussion of various items and then as a basic checklist. Of course, you will have your own items to add and may not need some of mine, but I believe these lists will provide a good starting point for developing your own well-organized master plan.

PREPARE YOUR ROOM

I often refer to attending school as children's "work," and I frequently draw analogies between the many common behaviors and conditions that lead to success in school and at work. In any profession your environment affects your comfort and efficiency, and your interactions with other people affect the speed and accuracy of your work. As an adult, you have multiple options if you are uncomfortable or unhappy with your job. Students are stuck with whatever classroom environments their teachers create; your classroom environment can mean the difference between a room filled with cooperative, enthusiastic, motivated children or a group of apathetic nonparticipants and disgruntled whiners. Creating a dynamic classroom environment involves four basic elements: sensory details, seating arrangements, supplies and storage, and student information.

Sensory Details

Children are much more attuned to (and distracted by) the world's sensory elements than are most adults. Four of the five senses come into play in a classroom because students respond, often quite dramatically, to the way your room looks, feels, sounds and, yes, even the way it smells. You can do a great deal (considering the limited equipment and funds available to you) to address those four aspects of your classroom with an eye toward creating an environment that is functional, comfortable, welcoming, and inspiring.

Sound and smell are the easiest aspects to address, so let's tackle them first. If your school is noisy because of traffic, loud air conditioning or heating systems, thin walls, or rampaging students, you can create an oasis of calm in your classroom by playing soft music before and between class periods. Scientists have repeatedly proven that music can either encourage (classical) or discourage (heavy metal) thinking and that classical music can improve IQ test scores. Light classical music, jazz, or music designed to enhance meditation can all be used to take advantage of children's natural affinity for melody and percussion.

If music is playing when students first enter your classroom, they will definitely notice; and many of them will make their opinions known. This is your chance to teach them how to be intelligent critics. If they criticize your music choice, ask them to listen long enough to be able to articulate an intelligent opinion about the music. Some students will resist listening to music that doesn't include screaming vocals or ear-numbing electronic drumbeats, but if you ask them to give it a try just for a few minutes each day, they will soon become accustomed to it. (If you have a large number of vocal complainers, don't argue. Just turn off your music, politely tell them you are sorry they weren't interested in your experiment, and drop the subject. Move quickly to the next academic activity. Chances are good that the students will change their minds and decide to give your horrible music a short listen.) One teacher I know spent weeks trying to convince her high school juniors to listen to light classical music before class started and during exams.

Before long her students began complaining that the room was too quiet and that sounds were too distracting if she didn't play music during exams.

Music can also be a great tool for increasing student participation and motivation, but if you do play music, some student is bound to ask if he or she can change the radio station or listen to a popular CD. If your goal is to create a calm environment in your classroom, then I would suggest keeping the music choice as your domain, but include music in your student projects or allow students to have five minutes of music time at the end of any class period during which nobody disrupted and everybody completed the work assignments (you'll need to figure out a system for rotating choices, or a few students will dominate). I have had groups in which even confirmed nonreaders agreed to read difficult fiction in order to spend a few minutes at the end of the class period listening to their horrible, loud, screeching "really great music."

Now let's talk about smell, an integral part of any school experience. If you close your eyes and let your nose drift, I would bet you can recall at least one distinctive smell from your own school days. My strongest olfactory memory is of new books. I have always loved their smell. But not all school smells are pleasant. In fact, when you take twenty or thirty warm bodies, plenty of well-worn sneakers, several quarts of perfumed personal hygiene products, dust from chalk or dry-erase markers, residue from the custodial staff's industrial strength cleaners, and reams of old papers, you can end up with some nasty-smelling classrooms.

Fortunately, smell is the easiest aspect of your room to control, but buying a decent air cleaner is probably going to cost you at least $30 out of your own pocket, unless you can find a local business to sponsor you or unless your department budget provides teachers with a petty-cash allowance. Even if you have to fork over the dough from your paltry paycheck, your investment will pay off. Not only will your classroom smell nice, but you will find that you have fewer students sniffling during allergy season. And if you buy an air cleaner with an ultraviolet light, it will also kill many of the germs that congregate in classrooms during cold and flu season.

Do a little research before you buy an air cleaner. There are a lot of urban myths surrounding negative ion generation and ultraviolet radiation. Negative ions are not harmful unless they are created in overabundance, and most new air cleaners have built-in controls. When an air cleaner generates the proper amount of negative ions, your room will have a fresh, outdoorsy smell. If you smell a distinctive tangy odor instead, you know that you need to make an adjustment to decrease the negative ions. Ultraviolet lights in air filters are not placed where they can injure people's eyes or subject them to radiation, and they very effectively zap airborne germs and pollutants.

Now we're ready to tackle the feel of your room. Take a walk around the block and then enter your classroom. Notice whether it's too warm or too cold, whether the lights are so bright that they create glare on the desks. Are the walls a nice warm color, or have they been painted an ugly industrial gray or tan to hide the dirt? (I know, I know, you aren't supposed to paint your room. But there are ways to get it done if you are creative. And if you do decide to paint, consider buying a paint that does not give off gases. They are called low-VOC paints; read about them at the BioShield Paint Web site (www.bioshieldpaint.com) or ask your local reference librarian for help in locating information.

Does your classroom feel inviting? Is this a place you'd like to sit for a few hours every day? Wander around and visit some other classrooms. Compare the way they feel to the way your classroom feels. Then see if you can figure out what makes them more or less inviting. If your room is stuffy and overheated or too cold and drafty, find your school's maintenance supervisor and ask for his or her advice. Some school districts are inflexible about the dates that schools must use heating or air conditioning, regardless of the local weather conditions. And some buildings have a central ventilation system that doesn't allow for individual room settings. But if you explain that you are trying to make your room as comfortable as possible for your students, your maintenance professionals will probably find a way to help you; it has been my experience that they appreciate being recognized for their knowledge and training, and they are eager to help you if you approach them with a respectful and patient attitude. At one school, the custodians placed a transparent blue film over the fluorescent lights to reduce the glare and create a more natural color of light. At another school, when I asked about full-spectrum fluorescent lights, the head custodian said, "You tell me what kind of lights you want, and I'll go find them." When I painted my room one weekend—honestly, I didn't know I wasn't supposed to—the custodians shook their heads but agreed to pretend not to notice. (I didn't paint it a wild color, just a nice warm peach with light blue accents, and all the paint was provided by a professional painter who did the painting for free.)

Of course, your room should look inviting and interesting. In addition to the standard posters, maps, and magazine articles, try tacking up photos of students from your old high school yearbooks, copies of your childhood report cards and homework assignments, six or seven different calendars, restaurant menus, theater playbills, jokes, flags, banners, colorful mobiles, plants (real or fake), and athletic memorabilia. Think of theme restaurants you like: the decor has nothing to do with the food, but we still like to sit in surroundings that are beautiful, interesting, or amusing. Put a fake palm tree and some floor pillows in a corner of your classroom, and kids will clamor to be able to sit there and read. (Don't ask permission to do this. Just do it, and if you get in trouble, apologize profusely. If you can prove that student behavior or grades have improved because of your decor, administrators are much more likely to give you permission to keep it.)

Does your room have some eye candy for those students who really need a daydream break now and then? Research supports what many teachers instinctively sensed: that even when students aren't paying attention to your lessons, they will still absorb the information you have posted on the walls around them. Motivational quotations are especially effective. There are books devoted exclusively to memorable quotations, so you will be able to find some that will suit your students. In the meantime here are a few of my favorites to get you started. Be sure to write them in very large letters so that students can read them from a distance:

The hallmark of a second-rater is resentment of another's achievement.

—Ayn Rand

If you don't decide which way to play with life, it will play with you.

—Merle Shain

Nobody can make you feel inferior without your consent.

—Eleanor Roosevelt

If you can imagine it, you can achieve it;
If you can dream it, you can become it.

—William Ward

Great spirits have always encountered violent opposition
from mediocre minds.

—Albert Einstein

He who angers you enslaves you.

—Author unknown

*The hardest thing about success is finding somebody
who is truly happy for you.*

—Bette Midler

*There are two tragedies in life: one is to lose your heart's desire,
the other to gain it.*

—George Bernard Shaw

*If your only tool is a hammer,
you tend to see every problem as a nail.*

—Author unknown

*One often learns more from ten days of agony than
from ten years of contentment.*

—Merle Shain

*Light came to me when I realized I did not have to
consider any racial group as a whole.*

*God made them duck by duck, and that was the
only way I could see them.*

—Zora Neale Hurston

Rudeness is a weak person's attempt at strength.

—J. M. Casey

*A life spent making mistakes is not only more honorable
but more useful than a life spent doing nothing.*

—George Bernard Shaw

The only real failure is the person who refuses to try.

—Author unknown

*Hold fast to dreams, for if dreams die,
life is a broken-winged bird that cannot fly.*

—Langston Hughes

Keep away from people who try to belittle your ambitions.
Small people always do that, but the really great
make you feel that you, too, are great.

—Mark Twain

We are each given the same twenty-four hours each day.
How we choose to spend our time makes the
difference between success and failure.

—Kenneth Brodeur

Just because you're right doesn't mean I'm wrong.

—My mom, Alyce Shirley Johnson

Seating Arrangements

Student seating arrangements have a tremendous impact on students' motivation, behavior, and interactions with each other as well as with the teacher. The shape and size of your classroom will limit your options, but two considerations should take priority, regardless of what arrangement you choose: vision and access. While seated, all students must be able to clearly see the board, any screens used for various projections, the TV or VCR monitors, and the clock. And you must have quick and easy access to every student in your classroom. You will have far fewer discipline problems if you arrange your student seating so that you have a clear pathway to each student, with a maximum of two people between you and a given student at all times.

Creating access can be a challenge in a small room, especially in narrow mobile classrooms (I think such classrooms should be illegal). In a smaller room, you may have to create three or more separate areas in order to have desks only three deep. Before you arrange your room, try sketching a few different ideas on paper. If you have a small room, you might consider eliminating your own desk if it's big and bulky and you have sufficient storage shelves and filing cabinets. A small mobile computer desk and a small worktable might allow a more effective use of space, and you can easily move them if you decide to rearrange.

Psychology plays an important role in seating: a round table indicates that all participants hold equal status, whereas a rectangular table usually has a chair at the head for the leader. Large tables with chairs that face across are conducive to communication and discussion. Chairs lined in long straight rows facing a stage (think of church pews or seats in a theater) create a clear distinction between the speaker(s) and the audience.

You can use seating psychology to send messages to your students. Long, straight rows indicate that yours will be a traditional classroom, governed by strict rules and regulations. A large circle or concentric semicircles send a different message, usually indicating that you expect group discussions or other student feedback. Small groups of desks or tables alert students to be prepared to participate in informal exercises, small group activities, or teamwork exercises.

I take advantage of seating psychology by using different arrangements for different activities, but I have learned the hard way to avoid arrangements in which students face each other squarely from across the room. At one school where gang activity was a serious problem, both boys and girls would stare down students who sat directly opposite them when their desks faced each other head-on. Turning desks so that they face each other at even a slight angle can eliminate this problem; it's easy to judge whether you've got it right. Sit in one of the student desks in the front row. If your gaze is directed squarely at another student's desk, then shift your desk so that the direct line of your gaze includes several desks or a wall.

The only time I use straight rows of desks all facing the same direction is when we have an important test. Students understand that when they see test formation, they should sharpen their pencils, stow their possessions, and be prepared to work quietly. I don't like long, straight rows except during test periods, however. Students tend to misbehave or daydream when they are seated in rows of six or seven, because no matter where I stand, several students are far away from me. Worse yet, students can't hear or see each other. Students seated in the front and back of the room can't hear each other's comments, questions, or answers during class time. Everybody has trouble hearing when students read aloud during class because students are either reading into a void in the front of the room or into the backs of other students' heads—not conducive to creating a dynamic environment for learning, participation, or discussion.

In a classroom with a clearly defined front (a chalkboard or whiteboard and a projection screen permanently located along the same wall), my favorite arrangement is a modified semicircle or U shape (Figure 3.1). This allows everybody to see clearly while giving me quick, easy access to all students.

In a classroom with two possible fronts—(with boards or screens on opposite walls or a board on one end and screen at the other), I use two semicircle formations

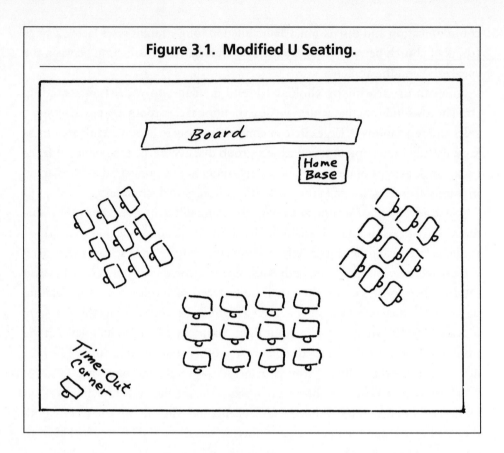

Figure 3.1. Modified U Seating.

(Figure 3.2), so that the focus shifts from one side to the other without obstructing students' vision or necessitating rearrangement of student desks.

For all small group activities, I place the desks into circles of three or four, depending. I try to separate the groups enough to allow for private discussions and eliminate distractions from other groups. (Some teachers ask students to arrange the desks for group activities, but I don't. If I have early birds, I may ask them to help me; but I have found that having students move the desks during class creates too much chatter and confusion. If desks are already arranged, students come in, sit down, and get to work.)

Although mobile classrooms will be illegal after I am crowned queen of education, at present we have to work with them. The biggest problem in trailer-style rooms is vision. If your board and screen are at one end of the room, some students are going to be forced to sit where they can't see clearly. If your board and screen are attached at the side of the room, I would recommend asking mainte-

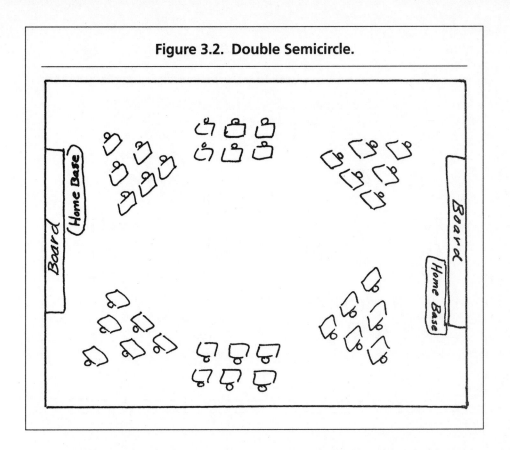

Figure 3.2. Double Semicircle.

nance to provide portable versions, especially if you teach math or science. If you try to line up the student desks lengthwise, facing a board mounted on a side wall, you are going to end up with all your students crowded into a small space and those on the ends won't be able to see well.

My approach to trailer teaching is to divide the students into two groups, one at either end of the trailer (Figure 3.3). While one group of students works independently at their seats, I instruct the other group using the overhead projector and whiteboard (moving the screen and board for each group so that they are positioned where all students can see them). Although I have to present the same lesson twice, it doesn't hurt anybody; and it actually helps those students who process information more slowly, allowing them to tune in to both presentations as needed.

One final note on seating: Should you create a seating chart? Some teachers swear by them, and some students swear at them. Alphabetical seating is popular because it helps teachers learn names, take roll, and coordinate activities that

Figure 3.3. Mobile Classroom.

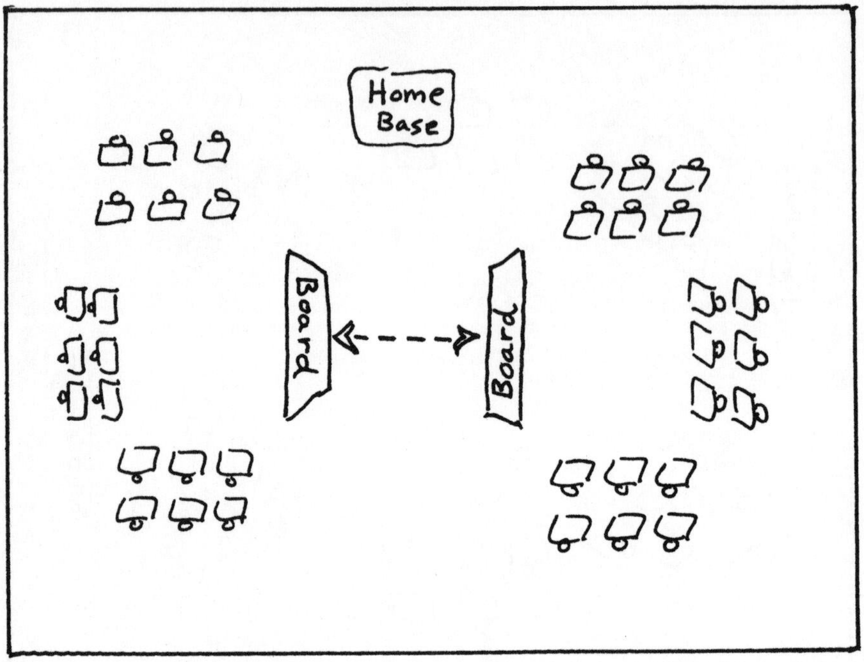

require students to line up and move as a group. Alphabetical seating arrangements can be helpful to teachers, particularly if they work with very young children, but such an arrangement can backfire with older students. Some students become irritated or apathetic after years of being assigned to the front or the back of every lineup; and some students will have been forced to sit year after year near students with whom they have serious personality conflicts. During junior high and high school years, personality conflicts can contribute to serious behavior problems. Unless your students are quite young or you already know them and their personalities, I recommend starting without a seating chart.

One technique that works well for me is to announce at the start of each semester that I will not assign seats as long as everybody cooperates with me and we don't have a lot of discipline problems and disruptions. Some students find it boring to sit in the same seats every day, whereas other students prefer the emotional security of sitting in the same seat in a particular classroom. I ask students who prefer to sit in the same seat each day to select a seat; those seats are then assigned and cannot be used by others, even if they are temporarily vacant due to absences. All the unclaimed seats are up for grabs. If discipline becomes a problem, I warn the students once. Then I create a seating chart that stays in effect until the end of that quarter or semester.

If you decide to use a seating chart, I would recommend taping name cards to the desks the first time students must sit in assigned seats, so that students won't sit down in one seat and then have to move to another. Better yet, stand in the doorway of your room to greet your students as they enter, and direct them to their assigned seats. Students, especially adolescents, are much more receptive to sitting in an assigned seat if they don't have to move after they have selected a seat. Changing seats after students are already seated can create confusion, animosity, and a poor rapport between you and your little scholars.

To head off most complaints, explain that you have created a seating chart in order to help your students be successful people, not simply because you enjoy being the boss. Tell them that you have put a lot of thought into the plan and that you believe it will help them succeed. If students complain about their seats, ask them to come talk to you after school—not after class. If they care enough to stay after school, then I would suggest you strongly consider changing their seats. Often students will ask for a new seat because somebody is bullying them or they don't want to sit near a former friend. Some students don't want to sit by their own best friends because they know they won't be able to concentrate and they know they won't be able to resist the temptation to whisper or pass notes when they should be paying attention.

Supplies and Storage

Choose a spot as your home base—the spot you will return to before and after class and during breaks between activities. You may choose to put your desk at home base, or you may opt for a lectern or podium on which to store daily lesson materials, leaving your desk elsewhere. If you use your desk as home base, be prepared. Unless you mark your territory and strictly enforce your no trespassing rule, students will buzz about your desk; because they are children, they are going to be curious about everything in, on, around, under, and behind your desk. They will sit in your chair and spin or rock. They will open the drawers just to see what's in them. They will jingle your key chain and look into your purse or briefcase.

Student curiosity is the primary reason why so many teachers choose to make their desks off-limits. During school hours they sit at a work table or a small desk between activities, away from their desks and all those temptations.

Some teachers like to place their desks in the corner of the room farthest from the door. Others prefer to put their file cabinets and supply shelves in the far corner of the room but keep their desks near the door, where they can more easily monitor student activity. Regardless of the arrangement you choose, you will need to create one area where you can keep confidential files, student grades, exams, and lesson outlines and make that area strictly off-limits to students. Hang up a sign if you need to, warning them to keep their hands off. If a student ignores the warning, act quickly and forcefully. This is the one time you do want to reprimand a student in public. You don't have to punish the student, but you do have to make a big deal out of the incident; otherwise, you give your students the message that you don't really care if they snoop and pry.

Even if your desk is off-limits, if it has actual working locks and keys, lock up anything that can be thrown, spat, flung, or shot at or stuck to other students such as paper clips, rubber bands, tape, and tacks. Be especially careful with black Sharpie markers; they are irresistible to children and will disappear faster than most other supplies. If your desk doesn't lock or you don't want to worry about keys, buy a plastic bin with a solid latch to keep extra staples, paper clips, rubber bands, markers, and so on.

I have tried both arrangements—using my desk as my home base and keeping my desk private and using a lectern or podium during lessons. The second method works better for me. I don't stand at the podium and lecture. I move constantly. But having a podium limits my space, which forces me to stay organized, and I can move quickly from one activity to the next. Each morning I place the lesson plan and necessary materials at the podium. Between activities and class periods, I may make quick visits to my desk; but if students are present, I stay at the podium so that they can ask questions or request my help.

My own desk is off-limits to students at all times. I place my desk diagonally across one corner of the room, with a file cabinet behind my chair to store student records, exams, and other confidential materials. One corner of my desk meets the wall, blocking access from that side. I place a visitor chair against the other side of my desk and allow an opening just wide enough for me to walk past to my own chair. I place a computer workstation, another file cabinet, or a bookshelf behind my desk so that I create a small entrance to my personal area. This setup reinforces

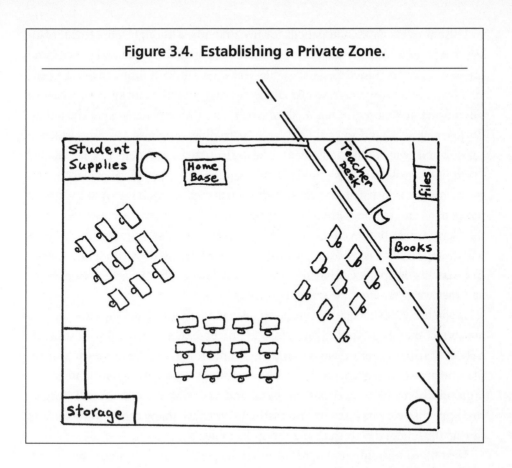

Figure 3.4. Establishing a Private Zone.

my no trespassing rule by creating a physical barrier between my private territory and the rest of the room.

Once you have situated your desk and storage units, find a small shelf or table for student supplies. Keep this student supply table near your home base so that you can monitor student use and restock as needed. Your supplies will vary according to your students' age and the subjects you teach, but I recommend a few supplies for every classroom: a box of tissues, a bottle of hand cleaner, a small mirror (children get things in their eyes), and a box of Band-Aids. If you choose not to provide a bottle of hand cleaner year-round, I would suggest that you consider supplying it during cold and flu season. Ask your students to use it after they have sneezed or used a tissue to blow their noses, especially those students who have a cold. Use it yourself between classes, especially after handling student papers. You will cut down on absences, including yours.

I also provide paper and pencils for my students. Although some teachers insist that parents or the school district should pay for all the paper and pencils, and the same teachers sometimes make a big deal when students forget to bring a pencil, I believe that we could save our energy for bigger battles and keep a package of lined notebook paper on hand, along with ten unique pencils (sparkly, polka-dotted, engraved, and so on). For classes with older students, I also provide ten unique and easily identifiable pens. I keep the pencils and pens in a jar labeled "Writing Utensils to Borrow" and assign a student to be the official pencil counter for each class or instructional period. The pencil counter's job is to make sure that ten pencils and ten pens are in the jar before students leave my classroom. This may seem trivial, but if you don't designate a pencil counter, your pencils and pens will disappear; it's easy for students to forget they borrowed a writing implement. But students do appreciate having a pen or pencil when they forget to bring theirs, and they waste far less time settling down to work.

If you feel very strongly that students need to bring their own supplies and you are certain that their families can afford to purchase them, then sell your students a sheet of paper or rent them a writing instrument and use the money to buy replacements when needed. But I'd think twice about wasting your time and energy arguing with children over pencils, pens, and paper. Many of them will "forget" their pencils every day just to procrastinate. We have many other opportunities during the school day to teach them responsibility.

Next fill your supply cupboard (or buy a big plastic bin) with trash bags, Band-Aids, Neosporin, disposable gloves, disinfectant cleaner, disposable antibacterial wipes, paper towels, a whisk broom, and a dust pan. When kids make a mess, unless they are very young, don't clean it up for them. Have them put on the gloves and get to work. (I know, I know, schools should supply these things; but if they don't, get them yourself.)

Set one wastebasket near the tissue box on your student supply table and another near the door to your room (buy an extra one if you have to; your room will stay much cleaner). When wastebaskets are convenient, people are more apt to use them.

Student Information

You can train your students to check certain locations for information each time they enter your classroom. For example, if you reserve the upper right-hand corner of your chalkboard or whiteboard for the daily agenda and make sure you post the agenda well before students enter the room each day, you won't have early birds hounding you with incessant "What are we gonna do today?" questions while you are trying to prepare for class. When students enter the room and ask you what they're going to do, point to the board and smile. Soon they will learn to look for themselves.

Make sure you post your agenda where everybody can see it. If you are very organized, you may choose to list details and specific times for specific activities. I prefer to make my agenda more flexible to allow for unforeseen circumstances. Sometimes students zip through an assignment that I thought would provide a challenge; at other times they struggle with something I thought would be quite easy. So I make a simple list of general activities. Monday's agenda might read: Independent Reading, Spelling Quiz, Vocabulary Review, Journal Writing. Another day's agenda might say: Pages 56–62 in Lit Text, Lit Worksheet, Group Discussions. Usually I post the following day's agenda before I leave the classroom at night so that it will be ready for even very early students. Some schools require custodians to clean all the boards, so if you post your agenda early, be sure to ask your custodian not to erase it.

Another option is to buy a portable erasable whiteboard, write your agenda with dry-erase markers, and post it above the student-supplies table. If your board is large enough, you might consider listing today's agenda, with a brief outline of the previous and next day's agendas for students who were absent or who like to plan ahead.

Having a daily agenda helps students focus, but some of them need a bigger picture. Using poster board or giant construction paper, I create a classroom calendar big enough to be legible from across the room and hang it high enough so that it's clearly visible when students are seated. I mark all holidays, reviews, quizzes, exams, and special events. Quizzes are noted in blue marker, exams in red (for each quiz or exam, I count back three school days and post a reminder on that day for students to study and review). Special events such as graduation, picture day, and homecoming are marked in purple.

In addition to eliminating complaints from students that they didn't know about a test (no matter how many times you announce a test, somebody will forget), a classroom calendar provides a visual record of progress for students who feel overwhelmed by the length of the school year. Your calendar can also be a good motivational tool. One successful technique I have used is to place a star on the calendar for each day that I did not have to ask somebody to stop disrupting class; when a group earns fifteen stars, students earn a reward such as fifteen minutes of free time, a chance to play educational games such as Scrabble, or a class visit to the library for thirty minutes of free reading. The only disadvantage of using stars to motivate classes is that you need a separate calendar for each class if you teach multiple classes. On the other hand, making separate calendars can inspire students in one class to work harder so that they don't fall behind another class. Although I don't like to focus on cutthroat competition, I do try to use positive peer pressure as long as students don't turn the process into a tool for humiliating each other. This is where your excellent teacher judgment comes into play.

Perhaps you're thinking you should make a list of rules and post them on the wall where everybody can see them and be reminded how to act. My recommendation is to nix the rule list. Kids know how they are supposed to act, unless they are in kindergarten or first grade, because they have already gone to school, where every teacher has at least one rule. Most have a list. Some have incredibly long lists. Hang on to your list of rules. Don't hang them on the wall to remind students how to misbehave, and don't launch into a big discussion of rules on day one, even if your administration instructs you to spend the first day of class going over your classroom rules. Save that discussion until a week or two into the semester to allow for new students and shuffled students. On your handout to welcome the class, include the most important rule and let students know you will discuss other rules in depth later on, after you have a chance to get to know each other and are sure that everybody is here to stay.

I don't hold back my rules out of pure orneriness or whimsy; I hold back for a reason. My niece Lila explained it much better than I could. Excited about her first day of high school, Lila confided that she couldn't sleep for two days before classes started. She couldn't wait to be a freshman. I called her after the first day of school and asked how she liked being one of "the big kids." She responded with a long, melodramatic, teenage-girl sigh.

"It was sooooooo boring," Lila said. "All we did was listen to a bunch of rules six times in a row in six different classes. It was just like kindergarten. I thought it was going to be different in high school. Now I don't even want to go back tomorrow."

Lila made a good point. Unless they are in the first grade, students know exactly how they are supposed to act in school. Aside from boring and alienating them, a teacher who reads the rules on the first day can cause other problems. When new students join your class, you have to repeat the rules for their benefit, which will bore the other kids who have already heard fifty million rules. Or you could hand them a printed copy of your rules, which they may glance at before throwing it in the trash or stuffing it into their backpacks. You could ask the new students to stay after class, which will irritate them because they have better things to do and because they heard the rules yesterday from the other teachers. Or you could cross your fingers and hope they behave.

You may think I'm splitting hairs, but it has been my experience and the experience of many successful teachers that the first day of class sets the pace for the rest of the year. On day one concentrate on grabbing your students by their overactive brains. Get a good grip. There will be plenty of time to talk about rules later on. (Chapter Five includes suggestions for creating workable rules and discipline codes, and Chapter Four contains specific suggestions for making day one a success.)

PREPARE YOUR PAPERWORK

Your classroom is looking good and smells nice too. Your supplies are stowed safely away, and your student desks are arranged to give you easy access to each little darling who will soon be sitting there, looking to you for knowledge and inspiration. It's time to get your paperwork in order and put out the welcome mat.

Paperwork problems can overwhelm a teacher who isn't organized. You can do much to prevent those problems, improve your efficiency, and save hours of time if you design a workable file system. Your individual circumstances will guide you, but I would like to offer some suggestions for techniques that have served me well.

Place an In-Basket on Your Desk

Place an in-basket on your desk that is deep enough to hold at least one hundred sheets of paper or thirty student reports or file folders. Instruct students to place all items for you in the basket—not on your desk, your chair, or on top of the file cabinet. (If they have an item too large to fit into the basket, they must deliver it to you in person.) Also enforce a strict policy that makes it a classroom felony for a student to remove anything from the in-basket, including his or her own paperwork or folders. If students must retrieve something from the in-basket, they must ask you for assistance, in order to protect the privacy of other students and to avoid misplacing, disarranging, or losing important paperwork. At the end of each hour or class period, collect all student papers from your in-basket and stow them in the proper color-coded file folder until you have a chance to organize or grade them.

Create Daily Lesson Folders

Keep one brightly colored folder for each hour or subject with daily lesson plans, assignments to grade, graded papers, and personal notes for students. If you need to take papers home to grade, tuck them into this file folder (if you teach multiple classes or subjects, keep your file folders in a binder that you use only for this purpose). After you have graded papers at home, return them to the file. Add your lesson plans or notes for the next day, and you have everything in one place for easy access.

Prepare Your Own Emergency Plan

Accidents and illnesses happen, as do fires, earthquakes, and other disasters. Your school will have emergency procedures and instructions to follow during drills or evacuations. Place this information in a three-ring binder that has pockets to hold papers and a place to store a pen or pencil. Put a copy of your roll sheets in the binder, along with your own contact information (address, phone number, name and phone number of a relative or friend). When an emergency occurs or a practice drill is announced, grab your binder and lead your students to safety. And in the event that you are called away without notice, your supervisor can easily find information to contact your family or friends.

Prepare a Substitute Folder

Include a copy of your roll sheets and three full days of lesson plans for use if you have an unplanned absence. If you know you will be absent, you may choose to provide lesson plans that continue your present unit of study, with associated activities. But be aware that not all substitutes are created equal. Some of them will follow your instructions to the letter; others will do nothing or create their own lesson plans.

Once, when I became ill with the flu, I came into school one evening to write out detailed lesson plans for my remedial freshman English class, which was reading *Romeo and Juliet.* Reluctant readers, the students had agreed to read only because I promised they could watch the movie afterward. I provided the sub with page numbers, worksheets, journal-writing assignments, and a review worksheet. I specifically asked her not to show the movie until after the students had read the entire play. When I returned after three days, I found that the sub had ignored my lesson plans and shown the movie during her first day. During the subsequent two days, she held discussions and ignored the worksheets and journal assignments. When I filed a complaint about the sub, she countered by saying that I was "too control-ling" and that she should be allowed to design the lesson when she was subbing, al-though she had no teaching license and her major field of study was science, not English or literature. After that I created a series of independent lessons that would provide students with practice of important skills but did not necessarily coincide with our current unit. When I have an unfamiliar sub or if I am called away sud-denly, the students aren't thrown off track or bored by useless assignments.

While we're on the subject of subs, know that some schools permit teachers to re-quest certain subs. If you find a good sub, ask if you might have her phone number so that you can call and check her availability when you know you're going to be ab-sent. Having one or two regular subs can be a real benefit. Students enjoy seeing a familiar face, and they often behave better for somebody they like and trust. And you can relax, knowing that your students won't be wasting their time while you're away.

If you work with students who are not emotionally secure, they may act out while you are gone, even if they have an excellent sub. Instead of punishing those students severely on your return, hold a class discussion about the subject. Ask kids to describe their feelings and think about why they misbehave when you are gone. Remind them that their behavior is a reflection on you; you are very proud when they can behave well for a sub. Suggest some alternative positive behaviors for stu-dents to use if they feel stressed or upset about your absence. They might ask to go visit with a familiar counselor, coach, secretary, teacher, or administrator for a few minutes (you might want to discuss this with the adult staff members involved to prepare them). They could write you a note or make an entry in their journals. They could offer to help the sub by taking roll, erasing the boards, or passing out papers. Of course, if a particular student continues to behave disrespectfully after your discussions, the student will have to face some consequences. But try to make those consequences applicable to the behavior, such as a written apology to the sub, and not simply punishment.

Fill a Folder with Fun Lessons

Do a little research and find some quick, fun, entertaining or challenging lessons. Trivia quizzes, brain busters, riddles, word games, and IQ tests are big hits with stu-dents of all ages. When your students zip through a lesson faster than you expected, when they behave especially well, or when they do something to make you proud, take a few minutes at the end of the hour or day to reward them with a fun lesson. Every bookstore has a section of books with educational games and puzzles, or you can create your own. You can also find a lot of suggestions on the Internet or in the Appendix of this book.

Create a Makeup Work Folder

Buy an accordion-style folder with alphabetical divisions and write "Makeup Work" in large bold letters on both sides. If you teach more than one group, buy a separate accordion-style folder for each class. Whenever you distribute any paperwork or assignment, pencil in the last name of absent students on the assignment and place it in the folder under the appropriate letter. If you cover material in the textbook on that day, make a brief note of what you covered and make copies of the note for each absent student. When students return to class, their missing assignments will be readily available, saving you the time of searching for copies and explaining what they need to read to catch up. Elementary-level students may need help remembering to pick up the papers and may require help doing the assignments, but you should expect older students to pick up their assignments and get them done. Make clear that students are responsible for making up the work, although you will be happy to answer any questions they may have or suggest sources for information or assistance.

Fill out Library, Hall, and Bathroom Passes

Fill out the basic information (your room number, destination, any specific instructions) on library, hall, and bathroom passes. Don't sign the passes, and be sure to number them so that students can't steal them. Then keep the passes tucked or locked away in a folder with a simple tally sheet showing what numbers you have issued. When you need to send somebody out of the room, you won't have to waste so much time filling out the passes. Usually I have students fill in their names and the date, then I sign the pass. With this system, you don't have to stop teaching, locate a pass, and make everybody else wait while you fill it out and sign it. (Because some schools have elaborate policies concerning passes, we'll discuss this issue in more depth in Chapter Five.)

Copy Your Roll Sheets

Make two or three spare copies of your roll sheets as soon as you get them, and use them to create your own records for rewards, attendance, seating charts, teams for group projects, birthdays, field trips, fire drills, and other occasions for which you might need a list. I take a copy of my roll sheets home to use when I am creating lessons, such as vocabulary worksheets or quizzes, in order to use my students' names in sentences. They always perk up and smile when they read a sentence that contains their own or a classmate's name (be sure to check off names and use everybody's name at least once in order to avoid hurting feelings or giving the impression that you have favorites).

Buy Plastic Crates for Student Folders

This is my all-time favorite time saver and organizer. I buy a different color plastic file bin for each class I teach, and I label a file folder for each student in a particular class. For each class I use a separate color or folders cut on the same tab—all left one-third tabs, for example—so that I can easily identify folders and match them with the proper bin. If I can't find any colored file folders and I have to use all manila folders, I use a marker to draw a colored line across the tab, all red for one period, blue for another, and so on. (Note: at the start of the year, the folders will be slim, so you may elect to store two or three different groups in the same bin until the folders fatten up. Then you can transfer them to separate bins.)

Using my roll sheets, I lightly pencil in student names on the folder tabs, or I use adhesive labels so that I can reuse folders when students transfer into or out of my class. During the first days of school every term, I distribute the folders as students are taking their seats and doing their first work activity of the day. I quickly see who is absent and keep those absent students' folders on my lectern, where I can insert copies of any handouts or reading assignments for that period.

When I return their homework or assignments, students have the option of taking the graded papers home to show their parents or placing them in their folders. I always suggest that students keep important assignments, quizzes, and tests in their folders for future reference and as a record in case of report card questions. Some students take their paperwork home and keep their own records, but many students (and parents) are so disorganized that they will lose anything you give them. I place the paperwork of absent students in their file folders so that I don't have to carry them around or risk losing them. When students return, all of their graded assignments are waiting for them.

Personal folders help students learn to organize their work and make it easier for them to locate study materials prior to exams. Because the folders are personal, many students like to decorate them. I allow them to draw or write whatever they like on their folders, except for vulgar, obscene, hateful, or gang-related words and symbols. Some teachers prefer to prohibit decorating to create a more businesslike appearance.

Create Assignments for Rude People

If you teach people who are ten years or older, label a file folder "Assignments for Rude People." Fill this folder with five or six lessons that are challenging and pertinent to your subject matter. Meet with your librarian and let him or her know that you may send a student to work independently from time to time but that you do not expect the librarian tolerate any misbehavior. Fill out a library pass with everything except the date and student's name and write: "Rude Person Study Time" on the pass. Put your file where you can easily find it, and hope you won't have to use it.

If the day arrives when you have a student who repeatedly misbehaves just enough to trip your trigger but not badly enough to warrant a visit to the principal, if you have a sneaky student who repeatedly instigates bad behavior in other students, if you have identified a problem child ringleader but can't catch him or her in the act, if parents and principals can't seem to convince a child to act respectfully, and if your private discussions and warnings don't work, you have a rude person on your hands.

Don't argue or warn this rude student. Simply select the appropriate lesson from the folder, remove the other assignments, and hand him the Assignments for Rude People folder. Let the student see the label referring to him as rude. Even if he pretends to think it's funny, he will be pretending. Show the student the library pass and inform the student that he must return the signed pass and the completed assignment to you approximately one minute before the end of that class period. Explain that if he doesn't return at the end of the class period, you will be obligated to report the student as cutting and then the school's disciplinary system will take over. Walk the student to the door of your room, wave good-bye, and shut the door firmly.

When the student returns with the completed assignment, say, "Thank you," and tell him you hope he will decide to control his behavior so that he can remain with the class in the future. Most students will stop their disruptive behavior if they lose their audience, because they usually aren't capable of doing all their assignments independently. If you have a whiz kid who aces the assignments on his or her own, you have identified the root of the misbehavior—boredom—and you can take steps to create lessons that will challenge the student.

Note: if the student refuses to go to the library or won't accept the Assignments for Rude People folder, simply return the folder to your file cabinet and take out your Misbehavior folder. Fill in the student's name on the referral form, call security for an escort, and go to the nearest classroom to alert the teacher that you may need reinforcements. After security removes your student, return to your lesson without any further interruption or discussion with your remaining students. If they seem to be on the verge of an outbreak, look very slowly around the room and say, "Does anybody else need to leave?" My prediction is that nobody else will need to leave. If they do, repeat the procedure. (See Chapter Five for a more thorough discussion of disciplinary techniques.)

Prepare a Misbehavior Folder

Usually students wait until several days into the school year before they become truly disruptive. But sometimes you'll have an overachiever who will decide that the first few days of school would be prime time to act like a maniac. If a quick step out into the hallway for a talk isn't an option (if a student curses at you, touches or threatens you or other students, for example), you can remove the student who is out of control, lose the minimum amount of precious class time, and send a very clear message to the rest of your students that you will not tolerate outrageous behavior for even one minute in your classroom—*if* you have prepared a Misbehavior folder before the school term begins.

Fill out one or two disciplinary referral forms with as much information as you can, except for the date and the student's name. Where it asks you to describe the incident, write: "Student disrupted class, interrupted my teaching, and made it impossible for others to learn. I called security to escort the student to the principal's office. I will provide full details as soon as possible. I request a student-principal-teacher conference before the student returns to my classroom."

Place these partially completed forms into a folder labeled Misbehavior where they will be readily available at the first sign of serious disruption. The first time you pull out that folder, whip out the form, and send your obnoxious student packing, other students will get the message that you are prepared and serious about teaching. Your principal will require specific details, and you will have to follow up on the incident; but if you have a form prepared ahead of time, you will have provided enough information to remove the student from your classroom quickly, preventing more serious problems, and establishing your control without wasting time or losing face by engaging in a prolonged argument.

Get a Grip on Grades

Create a system for your paper grade book (keep a paper book for backup even if you use a computerized grading system because systems crash and some students are accomplished hackers). Don't write in your grade book during the first few days (or weeks if you work at a disorganized school). Instead, make a couple of copies of the first page of your grade book and use that to keep track of students' progress until after the administrative shuffling has ended and you have had the same students for a few weeks. Then enter the names in your grade book in alphabetical order. Enter the same names in the same order in your computerized grade book, so that student number one and student number fifteen are the same in each book. This will save you time later on.

With a little creativity, you can design a system so that your paper grade book functions as a record of attendance, participation, and extra effort, as well as a record of graded assignments. When students are absent, for example, you might outline the box for a specific graded assignment in red so that you can see at a glance which students were absent when you gave that assignment. (Some students will claim they were absent; if you don't mark it in your grade book, you will have to track down your attendance sheets and compare them to your grade book. You don't have time for such silliness.)

When absent students make up the missed assignment, you can enter the grade into the box, but you still have a record of absence. If the student doesn't turn in the assignment by the makeup deadline, you can enter a red zero to remind you and the student that the assignment was not completed by the deadline.

If you include a column in your grade book for extra credit and one for negative credit, you can add or subtract points for students who do extra work and for those who cause extra problems and stress when you are trying to teach. This is one way to reward students who cooperate and work hard but may not be geniuses. They can earn points every day for putting forth real effort and acting like decent people. Likewise, smart-mouth, disruptive whiz kids can earn negative points so that they don't walk away from your class with an A just for being intelligent, in spite of the havoc they may have wreaked among their peers who were struggling to learn while they were entertaining themselves. (I usually enter negative points in pencil so that if a student decides to grow up a bit and stop causing trouble, he or she can earn full credit for being brilliant.) I realize that some people object to such subjective grading, but I submit that all teachers are subjective to some extent and at least this method is honest and transparent.

Some teachers assign each student a number in the grade book (if you teach multiple classes, it's a good idea to use a combination of letters and numbers so that you avoid mixing up student papers from different classes). Instruct students to write their assigned numbers in the upper left- or right-hand corner of all papers they turn in. You can then place the student papers in order as you collect them and identify any missing numbers immediately. Read out the missing numbers to alert students that you do not have their papers, and place all the papers in a folder, making a note of the date and any missing numbers on the inside cover of the folder. When students turn in a late paper, make a checkmark and write the date, creating a record of all missing or late papers. This method prevents lost papers, avoids arguments about whether students turned in assignments, and makes it easier for you to enter grades or notations for missing assignments into the grade book. If you have a particularly argumentative group, you might consider stapling papers together after they are collected as proof that those papers were collected on time.

Grading is one area in which computers truly are worth the headaches they sometimes cause. Even if you have to buy the software yourself and borrow a computer, find a way to use computerized grading. Your investment will save you time, energy, and frustration. Entering the student information to get started can take hours, but once you have the data in the program, you can manipulate it to change the weight of specific assignments and tests, provide periodic status reports, and be prepared to produce report cards quickly and accurately.

Electronic grading has another advantage. Because you can print out reports for an entire class or for an individual, you can quickly see how well your students are doing as a group. You can adjust your teaching, review specific problem areas, or add additional graded assignments as needed. You can also show a student his or her individual progress. Students who skip assignments are often shocked to see just how much one grade can raise or lower their average. If a student has skipped two heavily weighted assignments, for example, you could show him what would happen to his grade if he had done the minimum amount of work and earned a C on one of those assignments. You can also print out interim progress reports to give fair warning to students who are in danger of earning poor grades, as well as an incentive to students who are working hard. Seeing their grades in print is a powerful motivator for most students.

Draft a Master Lesson Plan

Many schools require teachers to file lesson plans weekly or monthly. Even if lesson plans aren't required, effective teachers take a longer view and create a rough draft of their plans for the entire quarter, semester, and year. If you teach high school and have multiple preparation periods, then mapping out your lesson plans for the year is even more important because you will have more planning to accomplish during your precious preparation period. Working from a master schedule enables teachers to adjust their daily lesson plans as needed, to allow for variations in student progress, changes in required curriculum, standardized tests, weather emergencies, and so on. And sleeping at night is far easier when you don't have to worry about what you are going to do in the morning.

My preferred method is to make copies of a monthly calendar template so that I have one page per month. Then I consult the school calendar and mark every noninstructional day in red: holidays, teacher in-service days, midterm and final exam days, open house, and picture day. I also use red ink to block out days on which many students are likely to be absent or obsessed with some important social event such as homecoming, prom, baccalaureate, sports tournaments, college days, prearranged field trips, and so on. For those social event days, I plan a flexible lesson that will count for grade credit for students who are present but will not include essential information that absent students will need in order to complete future assignments or exams. And I do not require that absent students make up the missed work, if their absences are excused. I simply place an X on the wall chart to indicate that the assignment was done. Students don't receive or lose credit for the assignment; they earn an X that has no value. (I don't announce my plan to the class, because I don't want students to skip class, thinking that they won't be penalized for missing the assignment.)

Next I highlight quarter, semester, and final exam days in green ink. One week before each major exam, I back up and schedule a day or two for review of material that will be on the exam. Then I plan two days without homework following the exam so that I will have time to grade and return exams quickly. Now I have a rough idea of how many instructional days are available for the various units in my curriculum.

It's time to put away the pens and start using a pencil so that I can make changes later. On a separate sheet of paper, I make a list of all the elements I intend to teach during the year. Because I teach English, my list includes journal writing, informal essays, reports, research papers, poetry, short stories, plays, novels, literary analysis, grammar, parts of speech, spelling, vocabulary, analogies, and so on. I break my master list down further by assigning each element to a specific number of units to cover in each quarter.

Now that I have a rough outline of various units, I can figure out how much time to devote to a specific skill each day or week and how many weekly or monthly quizzes will be appropriate. Because some schools require a specific number of graded assignments during a given period, I can easily check to see that I will have enough.

How you divide your time is purely your choice, but in my experience students of all ages and abilities do better when practice exercises and quizzes take place on a regular schedule—vocabulary exercises every Tuesday morning, for example, with a quiz on Friday. Regularly scheduled activities will also help you create lesson plans when you are ill, overwhelmed, under stress, or exhausted. Likewise, having students begin each day with the same activity will improve behavior and help students settle down more quickly. You should post this beginning activity at the top of your daily agenda as a reminder, even though students will quickly learn the drill. Choose a calm, brief activity that will engage students immediately while you take roll and do necessary record keeping. Some good activities include reading independently, learning daily grammar tips, taking notes from selected pages in the text, completing a worksheet, writing in a journal, copying vocabulary words from the board and looking up definitions, writing a brief summary of the previous day's reading, thinking silently for five minutes about a controversial quotation or ethical question that you have posted on the board and that students will discuss at the end of the thinking period.

Design a Handout to Welcome Students

Design a one-page Welcome to My Class handout that includes a short course outline, truly important information, a few tips for success in your classroom, and an abbreviated overview of your most important rules and procedures. If you don't like the title "Welcome to My Class," try something more formal, such as "Course Outline and Objectives." (Note: please don't title your handout "Classroom Rules and Procedures." If you do, you will create a dynamic of teacher versus student from the start because so many students are resistant to rules of any kind.)

To give you one example, Exhibit 3.1 is the handout I use to welcome my high school English classes.

Exhibit 3.1. Handout: Welcome to My Class.

Welcome to Miss Johnson's English Class!

Course Outline and Objectives: This class is designed to improve your communications skills through reading, writing, vocabulary, and grammar exercises; group assignments; and individual projects. We will read a wide variety of literature. Assignments will include timed responses, journals, essays, research reports, and literary critiques.

The Rule: Respect yourself and other people. No insults based on ethnic background, skin color, native language, gender, sexual preference, religion, body shape, or body size will be tolerated. It is unfair to erase somebody's face. We all have the right to be treated with respect.

Standard Procedure: I expect you to be seated and ready to learn when the bell rings. Likewise, you should expect me to be ready to teach.

Attendance: My job is to make this class enjoyable and informative. I will never intentionally embarrass you. Your job is to come to class. Be there or be square.

Tardy: Don't you hate waiting for people? I do. Don't be rude. Be on time.

Study Materials: Imagine how you would feel if you made an appointment to have your car fixed and when you took it to the shop, the mechanic said, "Oh, gee. I forgot to bring my tools today. Sorry." Not cool. Bring your learning tools to school.

Homework: We won't have homework every night, but when we do, it's your job to do it—by yourself, using your own personal brain (it is perfectly acceptable to get help or share ideas with friends). If you have problems or questions, call me at 555-1212.

Makeup Work: When you return to class after any absence, it is your responsibility to check the makeup folder on my desk. You will have three days to complete the work. If you need more time, talk to me.

Discipline: I prefer to deal directly with you instead of calling your parents. You are responsible for your own behavior. You behave yourself, and I'll behave myself.

Fun: We will have the maximum amount of fun allowable by law. Please bring your sense of humor to class.

PREPARE YOURSELF

With your room and your paperwork organized and ready and your philosophy of teaching fresh in your mind, you can now focus on physically and mentally preparing yourself to grab your students by their brains when they walk into your classroom. Don't worry about feeling nervous. Almost all teachers get nervous before the start of a new semester or school year, even experienced teachers. (Sometimes the veteran teachers get more nervous than newbies because they know exactly what they are getting themselves into!) Don't panic. Most of the time, students will cooperate if they know exactly what you expect them to do. Therefore, you must know exactly what you expect them to do.

Plan Your Procedures

If you are ill-prepared and forced to create procedures as you go along, students will follow your example and create their own. So brainstorm every routine activity that will occur in your classroom, and establish a procedure for performing it. (Sit in your classroom as you brainstorm so that you will be reminded of physical obstacles or space limitations.) For example, how do you want students to request permission to do the following: use the bathroom, line up when the entire group needs to leave the room together, conduct themselves in the hallways, ask or answer a question during your lectures, turn in late assignments, request help during classroom activities? Make brief notes or use index cards to remind yourself of each procedure so that you can quickly teach it to your students. (You may have to repeat some procedures many times before students catch on, so it's a good idea to have written instructions to remind you to be consistent.)

Decide how and when you are going to teach your procedures. Some teachers like to teach all of their procedures as one lesson and add a short refresher course when it's time to implement a specific procedure. If you teach your students your procedure for walking to the library as a group, for example, but don't take them to the library until three weeks after school starts, many students will have forgotten what they are supposed to do. Some will forget the instant after you tell them, which is another good reason to write your procedures down. You can copy your procedure cards individually or as one list and distribute a copy to each student to keep in his or her folder as a reminder.

Design Your Discipline Code

Write down your discipline code. If it's too long or complicated to fit on an index card, you may find it difficult to communicate to students and even more difficult to enforce. When I first started teaching, I did the rule thing. Sometimes I created rules; sometimes I included students in their creation. But in every case for which I had a list of rules, I had to make a list of consequences and then a list of increasingly punitive consequences for the students who broke the rules. I had to figure out a system for keeping track of offenses, consequences, follow-up conferences, and referrals to the office. Quite often I found myself bending a rule because of special circumstances; for example, a boy missed school to attend his grandfather's funeral, so I broke my zero tolerance policy on late assignments and allowed him to turn in a project two days late. Other students then appealed for extensions based on their own "emergencies," putting me in the position of deciding which emergencies were important and which weren't. Everybody was upset and nobody was happy, including me.

After that incident I read more books on classroom management, but I couldn't find the perfect discipline plan. So I branched out into psychology books, as well as books devoted to salesmanship, leadership, and the art of persuasion. I tried different tactics with different groups and finally settled on one universal approach that has served me well with every group of students I've taught, from at-risk high school freshmen to university graduate students. After our welcome and get-to-know-you days, I lay out the ground rules for student conduct in my classroom. I make the following speech:

> You are individual people with individual lives and needs. And life presents surprises and obstacles to us all. So I am not going to create a set of rigid rules and then argue with you about enforcing them. I reserve the right to make judgments as needed in my classroom, taking into consideration several factors: the weight of a given assignment or exam, your own skills and attitudes, the amount of effort you expend in my class, how well you cooperate with me and other students, and so on. But I do have one rule that applies to every person in the room, including me, and it is absolutely unbreakable.
>
> The rule: respect yourself and everybody in this room—no put-downs of other people based on their race, religion, ethnic back-

ground, skin color, native language, gender, sexual preference, intelligence, body shape, or body size.

Those characteristics are not chosen by people; we are born with them. Yes, you can change your religion when you are an adult, but most children are required to accept their parents' religion; to criticize them for respecting their parents is wrong. Criticizing or insulting people for things that are beyond their control is not fair. It is not respectful, and I will not tolerate it in my classroom. You may comment on other people's behavior as long as you voice your observations in a respectful manner. If you believe somebody is being cruel or insensitive, for example, you may say, "I think your behavior is cruel" or "You are being really rude." You may not, however, call the person a stupid jerk or blame their bad behavior on their gender or skin color. Which brings me to the subject of prejudice.

There are many, many forms of prejudice, and most of us have our own opinions and ideas about the world. You are entitled to believe and think whatever you choose. You are not entitled, however, to express your opinions in a manner that may insult, degrade, embarrass, hurt, or humiliate other people. Prejudices are like underpants: most of us have them, but it's tacky to display them in public, especially among people we don't know well.

Students may laugh, but they get the message. I always ask if anybody believes my rule is unreasonable. Nobody ever has. And since I have started using my one-rule policy without a list of specific offenses and consequences, I have had far fewer discipline problems. Again the connection between expectation and reality proves true: I expect students to take responsibility for their behavior, and barring the occasional inevitable exception, they do.

Rehearse Your Warning Speech

If you can find a willing volunteer, it may be helpful to rehearse the warning speeches you will deliver to mildly disruptive or defiant students who may need a quick trip to the hallway outside your classroom for a brief one-way discussion. You will do the talking, saying something along the lines of "Your present behavior is not acceptable in my classroom. You have the right to fail my class, if that is really what you want to do. But you do *not* have the right to interrupt my teaching or somebody else's learning. And you do not have the right to waste my time trying to get me to argue with you over silly things that don't matter. So why don't you take a minute out here to consider your options. When you are ready, please come back and take your seat. Thank you."

(Some teachers prefer to have students return when they are ready, while others insist that students remain outside until the teacher decides it's time to return.)

Check Your Wardrobe

Make sure that you have at least a few changes of clothing that are comfortable, easy to launder, and somewhat attractive, because students have to look at you all day long every weekday. At various times during discussions of what makes an effective teacher, students have suggested that teachers pay more attention to their clothing. You don't have to be a fashion plate, but as one student put it when he was describing a teacher he did not like, "It's a drag to have to look at somebody who looks like they just keep all their clothes in a pile on the floor." When I mentioned that I often speak to new teachers, he said, "Tell them not to wear the same outfit every Monday. It's like having those stupid underpants with the days of the week on them. School is boring enough without having to look at the same shirt every single Monday of your life." That's one young man's opinion, for what it's worth.

I've already suggested comfortable shoes, but your feet are important enough that I'm going to repeat the suggestion. If you are twenty-one and still indestructible, your feet may not notice the stress, but most teachers welcome as much comfort as we can find when it comes to shoes. Sore heels and achy arches can really ruin your day.

Find a Friend

Make a reciprocal chill-out pact with a teacher whose room is near yours. (If you can't find a friendly teacher, find an administrator or counselor, but find somebody.) Occasionally you will have a student whose behavior doesn't warrant a referral to the office or an official warning but who nevertheless jangles your nerves beyond your breaking point. And, unfortunately, once in a while you may find yourself having a bad teaching day. Make an agreement with your ally that either of you may send a student to sit in the back of the other teacher's class for a short time, to allow you and the student a break from each other. And if you realize that you are about to slip over the edge, you may ask the teacher to supervise your classroom for a moment while you supervise your colleague's. You may not have to make use of your chill-out option, but if you need to, those few minutes can save the day with a minimum of fuss and paperwork.

Meet the Support Staff

Seek out and introduce yourself to the maintenance crew, the audiovisual and computer gurus, the attendance monitors, the detention coordinator, and the custodian who is responsible for your classroom. Also, take time for a quick chat with your school librarian, classroom aides, and all the many secretaries who keep your school running. Recognize that these are valuable people without whom your job would be much harder. Ask if they require specific things from you or if you can do things to make it easier for them to respond to your requests. Knowing your classroom custodian and treating him or her with respect is not only the right thing to do, but you will find that a good custodian can provide advice, assistance, and an occasional miracle during the school year. And incidentally, it makes an incredible difference when stress levels rise to walk into the school building and find yourself greeted with smiles and encouragement from the adults on staff.

Check Your Classroom

Sit at your desk in your classroom and take a good look. Make sure that everything is in place for the first day of school. Review your checklists and the index cards containing your procedures and discipline code; give your supplies and student folders a final inspection. Then turn off your teacher brain. Go home and be a regular human being.

Take a Break

Give yourself a break, even if it's only for a few hours the night before school starts. Go out to dinner, rent a video, take a long hot bath—do something that is not connected with teaching. You may be tempted to stay at school as long as your security office will allow, but if you spend the weeks before school planning and preparing and the few days before school arranging your room, shuffling roll sheets, grade books, curriculum outlines, textbooks, and file folders, you will need at least a short break if you expect to greet your students with a smile on the first day of school. You deserve the break, and they deserve the smile.

Exhibit 3.2 provides the short version of the three checklists to help you get ready.

Exhibit 3.2. Three Checklists.

Your Classroom

_____ 1. Sensory details

_____ 2. Seating arrangements

_____ 3. Supplies and storage

❑ Home base   ❑ Private files   ❑ Teacher desk   ❑ Student supplies

_____ 4. Student information

❑ In-basket   ❑ Agenda   ❑ Calendar   ❑ Student-supplies table

Your Paperwork

_____ 1. Place an in-basket on your desk.

_____ 2. Create daily lesson folders.

_____ 3. Create a personal emergency plan.

_____ 4. Prepare a substitute folder.

_____ 5. Fill a folder with fun lessons.

_____ 6. Create a makeup work folder.

_____ 7. Fill out library, hall, bathroom passes.

_____ 8. Copy roll sheets.

_____ 9. Buy plastic crates for student folders.

_____ 10. Create assignments for rude people.

_____ 11. Prepare a Misbehavior folder.

_____ 12. Copy blank page from grade book.

_____ 13. Draft a master lesson plan.

_____ 14. Design a welcome handout (make copies).

Yourself

_____ 1. Plan your procedures.

_____ 2. Design your discipline code.

_____ 3. Rehearse your warning speech.

_____ 4. Check your wardrobe.

_____ 5. Find a friend.

_____ 6. Meet your support staff.

_____ 7. Inspect your classroom.

_____ 8. Take a break.

Make the First Week of Class a First-Class Week

We all know what's supposed to happen on the first day of school. You take roll, cover the ground rules, and get on with the task of teaching. Perhaps your school district is extremely well organized; the weather and rush hour traffic cooperate; and everything goes according to your careful plan.

But for far too many teachers, what actually happens on day one is closer to this: the bell rings and students continue to trickle in, late because their parents had car trouble or got stuck in traffic or because the elementary school pupils decided they weren't going to school after all and Mom or Dad had to carry them to your classroom and spend five minutes peeling them off their bodies. A few high school students got lost in the labyrinth of hallways or spent ten minutes searching through their backpacks for their class schedules. Somebody in junior high is really, really sorry, but she has to use the restroom right this minute because she had a soda for breakfast; and some very small person throws up in the corner and cries because he is embarrassed and because school is very scary indeed.

Teachers are trained to carry on in the face of challenge, so you finally get everybody seated and listening. But the intercom interrupts your introductory remarks several times to announce changes in the bus schedule and remind students that free lunch tickets are available. Your students stop being scared and start to fidget. You hurry to begin explaining the rules and procedures for your classroom. Halfway through rule number one, somebody knocks on the door to explain that two students are in the wrong classroom. They should be in B103, not C103. You send them on their way and start again. You're on rule number two when a knock on the door interrupts, and you open the door to find a scared-looking girl who blushes and stammers that she thinks maybe perhaps somebody, um, told her she is supposed to be in your room. You hurry to your desk to retrieve your roll sheet and find that she is indeed listed. You direct her to an empty seat and call the class to attention. They respond reluctantly, and you resume your recitation. Another knock. This time it's a boy and a girl; neither child is blushing. They glare at you and thrust their schedule cards in your direction, as though it were your fault that the computer goofed and they won't be in the same first-period class with their best friends. Again you check your roll sheets, hoping the names of the two newcomers won't be there. But they are. And so it goes.

DAY ONE: START WITH A SMILE

You can do much to ensure that your first day goes well, regardless of accidents, delays, and interruptions, by putting the focus on your students and not yourself. Instead of starting with an activity that requires all your students to sit and listen to you, make a student activity the first item on your agenda. Choose an activity that is simple but engaging. For example, provide large index cards and markers and ask students to create a tent-style name card for their desks. This activity is good for difficult or very talkative groups, and you can learn a lot about students from the way they write their names on their cards. Big bold letters usually indicate an attention seeker who either has confidence or would like to. Tiny letters may indicate shyness or lack of self-esteem.

Other options include placing name cards or file folders labeled with students' names on the desks before they arrive and asking students to find their names and take their seats. You might give them a questionnaire or ask them to write a paragraph telling you what they hope to learn in your class and what their favorite and least favorite school subjects are. Remember that older students may have six or seven classes during one day and that several teachers may ask them to write, so keep your assignment short and easy. Your goal is to get to know your students' personalities and general abilities, not to intimidate, threaten, or bore them.

The specific activity you assign isn't as important as getting the students busy so that if you are interrupted, they can continue their task while you are momentarily distracted. In addition to capturing their attention, an introductory activity reduces the chances of misbehavior because students won't be bored and won't feel on the spot as they often do when they file into a quiet classroom and sit facing an unfamiliar teacher. A student-focused activity also allows you a chance to check out your students while they are otherwise engaged. You will immediately get a sense of which students are shy or unsure of themselves, which are gregarious and inclined to socialize, and which ones are reluctant to cooperate.

How you deliver instructions is very important. Remember, your students are going to form their opinions of you and your teaching style within the first few minutes of your first meeting. You will project a very different persona depending on whether you are seated at your desk, perched on a stool, roving about the room, or standing in the doorway. Students will respond to the pitch, volume, and tone of your voice; your choice of words; and especially your facial expression. How you choose to greet your group is up to you, but keep in mind that human beings are naturally inclined to respond to a genuine smile with a smile in return. Ignore those old farts who warned you not to smile until Christmas. There is a huge difference between being kind and being weak, and your students know that difference quite well. Also keep in mind that distance is important when you want to establish authority. If you stand behind your desk or podium, you will be placing a physical and psychological barrier between you and your students from the start—good for maintaining distance or creating a separation between you and your students but bad for developing rapport and creating an environment of mutual respect.

My recommendation is to rove around your room if you are confident and experienced in establishing control. If you are inexperienced, young, small in stature, or nervous, I would recommend standing in the doorway to your classroom or just outside the doorway as students enter. Smile, welcome each student to your classroom, and give very brief instructions for beginning that first activity. (Don't forget the visual learners: it's a good idea to write the instructions on the board as a reminder. And young or immature students will respond faster and better if you model the activity for them.)

Standing near the doorway has several advantages. First, it establishes that students are entering your territory as they cross the threshold to your classroom. Second, it sends a clear message that you are in charge of your territory and that you are allowing them to enter. This helps students understand that entering your classroom is a privilege and not a right. Third, your physical presence forces students to slow down and enter the room individually, which greatly reduces chattering and focuses their attention. One teacher, rather small and slim, said that he not only stands in the doorway but shakes the hand of each student who enters his room. He introduces himself by name and welcomes the students to his room. "They know right away that I am the boss and it is my classroom," he said, "but they don't feel threatened."

I like to begin with a questionnaire called "Getting to Know You" that I distribute as students are taking their seats. It gives me an opportunity to walk among them and get to know a bit about their personalities. (My version was designed for high school students, but you could easily adapt this for younger children by replacing or rewording some of the questions or doing this activity it as an oral exercise.)

This questionnaire may seem like a silly assignment to the students, but it accomplishes some serious objectives. First, it makes my students smile, which breaks the tension that often occurs when they are placed in a room with peers they don't know or don't like. Second, it occupies them while I check out their hair, clothing, jewelry, body language, and interactions with each other—things that give me clues to their economic backgrounds, social groupings, and so on. Third, their answers reveal quite a bit about their personalities and learning styles:

Item number three gives me a hint about the student's learning style—auditory, visual, or kinesthetic.

Some students can't think of a single good thing about themselves (number six), which alerts me to possible problems stemming from low self-esteem or lack of confidence.

Students who select d as their answer for question number nine (reading) may have reading problems, scotopic sensitivity syndrome, or dyslexia.

Responses to number ten often indicate personal problems or concerns.

You don't have to be a psychologist to recognize the anger in the response I received from one boy. He wrote that he'd like to be invisible so that he could kill his

Exhibit 4.1. Questionnaire: Getting to Know You.

Name _____ Class Period _____

Instructions: Fill in the blank or circle the best answer for you. This is not a graded exercise.

1. My favorite sport or game to watch or play is _____.

2. There are a lot of things I would do for $1,000,000. But one thing
   I'd never do is _____.

3. In my free time, I would rather
   a. Watch a movie
   b. Listen to good music
   c. Play a sport or game
   d. Read a book or magazine

4. If a wizard bopped me with a magic wand and said he was going to
   change me into an animal, I'd want to be a/an: _____.

5. I'd choose to be that animal because: _____
   _____.

6. The best thing about me is: _____.

7. If I had to choose just one, I'd rather be
   a. Good-looking
   b. Popular
   c. Smart
   d. Talented

8. Usually, my homework habit is this:
   a. I do my it and get it over with.
   b. I put if off until the last minute.
   c. I sometimes forget all about homework.
   d. I just ignore it.
   e. If I don't have time, I copy off my friends.

9. I'd rather
   a. Read silently
   b. Read out loud
   c. Listen to someone read
   d. Do just about anything *except* read

10. If I could be invisible for one day, I'd: _____
    _____.

parents without getting caught. I interpreted his response as a joke, an attempt to shock me, or a cry for help. As it turned out, it was a cry for help. He continued to write about his family in his journal and eventually agreed to talk to a counselor, who helped him learn to cope with his stressful and difficult life.

While your students complete their first activity, you can take roll and handle any unforeseen tasks that may arise. Now it's time for you to greet your class. But don't distribute your Welcome to My Class handout yet. Talk to them first. Walk around a little. Let them have an opportunity to stare at you without appearing to be rude. Tell them how much you look forward to working with them. Tell them how much your like your subject (or grade level) and why you chose to teach it. Tell them what they are going to learn during this school term, but don't go into great detail about what you will cover during the year. Keep your introduction short and simple.

GRAB YOUR STUDENTS BY THEIR BRAINS

It's time to grab your students by their brains. They expect you to go over your rules and perhaps discuss the consequences for a variety of misbehaviors. Your school administration may even require you to discuss your rules or the school's rules during the first day. This is one time when I would risk ignoring those instructions because students already know how to behave. Even in the unlikely case that they haven't been to school before, their parents or other adults have repeatedly told them to sit down, be quiet, stop hitting or teasing each other, mind their language, and act polite in public. So I hold off on talking about rules until the second, third, or fourth day of school. I usually say something like "We are supposed to go over the rules and regulations today, but I would like to save that for later this week because right now I'd like us to get to know each other." Then I do something to grab their attention. I entertain them with a slide show or a film excerpt, shock them with statistics about things that affect their lives, tempt them with a word puzzle, challenge them with a difficult question, or inspire them with a motivational pep talk. I do anything except what they expect me to do, which is talk about rules, regulations, course requirements, objectives, standard procedures, and zzzzzzzzzzz.

Scholarly teachers can pass out copies of a recent newspaper editorial on a topic that is related to the subject you teach. Ask your students to read the editorial and jot down their responses in one or two brief paragraphs. This quick assignment will give you a lot of information about your students' academic ability: reading rates, reading comprehension, and writing skills. It will also give you information about their personalities: their confidence in expressing their own ideas, their attitudes and opinions, their willingness to cooperate with your requests.

If you're an English or drama teacher, or a ham, recite Hamlet's "to be or not to be" soliloquy and ask your students what it means. Music teachers, English teachers, or social studies teachers might quote a pop or rap song and ask students what they think of the lyrics. A history teacher might ask students to write down a list of the three most important inventions that humans ever created. In art class ask students to sketch their self-portraits as they look now or as they think they will look when they are seventy years old.

If you teach younger children, get them involved with a game, word puzzle, song, or art activity. Make sure they understand that the activity is not for a grade, but is meant to warm up their brains and help you get to know them.

STOP THE TEACHER-VS.-STUDENT ATTITIDE IN ITS TRACKS

There is an old navy saying, "Kick butt first, take names later." Boot camp instructors use that approach to keep new recruits on their toes and to quickly establish who is in control. I use a modified, gentler version of that boot camp strategy, but my purpose is the same: I want my students to understand immediately that they are welcome in my classroom but that it is *my* classroom and I am in charge. Also, I want to establish an environment in my classroom wherein students are working with me and not against me. I do not allow students to manipulate me into a teacher-versus-student stance. Instead, I try to show them that we are both on the same side, that we will work together to tackle the curriculum and have as much fun as possible while doing so.

Depending on your personality and philosophy, you may choose to do something entirely different from what I do. What you do isn't as important as whether it works. But until you have students on your side, you can't teach them anything; you will be too busy trying to establish discipline and enforce your rules.

Getting students on your side isn't that hard. I have yet to meet a child who wanted to be a failure or who wanted to be disliked. Those things aren't natural. But many children, especially teenagers, act obnoxious and unlovable when they are afraid, and children are afraid of so many things. In school they have two particular fears: that people won't like them and that they won't be able to pass your class. Even smart kids worry about those two things, so I address their fears in my welcome. My speech goes something like this:

Welcome to my classroom. My name is Miss Johnson, and I'm very happy to have you in my class because I like teaching school. I want to help you become more effective students, which will help you be successful people. I'm not here to pick on you or try to flunk or boss you around. I promise not to embarrass you or humiliate you in my class. But I will expect you to think. If anyone dies from overthinking, I will take full responsibility for your death. Now how many people would rather go to the dentist than read out loud? Raise your hands please.

There are always hands. So I say,

Relax. You never have to read out loud in my class if you don't want to, so quit worrying about that right now. I don't want you to hate coming to my classroom. I want you to enjoy reading and writing and discussing the books and stories and essays we're going to read this year. I want you to learn to analyze other people's ideas, compare different ideas, and express your own ideas in an intelligent and articulate way. The more command you have of your language skills, the more successful you will be in school, in your work, and in your personal life—especially your love life.

They giggle. They think I'm joking, but I'm not. I explain:

I'm serious. Think about it. We use words to get many of the things we want in life. Of course, you use words to answer questions in school. But you also use words to ask somebody for a date. Or to explain to somebody why you don't want to take drugs or take off your clothes. Or to convince your parents to let you shave your head or borrow their car. And later on you'll use words to make your future mother-in-law like you—and if you don't think that's important, you're in for a big surprise.

And speaking of surprises, it may surprise you to learn that everybody starts my class with an A. Whether you keep the A or not is up to you, but I will do my best to help you keep it. And I promise you that if you come to class regularly, cooperate with me, and work hard, you will pass this class.

But before we start talking about what we're going to do this term and all the rules and regulations and all that other official stuff, we have something very important to do. I am going to learn everybody's name right now. You are not just numbers to me. Each one of you is a special and unique person. I already took attendance, but I'm going to go over the roll sheet now, and I want you to raise your hand when I call your name. Please correct me if I mispronounce it, and let me know if you prefer to be called by a nickname.

I can't count the number of students who have thanked me for learning to say their names correctly or allowing them to use a nickname because they have been teased unmercifully about their given names.

As I call each name, I take a moment to look at the student who responds, to give my brain time to match the face with the name. Then I go down the list once more. This time I try to identify the students before I call their names. This repetition doesn't bore them, because they are interested in knowing the other students' names.

Next I pass out 3-by-5-inch index cards (larger cards work just as well) and ask students to provide some information. (I use a different color card for each class so that I can easily identify where a card belongs, and I can take that group's cards home with me for phone calls or parent communication activities.) Because so many kids are visual learners, I write the information I'm asking for on the board:

Name:

Full address:

Phone number:

Birthday:

Name of parent/guardian:

Student ID #:

Note: be sure to keep some blank cards on hand for students who transfer into your class later, so you can add them to your files.

THE CARD TRICK

As my students fill out their index cards, I write the names of any absent students on blank cards for them to fill out if and when they show up. Then I walk around the room, between the aisles, with my roll sheet in hand. I mentally test myself to see whether I can remember the students' names. If I get stuck, I sneak a peek over students' shoulders to check the names on their cards. When they finish filling out the information I requested, I ask them to turn the card over and write a little bit more on the back of the card.

I explain:

> I want you to tell me anything I need to know to be a good teacher for you. If you have dyslexia or a speech problem or epilepsy or just hate reading, let me know. If you have a job, I'd like to know where you work. If there is something special you'd like to do in this class, let me know. And something very important: most of my phone calls home will be about good things because I'd rather brag about you than complain, but once in a while I may have to contact your parent or guardian. I had one of those fathers who would smack me in the teeth if I got in trouble in school, even if I was innocent. If you have one of those adults in your family, just give me a heads-up. I don't need the details. Just give me the name of an adult you want me to contact.
>
> And speaking of trouble, there is something else you need to know. If I have a problem with you in my class, I am going to call you first, not your parents. You're big boys and girls, and you are responsible for the things you say and do. I'm sure your parents have taught you how to act right, so I expect you to act right. If we need to talk about the way you act, I will call you. I want your real phone number on the card, not the number of the local pizza delivery, so I can call you if we need to talk. If you and I can't settle things, then I'll have to call your parents or guardians, but I'd prefer to work things out between you and me.

I give the students a few minutes to make the notes on the back of their cards (and for me to memorize more names), then I collect the cards. Instead of letting them pass the cards to me, I walk down the aisles and take each card individually. This serves two purposes: it brings me closer to them, which makes them nervous and more likely to behave, and it gives me another chance to match each name with the student's face. As I accept each card, I say, "Thank you," and repeat the student's name aloud. Once I have collected them all, I go to the front of the room and flip through them quickly, mentally testing myself. If I can't identify a particular name, I ask the student to raise his or her hand. Then it's time for the first test of the school term.

THE FIRST TEST IS ON ME

After a quick look at their index cards, I tell the class it's time for our first test. Invariably, they gasp and groan and mumble.

"Relax," I say, "this test is for me. I am going to go down the roll sheet and see if I have learned everybody's names. If I get them all right, I win. If I miss one name, you all get an automatic A on your first test, and you don't even have to lift a writing utensil."

Of course, I have no test prepared for them, but they don't know that. And I have grabbed them. Even the kids who are too cool for school are intrigued. They are certain that I will make a mistake, and they will receive that freebie A. Sometimes a sharp student asks what I will win if I remember all the names correctly. My response, "I win everything," delights them. They can hardly stand the excitement as I work my way down the roll sheet, identifying them one at a time. (If you decide to try this, and your first activity was making name cards, be sure to have kids turn their cards facedown so that no one can accuse you of cheating.)

So far I have managed to pass the name test every time. Usually somebody asks me how I can do it. I love when they ask that, because I love to tell them, "I remember your names because you are important to me as people. When I look at you, I see you, and I care about you." Even if nobody asks, I usually tell them that because it's true and I want them to know. I don't care whether they act cool and pretend they aren't impressed. I know that they are secretly thrilled to be considered so important. Who wouldn't be?

Sometimes I forget half the names as soon as one group of students leaves my room, but they don't know that and it doesn't matter. I have another chance to relearn their names the next day. When I do make a mistake and forget a name, as I know I will someday, it won't be a disaster. The students will be delighted at earning a freebie A and even more delighted at having caught a teacher making a mistake. It will be a good lesson for them to see that adults make mistakes too, and yet the world goes on.

You may be thinking, *What a waste of time! My job is to teach, not to show off my memorization skills.* I would argue that you will be able to teach much more effectively (and much faster) if you take the time to know your students before you begin your lessons. Names are much more than words; they represent us. In many cases children come to school empty-handed. All they have to bring with them are their names.

Or perhaps you're thinking, *But I could never learn a hundred names in one day!* If that's the case, and you haven't already done so, give your students sheets of 8-by-10-inch construction paper and pass around a few felt-tip markers. Ask them to print their first names in letters large enough for you to see from across the room and then fold the papers in half to make tent-style name cards that will stand up on their desks. Tell them that you have a terrible memory but that it's important to you to learn their names. They may act as though they don't care, but they do.

Spending a little while learning student names is worth your time and effort because it pays off. First, it demonstrates that you care about your students enough to be willing to take the time to get to know them. Second, people are much more apt to misbehave if they are anonymous members of a crowd. If you say, "You boys in the back, settle down now," or "You girls stop that giggling this instant," the boys are likely to go on punching each other's arms and the girls may put their hands over their mouths and go right on giggling. But if you say, "Jimmy Saunders, please keep your hands on your own desk, thank you very much," or "Shamica Abdul-Haqq, please be quiet so the others can hear me, thank you," Jimmy and Shamica are much more likely to cooperate.

Learning everybody's name sometimes takes the entire period if I have a large class. When that happens, I don't try to squeeze in any other activities. Just before the bell rings, I say, "It has been a distinct pleasure being your teacher today. I look forward to the next opportunity." Then I stand in the doorway and smile as my students file out. I wave and drawl, "Y'all come back now." Some of them laugh and wave; others roll their eyes and shake their heads at my silliness. But they leave my room smiling, and a group of laughing children is a lovely sight.

BE PREPARED FOR "TEST THE TEACHER"

So many factors affect student behavior that it's impossible to predict how students will respond to you. Your students may begin to test your tolerance during the first few minutes of the first day of class. A couple of kids seated farthest away from you may begin to pass notes or talk loudly while you're addressing the class. Some student may sit directly in front of you and start writing his name on his desktop. Somebody else may get up and boldly stroll across the room to talk to a friend.

What will you do if those things happen? Your reaction will set the tone for the rest of the school year. Remember, you are still establishing your teacher persona.

Don't let students draw you into a confrontation over trivial misbehavior, or they will all realize that they can distract you at any time they choose. Of course, you have to respond to their challenges, but you don't have to let them dictate your behavior. They expect you to yell at them, send them to the office, threaten to call their parents, or ignore them. So do something different from what they expect. For example, freeze in place and stare at the student, wide-eyed. Hold that pose for as long as you can (or for as long as the other students stay quiet, awaiting the outcome). If the student stops the misbehavior, say, "Thank you so much" and carry on. If the student continues, walk briskly to the door, open it, and say, "Please step outside."

If the student steps outside, you have several options, from having a quick chat and a handshake to sending the student to the office. By taking your confrontation outside, you have deprived the student of his audience, and usually that is enough to end the incident and establish your authority. You have also shown everybody in the room that they cannot draw you into a silly argument for their own amusement.

If the student refuses to step outside, call security from your phone or a neighboring classroom and get the student out of your room. Then continue with your agenda as planned. Don't let one or two rotten apples ruin your appetite for teaching. Remember your basic psychology: in a given group, the odds are good that at least one strong personality will challenge the leader just to see how the leader responds. If the leader demonstrates self-control, confidence, and courage, the challenger will usually back down—if given the opportunity to back down without losing face.

Don't take student misbehavior personally, especially at the start of a new school year or term. Children act in unacceptable ways for a lot of reasons, but you are very probably not the reason. Often, when students express anger, even if they express it in your direction, you aren't the real target. Here are just a few examples of student misbehavior in my own classes, along with the reasons why the students misbehaved. I learned those reasons because I didn't react by automatically sending those students to the office; instead, I made them sit down and talk to me or write an explanation for their behavior in their journals.

- A boy leaped out of his seat, overturned his desk, and started shouting and shaking his fists, then ran out of the room. He refused to explain his behavior, but one of his friends told me in confidence that a girl had been sitting across from the boy, crossing and uncrossing her legs seductively while staring directly at the boy, and he wanted out of the room because he was embarrassed and physically uncomfortable.

• A girl jumped up and hit the boy seated next to her, then refused to come out into the hallway to explain her behavior. He told me to forget about it. Thinking that perhaps the boy had taunted her, I told her to sit down and behave herself. Her response was to hit a different boy in the head. I saw no choice but to call the office and ask somebody to come escort the girl out of my room. Later the girl confided that she had wanted to be sent home from school that day because she had to make a bowel movement and was afraid she would be assaulted in the school bathroom (older girls had twice assaulted her in the restroom).

• A boy threw a dictionary at my head. (If you read *My Posse Don't Do Homework,* you'll recognize Emilio.) He wanted out of my classroom because he couldn't read; he was afraid I would find out his secret and embarrass him in front of the class.

• A girl walked into my classroom, took one look at me, and flopped down into a seat with bad attitude scrawled across her face. She refused to do anything I asked her, except to leave my room. After several visits to the counselor's office, the girl explained that her parents were recently divorced and she had been sent to live with her father and stepmother, a woman she detested. Unfortunately, I looked very much like her stepmother, and it upset her to be around me. (After I told the girl I understood her situation and offered to request reassignment to another teacher's class, she agreed to overlook my appearance and stay in my classroom.)

I could go on, but you get the picture. Don't take your students' behavior personally, especially when they don't know you well enough to hate you. Don't assume that every challenge to your authority is an intentional sign of disrespect. Unless a student insults you specifically and personally, assume that it is your status as teacher, adult, or authority figure that is the target of the disrespect. Continue to demonstrate the kind of respect you want your students to show to you— and themselves.

EMERGENCY DISCIPLINE DISASTER PLAN

We'll discuss discipline more thoroughly in Chapter Five, but during the first days of school, it's best to have an emergency plan ready, because sometimes individual personalities and circumstances combine to create a combustible classroom. If you have seriously troubled or unusually aggressive students, they may make it impossible for you to start the school year with a smile, as you had planned. Sometimes a handful of students is enough to ruin your entire master plan. If that happens, don't panic. Just switch to emergency mode.

1. Identify the outcasts and bullies in your classroom—both need your quick and professional attention. If you have outcasts, be alert for things that you can suggest to help them fit in. If you detect bullies, alert administration immediately and hold private discussions with students to find out whether bullying stems from insecurity (most common) or actual nasty nature. Tell insecure bullies that you will help them develop true self-confidence and strength of character so that they won't have to feel compelled to pick on people. Tread lightly but firmly with true nasty bullies (there's a very good chance they have true nasty bully parents). Explain that it's very important to you to do a good job as a teacher and that students feel comfortable to express themselves in your classroom but that you won't accept or tolerate insults, threats, and fighting.

2. Create a seating chart. Take a spare roll sheet, cut out student names, and shuffle them around on your seating chart until you are satisfied that you have a workable plan. Meet students at the door the following day and direct them to their new seats. If they complain, tell them they can talk to you about it after school—not during or after class because you want to take the time to really hear their comments and consider them. Most students will shut up. If they do come to see you after school, they are serious, so listen to them and try to accommodate their requests. Tell the class that at all times you reserve the right to change the plan as you see fit.

3. Deal with the disrupters. At the first sign of disrespect, disruption, or bullying, stop whatever you are doing and ask the loudest or most disruptive student to step outside the classroom and wait for you. If the student refuses to leave, call security to remove the student from your room. Do not argue or yell at the student. Go to your Misbehavior folder (the one that contains referral forms that are partially completed). Take out one of the forms and fill in the student's name, the date, and time. When security arrives, give them the referral form and explain that the student disrupted your teaching and refused to step outside for a talk. Ask security to escort the student to the principal's office. Let the student and the administration handle the incident. If you must file a report, simply say that you asked the disruptive student to step outside, he or she refused, and you concluded that the student needed to have a conference with the principal. (If the student takes off before security arrives, add a statement to that effect and give the referral form to the

security person.) Return to your classroom and resume your lesson. Do not say anything about the incident. Students will probably settle down. If more students act out, choose the loudest one and repeat the same procedure. You may have to send several students to the office, but unless you have a truly unusual group of students, you will find that after you have sent two or three students on their way to the office, the others will be much more inclined to cooperate. At the end of that instructional period, say, "Thank you for your cooperation and good behavior. I appreciate it very much."

If the student causing the disruption does step outside, step outside as well and close the door behind you. Remind the student that if he or she leaves the immediate area outside your door, you will be required by law to report the absence, because you are legally responsible for students' safety and well-being. Say nothing else. Go back into your room. Make eye contact with students who are still in the room. Do not smile. Go to your desk and log the student's name, date, and time inside the front cover of your Misbehavior folder for future reference. Tell the remaining students exactly what you expect them to do during the next five to ten minutes. Step outside and deliver a serious warning speech to the student (practice this speech, if necessary, so you will know it by heart). Tell the student you will give him or her time to think about which behavior to choose, because the consequences will depend on that choice. Remind the student that you do not want to involve him or her in the disciplinary system but that whether that happens is not your choice to make. Go back into the classroom and continue teaching.

If you have time before the instructional period ends, make sure that all students are on task and go back out into the hall. Ask the student if he or she has decided how to handle the situation. If the student apologizes, accept the apology. Say you are proud of the mature approach and say, "Thank you." Then ask the student whether he or she will promise not to interrupt your teaching or the learning of other students. Extend your hand to shake to seal this agreement. If the student shakes hands, open the door, smile, and usher the student back into the room. Continue teaching as though nothing had happened. Don't create additional publicity for misbehavior. Move past it quickly.

If the student refuses to shake your hand, don't say anything, just leave him or her in the hallway and go back into the classroom. Leave the student outside until the bell rings. Before the other students leave your room, say, "Thank you for your cooperation and good behavior. I appreciate it very much. I take my job seriously.

I want to help you be successful students. I will not allow anybody to stop me from teaching or prevent you from learning. I look forward to seeing you tomorrow."

4. If you do not have the support of your administration or security personnel, you can still respond strongly to determined miscreants. Find a librarian, counselor, coach, or supportive teacher who will agree to provide a supervised environment for your defiant student. Don't discuss the plan with the student. Simply hand the student a signed pass and a folder of assignments. Instruct him or her to report to the designated area, complete the assignments, and return the folder and signed pass to you at the end of the class period. If the student does not report to the area or does not return the materials to you, report the student as truant and prepare the necessary reports and referrals. Continue this procedure until the student requests permission to rejoin your class. At this time restate your expectations and welcome the student back. (Note: one teacher used this method and was surprised to find that the student asked to continue working independently in the library, where he didn't have so many distractions and lacked an audience to encourage his misbehavior. He didn't disrupt other students at the library, so the librarian agreed to allow him to work there except during special circumstances. On those days he worked at a desk in the back of a nearby teacher's classroom.)

THE REST OF WEEK ONE

Depending on your circumstances, you will want to schedule other appropriate activities for the first week of school. Of course, you will have your own agenda, but I would like to suggest eight essential activities that may help you create a dynamic classroom environment and also help you develop a good rapport with your students:

- Introduce your students to each other.
- Teach your procedure for oral responses.
- Find out what your students already know.
- Distribute your welcome handout and student folders.
- Delegate some authority.
- Demonstrate the power of choice.
- Help your students understand themselves.
- Teach your students to think about thinking.

Introduce Your Students to Each Other

Students are much more likely to treat each other well if they know each other's names, but many of the popular games designed to help people get acquainted are more effective with small children and adults than they are with older elementary, middle, and secondary school students. Why? Little kids are usually too innocent to be intentionally cruel, and adults are usually too polite or too concerned with earning a passing grade to insult each other. But preteens and adolescents are experts at humiliating and tormenting each other. Another consideration, which breaks my heart, is that many children are involved in or targets of gangs. What may seem to you to be a simple game designed to give students a chance to become acquainted may create an uncomfortable or dangerous situation for some of them. I would not recommend pairing students or forming small groups until you know the students in a given class well enough to be sure that your grouping won't cause problems.

One of the most popular introductory games in school (and college) is student interviews. You've probably played this game more than once. The instructor asks students to pair off and interview each other, then introduce their partners to the class. This exercise appeals to teachers because it's quick and simple. But for many students, this activity is an exercise in embarrassment and agony. Here are just a few reasons why so many students dread those peer interviews:

- Unless the teacher assigns pairs, a few students are always left out—nobody wants to be their partner. They feel rejected and unlikable. If the teacher forces people to join them, they feel even worse.
- Some students are so shy that having to speak in front of the class is a major trauma, especially on the first day. Children are quick to pick up on weaknesses such as lisps, accents, stutters, and blushing.
- Preadolescence and puberty cause all kinds of physical situations that embarrass children: budding breasts, acne, sudden voice changes, random facial hair, uncontrollable physical responses to stimuli. Sometimes the worst thing teachers can do to students is make them the center of attention.
- Poverty, religious rules, or strict parents may force a child to dress differently from the norm. Their clothing may embarrass them or create situations in which classmates ask them questions that they would prefer not to answer in public.

Don't abandon the idea of using a game to allow your students to get acquainted. A number of games don't require students to address the class or stand in front of the group. One of my college professors used a game that worked very well for adults, and I had great success when I adopted her game for use with my high school students.

The Adjective Game

1. Ask your students to think of an adjective to describe themselves at the moment. (You may have to remind them what an adjective is. I usually give a few alliterative examples, such as Rapping Robert, Talented Tiffany, or Friendly Freddy, and a few amusing examples, such as Hungry Sam or Melodious Ivan.)

2. Beginning in one corner of the room, ask the first student to say his or her name and adjective. Ask the second student, and so on, until you reach five. Stop there.

3. Stand near or point to the first student. Ask the class, "Who's this?" They will call out the name and adjective. Move to the second student and ask, "Who's this?" Continue asking until you have repeated the first five names.

4. Repeat the same procedure, stopping after each five names to begin back at your original number one. When you reach the last student, go back to the first student again and repeat every name.

5. This step is optional, but it's a big hit with my classes. As the students give their names and adjectives, I jot them down on a numbered list. Now I instruct the students to get a pen and paper and number the sheet from one to thirty (or however many students are in the class). Reading from my list in random order, I give an adjective. The students try to write the correct name to match the adjective. (I make a small numbered notation so I will remember the random order of the names in the "test.") When I have read all the adjectives and the students have listed all the names, I quickly go over the list, giving the correct names. Then I ask to see the hands of people who correctly remembered all the names, who missed one, who missed two, and so on. I award boxes of animal crackers or spiffy pencils to the students who correctly identify the most names.

Aside from being fun and giving the students a chance to learn each other's names and catch a glimpse into their personalities, this game also gives me important information. The students who remember the most names are the auditory learners in your group, the ones who will learn most quickly from oral instruction and who probably will do the most talking during class because they need to hear themselves speak in order to learn.

Don't be put off by kids who make faces and shake their heads at your silliness. If they have enough sense of humor to laugh at you, they'll probably go along with the game. But if you have a truly tough class, as I have had, and you see that the ringleaders are going to ruin the game or refuse to play, you'll have to make some quick choices. You can ignore the party poopers and play with the kids who cooperate, which sends the message that students who cooperate are going to get more attention from you than the ones who don't—not a bad message. You can ask the nonparticipants to step outside until the rest of you are finished, which is risky because they may refuse to go; this spells success in their goal of getting you to abandon your plans and fight with them—not a good precedent to set. You can stop the game without explanation and move on to the next item on your agenda, preferably a challenging worksheet or reading assignment, which might be a good choice because you will have made it clear to everybody that if they don't want to play, you have plenty of work for them to do—another good message. Trust your instincts.

Teach Your Procedure for Oral Responses

Even if you plan to teach a lesson on procedures, now is the time to teach your procedures for answering questions in your class. There are endless variations on the theme of student responses, but students have three basic options:

- Students must always raise their hands before speaking and cannot interrupt you or each other.
- Students may spontaneously respond to your questions or to each other's comments.
- Everybody, including you, must wait for a specific period of time (I'd suggest thirty seconds to two minutes) before responding. During the thinking time, they jot down their ideas.

Some of us believe we want students to raise their hands before speaking, until we start teaching. Then we realize that sometimes we want students to speak out quickly, such as during brainstorming sessions or when we are trying to generate enthusiasm or excitement about an idea or activity. During other activities, especially exercises that involve complex or abstract concepts, we might want students to take two full minutes to consider any question before making a response. Even if you opt not to use this method, I would recommend trying it as an experiment. If you allow time for students who process information more slowly and for your quick responders to consider their comments before speaking, you will find that the complexity and intellectual level of student responses rises and that you will hear from students who normally don't volunteer an answer.

If you begin with just one hand-raising option and teach that as your standard procedure, students will soon learn to respond as you have taught them. If you then decide you want them to respond in a different manner, they may not be able to make the switch. Therefore, I would recommend teaching all three methods, using a variety of exercises, and then announcing which method you expect students to use as you begin any new activity. One easy way to alert students (and remind them) is to make three posters:

Figure 4.1. Three Procedures for Oral Responses.

If you are creative, you might add illustrations; or ask an artistic student to make the posters. Then, when you begin an activity, prop the appropriate poster against the board or tack it to a wall where everybody can see it. For younger children, you might turn this into a fun project: students can make the three posters and store them in their desks so that they can put the appropriate poster on their desktops during a given activity.

I'd like to back up here for a moment and revisit the topic of silent thinking time. A psychologist who works with students who have learning disabilities shared an experience with me that changed my attitude about time. A teenaged boy came to the psychologist's treatment center and asked the psychologist to give him an IQ test so he could prove to his father that he wasn't retarded, as the school claimed he was. The psychologist administered a standard IQ test under normal conditions and the boy earned a very low score. He insisted that the score was incorrect and asked to be retested. The second time, the psychologist allowed the boy to take as much time as he needed to answer the questions. He spent more than triple the amount of time normally allowed—but the second time he scored in the genius category!

After hearing that story, I wondered how many little geniuses had been sitting in my classroom feeling stupid because I didn't give them sufficient time to process information. I instituted a new policy that required a mandatory thinking period before answering questions, except during very informal discussions, and the results were amazing. Students who normally didn't respond began raising their hands, and their thoughtful comments inspired deeper thinking from the quick thinkers. My own thought process improved, as well.

You may have to work your way up to a full minute of silence before students speak out. Sometimes even teachers find it hard to be quiet for thirty seconds. Most of us have been programmed to respond quickly, and faster thinkers have been rewarded for raising their hands immediately. Unfortunately, slower thinkers may have better ideas, but most have learned not to bother thinking because they rarely get a chance to share their ideas. In order to give everybody a chance to think more deeply, try establishing a rule that nobody, including you, can respond before the allotted thinking time elapses. Students are very receptive to this idea, especially if you allow them to take turns being the official timer.

Find Out What Your Students Already Know

Give the counselors a day or two to straighten out student schedules before you distribute your one-page welcome handout. During those two days, give your students a diagnostic exam or assignments that will let you judge their skills and abilities, their strengths and weaknesses. (Don't quench their enthusiasm by grading these assignments. Ask students to do their best, but don't assign grades; another option is to give every student who sincerely tries to complete the assignment full credit, so that you do not punish them for making mistakes.) Diagnostic exams and exercises enable you to adjust your lesson plans so that you don't bore students or frustrate them by giving them work that is too easy or too hard. On my diagnostic exam, I include sample questions from chapter tests, semester reviews, and final exams, to find out how much my students already know. If the results show that the majority of the class needs to back up and cover some old ground, we back up. On the other hand, if nobody misses more than one or two grammar questions, I eliminate the easiest lessons I had planned in that area.

Responses to reading are an excellent way to find out what your students know about your subject, in addition to giving you a good look at their logic and writing skills. Find an interesting or controversial essay, editorial, movie review, or feature article in a newspaper or magazine, and make copies for your students. Have them read the article silently and write a response to the content (for younger students, I require a paragraph or a page; for high school students, I require more than one page). This not only gives you information about students' analytical thinking and composition skills, it also gives them good practice for the kind of writing they will be expected to do if and when they attend college.

At one time I taught freshman composition at a four-year university. My freshmen, all high school honors students, had a terrible time coming up with their own theses; they wanted me to tell them what to say. When I returned to the high school classroom, I added many more open-ended writing assignments to my lessons, and my former students have reported that they were better prepared than many of their classmates to produce the kind of writing that college professors expected from them.

Distribute Your Welcome Handout and Student Folders

Once you are reasonably sure that the students in your classroom will be there for a while and you won't have ten new students the next day, it's time to distribute your one-page welcome handout and cover your ground rules (see Chapter Five for a more complete discussion of creating rules; Chapter Three contains an example in Exhibit 3.1). Read your handout to the class so that you are certain everybody has seen and heard exactly what it says. After you read one section, stop and ask students if they have any questions or comments. Make sure they understand exactly what you expect in each area.

After you have read the entire handout together, ask again for questions or comments. Tell your students that this is their chance to argue with you, if any of your rules or procedures seems unreasonable to them. If anybody has a comment, consider it carefully and make a decision on the spot or tell them you will consider their ideas and let them know what you think at the next class. Unless you are an unusually gifted teacher or you have an unusually cooperative and well-behaved group of students, don't open your rules to student input or votes. Giving up control of the rules may feel democratic, but you may find yourself giving up control of your classroom, which is not a good idea, even with intelligent or mature students. Somebody has to be the boss, and that's your job. Of course, it doesn't hurt to consider your students' comments and opinions. Listening to their ideas is a good way to avoid future misbehavior or mutiny.

If you have a well-behaved, cooperative group, you might reward students' good behavior by giving them a practice "exam" on your rules. I make handwritten overlays and use the overhead projector to ask questions such as these:

1. If you return to class after being absent, you should
   a. Interrupt the teacher repeatedly to ask if she missed you.
   b. Show everybody your scabs or scars or medicine.
   c. Get your work from the makeup work folder.
   d. Kiss your teacher and yell, "I missed you so much!"

2. If you arrive to class tardy, you should
   a. Make lots of noise so everybody notices you.
   b. Gasp and pretend that you just ran five miles to school.
   c. Slap all your pals on the back as you pass by.
   d. Take your seat quietly and get to work.

3. What materials should you bring to class every day?
   a. Candy, gum, CD player, spiders, and assorted bugs
   b. A pen or pencil, paper, and your textbook (if applicable)
   c. Your dog, a pair of smelly socks, and two sodas
   d. A coloring book, a comic, and a note to Santa

Students enjoy the "exam" and everybody laughs, which is very good because it dissipates tension and creates an immediate feeling of bonding among your students. Groups that laugh together develop a quick rapport, and they tend to cooperate more quickly and efficiently.

Distribute your individual student folders on the same day that you distribute your welcome handout, so that students have a place to keep the handout and any other paperwork you may distribute. A blank page beckons to many students, so be prepared to answer the question, "Can we decorate our folders?" This is one of those small things that some students will try to enlarge into an argument in order to derail the teacher train.

If you find it difficult to tolerate immature or mildly defiant behavior, then it might be a good idea for you to insist that the students not write anything on the folders except their names. I allow students to decorate their folders with anything except gang insignias, racial slurs, or obscenities. I explain that the primary purpose of the folders is not for them to display their talents and political beliefs. Their primary purpose is to act as an organizational tool: the folders make it easier for me to communicate with students; they save time for everybody; and they help students store important paperwork. If students choose to use the folders to display political statements or provocative drawings, I allow them that privilege as long as what they draw or write doesn't insult or intimidate others. For example, if they draw a marijuana plant, instead of creating a confrontation as they expect me to do, I say, "Oh, you like plants. Maybe you'll decide to study botany in college." Then I quickly pass on by so that they aren't sure whether I am stupid or just kidding. Either way, they get the message that I am the one who chooses the battles in my classroom and that I will not permit them to draw me into a petty argument that was designed to disrupt my teaching. (If a student persists in provoking me, we step outside for a quick chat; if necessary, I schedule a private after-school conference, at my convenience.)

Delegate Some Authority

Teachers tend to be nurturing souls. We like to help other people. But we also like to be in control, and many of us find it difficult to delegate any of our authority. Sharing your authority can provide huge dividends, however. By assigning jobs to students, you can conserve your precious time and energy for more important tasks. Student jobs also boost tender young egos, teach children how to handle responsibility, and encourage students to cooperate with you and each other. Some elementary teachers assign every student a specific task, with an important title to accompany the job: president of pencil sharpening, official attendance taker, and so on. High school teachers often take on student clerks or assistants who earn credits for providing administrative support during a particular class period each day. Even when a school doesn't have a formal clerking program, I often request that the office approve such arrangements; my requests have never been denied.

In my classes I always assign a student helper to take attendance, although I always check to make sure the report is accurate (so students can't be pressured by others to record incorrect data). For each class period, I have an attendance monitor and a backup for days that the monitor is absent (here's your chance to recognize the memory skills of one of your students who remembered everybody's names). I also assign a door monitor for each class period to answer the door during class time. Instead of allowing people to walk in and interrupt our lessons, the door monitor greets anybody who knocks and accepts any notes, messages, or paperwork that doesn't require my immediate attention. I have taught at schools where two or three student messengers knocked on the door each hour to deliver notes from parents about after-school pickup times, birthday balloons, informal school surveys, notices of club meetings, and so on. Having a door monitor cuts down on disruptions and sends a message to your students that their work is too important to interrupt for trivial reasons.

The student cleanup crew is one of the most important student posts. I always request volunteers first. If I don't get at least four volunteers, I split the students into teams of four and rotate their assignment. The cleanup crew is responsible for making sure that no debris remains on the floor or desks when the dismissal bell rings. Students occasionally complain about being expected to do what they consider "the janitor's job," but when I explain that the custodial crew's primary responsibility is to create a safe and hygienic environment, not to clean up after slobs, they get the message. And when they are responsible for cleaning up their own or other students' messes, they encourage each other to be neater and more considerate of classroom furnishings and materials.

Demonstrate the Power of Choice

When I was a college student, my psychology professor, Kenneth Brodeur, once gave our class the simple assignment of completing these two sentences: "I have to [fill in the blank]" and "I can't [fill in the blank]" with the first thoughts that popped into our heads. Because I was on active duty in the navy at the time, I wrote "I have to wear my uniform," and because I had been married too young to a boy who had married far too young, I was involved in a very unhealthy marriage. So I wrote "I can't stop fighting with my husband."

Professor Brodeur told us to cross out the word *have* from the first sentence and replace it with *choose*. Then he instructed us to cross out *can't* and replace it with *don't want to*. My new sentences read, "I choose to wear my uniform," and "I don't want to stop fighting with my husband." I objected to the new wording of my sentences, as did everybody else in class. But the professor insisted.

"Does somebody dress you in the morning?" he asked me. "Or does somebody hold a gun to your head and force you to put on that uniform?"

"Of course not," I said. "You're being ridiculous."

"And what happens if you refuse to wear the uniform?"

"You know very well," I said. I felt myself growing very angry. "You aren't stupid. You know I'd get busted."

"You don't want to get busted," said Professor Brodeur in a maddeningly calm voice, "so you choose to wear your uniform."

"Oh, go away," I said. "You are just arguing semantics." I was not about to give in so easily. Professor Brodeur circulated through the room and eventually returned to my desk to discuss my second sentence. I knew I was right. My husband was belligerent and stubborn (even more stubborn than I am!). He enjoyed nothing more than starting a fight so that he could bully his way into winning.

"Isn't there anything you could do to stop fighting with your husband?" Professor Brodeur asked. "Anything at all?"

"Well, I suppose if I acted like a robot and did everything he said, twenty-four hours a day, seven days a week, he might slack off a little," I said.

"You aren't willing to do that, are you?" Professor Brodeur asked.

"Of course, I'm not," I said. "I have a right to be a human being."

"Well, then, let's tell the truth," he said. "You don't want to stop fighting with your husband badly enough to do what you would have to do to make that happen." He strolled to the front of the classroom and wrote on the board, "There are five things you *have* to do to stay alive: eat, breathe, drink water, sleep, and go to the bathroom. Everything else is optional."

"But there are lots of things we can't do," I argued.

"That's right," Professor Brodeur nodded. "You can't change your ethnic origin or your height, but there are really very few things you cannot accomplish if you are truly motivated and willing to work. When you go around saying, 'I have to' and 'I can't' all the time, you are telling the world you are a victim, and the world will treat you the way you tell it to. If you don't like your life, change it. You have that power. Whether or not you use your power is up to you."

That was the single most powerful lesson I have ever learned. It helped me realize that I could indeed change my life, my behavior, and my attitude. I have used Professor Brodeur's model to motivate my own students. We complete our power-of-choice exercise during the first week of classes. Sometimes students ask if we can repeat the exercise after a few months, just to refresh their motivation, and I complete the exercise along with them each time, because it's one of those lessons that teach you something new each time.

If you decide to use this exercise, make sure that your students understand your purpose. Reassure them that it isn't a test, that they don't have to read their answers out loud or share them with anybody. You won't grade them on what they write; they won't even have to turn in their sentences. It's important for them to know that this exercise is for their benefit, to help them understand themselves better and to make them stronger people. (Of course, it will help you to teach them, but some of them may not be interested in helping you, so why mention it?)

Here are some typical starting sentences from students: "I have to do my homework, and I can't get an A in math." "I have to clean my room, and I can't wear my hat in school." "I have to go to school, and I can't cut classes." "I always have to baby-sit, and I can't lose weight."

Ask for volunteers to discuss their sentences with you, and allow the other students to consider theirs silently. Be prepared: some students will find this exercise very distressing, and for some it will take time and repetition. When you tell your students that they *don't want to* earn As or wear hats or cut classes, they will most certainly argue with you. And in some cases they may be right. If they give examples of goals that have legitimate limitations or physical impossibilities (a girl with severe astigmatism probably cannot become a commercial jet pilot, although some students may argue that it is possible; and a boy cannot have a baby, at least right now). Accept and acknowledge any valid answers. But the majority of *can't* sentences will not hold up to honest inspection.

You don't need to use a worksheet for this exercise, but if you'd like to use a handout, I recommend omitting instructions for changing the wording because some people read an entire worksheet before they begin writing. If students know that you are going to ask them to change words, the exercise won't be as helpful. Exhibit 4.2 is the handout I use.

Once your students understand and accept the truth of this lesson, they will have to admit that when they misbehave or fail in your class, it is because they *choose* to misbehave or fail. They don't have to let somebody copy their homework. They don't have to respond to another student's insult by offering an insult in return. They don't have to come to your class if they don't want to learn. And if they have a problem learning required material, they can ask you for help or arrange for a tutor or spend more time on homework. Unless they have a true learning disability, students have no valid reason for not passing your class, graduating from school, finding a decent occupation, learning to make friends, developing useful skills, and being successful people.

Help Your Students Understand Themselves

Young people are more interested in themselves and in each other than in any other topic. They are also most confused about themselves, and that confusion often leads to problems in school. Perhaps you are thinking, *Oh right. I need one more thing to add to my already overcrowded curriculum. Between school holidays, pep rallies, assemblies, and administrative busywork, I don't have time to cover my textbooks, much less try to teach psychology.* If you are thinking that, you are absolutely right. Teaching psychology isn't your job, so you may decide to skip this section. But if you have problem students who sometimes make you want to change professions, then you might consider discussing Abraham Maslow's theory with your classes. It will take only a few minutes, and it may save you many hours or months of aggravation.

At some time during your teaching training, you probably had a survey course, maybe two, in child or adolescent psychology. You've probably read at least one interpretation of Maslow's hierarchy of needs (Exhibit 4.3). I'd like to add my version to your repertoire. I first discussed this idea with a class of students who had serious problems resisting the lure of gangs, drugs, shoplifting, and sex. One day we began talking about why people do what they do, and I told them that during my college studies in psychology, I learned that we often do things because we need to belong to something. No matter how many times we promise ourselves that we will be independent and stand our ground, we end up giving in and doing things we regret. Then we hate ourselves.

"That's me! That's me!" One of my students waved her hand in the air. "I'm always going shopping with my sister and her friends, and they always steal stuff from stores and I say I'm not going to do it. But then I go right ahead and do it again, and I always wish I didn't. I swear I won't go with them again, but the next time they ask me, there I go, doing what I said I wasn't going to do. And I feel so bad, especially when I go to church and sit next to my grandma and think about how ashamed she would be of me if she knew."

I assured Tyeisha that she wasn't horrible; she was simply human, because human beings need to belong and be accepted by a group of people. That's why we join clubs and social organization, including gangs.

"How many of you have a family, people who love you, but you still feel like you don't really belong?" I asked my class. More than half the students raised their hands. "You aren't the Lone Ranger," I told them. "Lots of people feel left out, even in their own families. But we need to belong to something. So find something to belong to—a sports team, a hobby club, a karate studio, a church, a garage band, a choir, a group of sidewalk singers, a volunteer organization, an actors' group, even just a group of two or three kids that you eat lunch with or ride the bus with or walk to school with every day."

I explained that people who feel part of something are less inclined to join negative groups such as gangs, vandals, and shoplifters. My students were so attentive that I decided to introduce them to Maslow's theory. I outlined his theory briefly, and we discussed it. That night I made a chart for them to take home and keep where they could check it periodically to remind themselves to keep growing and

Exhibit 4.3. Maslow's Hierarchy of Needs.

Level 1, Physical. You need food, water, and shelter. If you're starving, you don't care whether you're wearing cool shoes. And you don't care whether your food is healthy. Food is food. Until these level-one needs are met, you can't move on to bigger and better things. If you don't have these basic things and need help, ask for it. Don't be embarrassed. Many people want to help you.

Level 2, Safety. Once your basic physical needs are met, you can think about things such as keeping warm, avoiding harm, and being healthy.

Level 3, Social. People (and lots of animals, like wolves) need to belong to a group and feel loved. You can have a family and still feel unloved. That may be why you hang around with people you don't really like or do things you know are wrong. Find something to belong to: a team, a club, maybe just of couple of kids you eat lunch with every day. Find some people who like you just the way you are. If you hang out by yourself all the time, you'll be a target for people who don't really like you but want to use you.

Level 4, Ego. Once we know we're loved, we start to look for ways to increase our self-respect, because we all need to feel important and appreciated. When you feel all right about yourself, you aren't afraid to try to learn new skills. You don't have to impress everybody else. You know it's more important to impress yourself.

Level 5, Self-Fulfillment. You have food, shelter, people who love you, and self-respect—now you're cooking! You don't waste time on unimportant things, such as gossiping about others. You are strong enough to walk away from a fight but you stand up for your principles. You nurture your talents, learn just for the fun of learning, help other people, invent things, create art or music or new ideas. You follow your dreams!

moving up the ladder of happiness and self-fulfillment. Many students reported that knowing about human needs helped them make better choices.

Depending on students' age and maturity, I may use more or less sophisticated vocabulary and more complicated examples, but I've never had a group who didn't understand this theory. In fact, the "worst" classes were most interested in discussing these ideas.

Teach Your Students to Think About Thinking

One day a high school junior challenged a classroom assignment. He wanted to know the point of doing the work. I asked him what he thought the point might be. He said, "To waste our time and give you something to grade." I was tempted to hush him up but decided to give him such a complete explanation that he'd never ask such a question again. As it turned out, the explanation blossomed into such a lively discussion of Bloom's taxonomy that everybody in class sat up and paid attention. The next day I presented the same lesson to my other classes, which all responded positively.

When I write "Bloom's Taxonomy of Cognitive Domains" on the board, I always hear whispers behind me.

"What's that?"

"I dunno."

I ask my students to try to figure out the meaning of the phrase. Usually, they recognize the word *domain* as a kind of kingdom, but *taxonomy* stumps them. I grab a thick dictionary from the shelf and announce that I am going to "look it up in my handy dandy pocket dictionary." Freshmen usually giggle; older students roll their eyes and make disgusted *tsk*ing sounds when I grab my dictionary. I ignore their ridicule.

Somebody usually says, "That's not a pocket dictionary."

I wink and say, "You gotta have big pockets."

I don't do those things just to be a clown but to model the behavior I want my students to practice. It works. Before long students grab their handy dandy pocket dictionaries to look up words they don't know during class.

After we define the terms, I tell the students that I'm going to share with them a lesson that teachers learn in college but don't usually pass on to their students. I tell them I think they should know why we ask them to do the things we ask them to do. So we're going to try some *metacognition*—thinking about thinking. I explain the different levels of thinking, giving one or two examples. I ask them to think of additional examples from different academic subjects for each thinking level, and I distribute a handout on Bloom's taxonomy (Exhibit 4.4).

After we discuss this handout and everybody understands the concepts, I give the students a handout (Exhibit 4.5) that shows how we use critical thinking skills in daily life. My students are amazed to see that all the "boring, useless stuff" they are learning in school—even analyzing Shakespearean sonnets—actually will help them when they begin their "real" lives.

The day after we discuss levels of critical thinking, I bring in items from newspapers for my students to analyze. We read an editorial commentary, a movie review, letters to the editor, and a review of a music album. I ask the students to see how much they can tell about the writers from reading their work and whether they accept those writers' opinions. We look at all of the ads in a particular magazine, and the students then decide what kind of people are the target audience of

---

Exhibit 4.4. Bloom's Taxonomy of Cognitive Domains: English Applications.

Recall (lowest level). Remembering information: reciting your ABCs, listing the parts of speech, defining the words *fact* and *opinion*

Comprehension. Understanding things: knowing the difference between a noun and a verb or between a fact and an opinion

Application. Using things you understand: filling in the blanks on a grammar worksheet with nouns or verbs, writing a list of facts or opinions

Analysis. Comparing different things: underlining all the nouns in a paragraph or deciding whether a sentence is a fact or an opinion

Synthesis. Creating your own ideas and projects: writing sentences that contain action verbs, writing a paragraph that states your opinion, writing a factual report

Evaluation (highest level). Making judgments based on knowledge: comparing three different sentences and deciding which one uses adjectives to create the best description, reading two different opinions on the same topic and deciding which opinion makes more sense, giving specific examples from the reading to support your choice

Exhibit 4.5. Using Bloom's Taxonomy: Your Own Life.

Recall. Remembering all the words to a song or all the foods on your grocery list, reciting the stats of a sports team, knowing the parts of an engine or stereo system

Comprehension. Understanding the differences between a receiver and an amplifier, knowing how a gasoline engine or computer works, realizing that some people are shy

Application. Installing a stereo or changing your car's spark plugs, making guacamole, filling out a job application with proper grammar, asking a shy person for a date without scaring him or her, fixing a toaster

Analysis. Deciding which job to accept, picking the best college for you, deciding whether to get married or have sex or have a baby; weighing the pros and cons of sending your kids to private school, joining a gang, or quitting smoking

Synthesis. Making a plan for your life and putting it into action, creating your own heavy metal band or rap group, starting your own business, writing songs, building a house, creating your own secret barbecue sauce recipe, making a budget based on your income, raising healthy children

Evaluation. Concluding that your present job doesn't offer the kind of future you want, reading the news and deciding whether it was presented truthfully, listening to all the candidates and choosing the one who will get your vote, figuring out the best way to discipline your kids, deciding what will be the best for your children if your spouse dies or asks for a divorce, figuring out what went wrong with your marriage or your car or your job and how you can improve your life that magazine, what political point of view the publisher is likely to hold, and what kind of people wrote the articles. This kind of analytical, critical thinking comes naturally to some students but will be a new and exciting introduction to some other students' own brain power.

And incidentally, after I teach my students to recognize higher-level thinking skills, they are on the lookout for assignments that push them to the highest levels.

One final note on this topic: please don't assume that your students aren't smart or mature enough to get this. I have discussed this subject with very low-performing students, disenchanted teenagers, and adults who don't speak English well; and they all understand at least the basic ideas. And they appreciate being treated as intelligent, capable people.

SHOW YOUR GRATITUDE

Every single day thank your students for coming to class and cooperating with you. They won't get tired of hearing how wonderful they are. If we expect children to continue their good behavior, we need to acknowledge that good behavior. And we need to take every opportunity to shake their hands, pat them on the back, and encourage them to continue demonstrating their self-respect. They will grow up to be just like us. They will treat other people the way we have treated them. So teach them to be ethical, compassionate, honorable people.

ONE DOWN, THIRTY-SOMETHING TO GO

Not bad—by the end of the first week of school, you know the names of all your students; they know all your rules; you have a good idea of what you have to work with; they understand that you hold them personally responsible for their actions; and they know what they will have to do to pass your class. With a little luck, they also understand themselves a little better and have at least a basic understanding of the different levels of thinking and how they will need to develop the highest-level thinking skills.

Now you can create lesson plans that suit your classes, but don't get too specific just yet. If you plan your teaching days down to the minute, the administrative tasks and unavoidable interruptions (inoculations, club photos, field trips, career counseling, college days, armed forces information day, and so on) will drive you crazy, and driving you crazy is your students' job. You wouldn't want to spoil their fun.

Discipline Is Not a Dirty Word

O nce in a while, I walk into a room filled with teachers who are expecting me to provide a workshop on classroom management. I stride into the room late and take my place at the podium. I glare at the teachers and gesture toward a couple of people in the back. "You two back there, stop talking," I say. I nod at another pair and say, "I'd like you two to move over here." I point to some other location. Then I say, "No, wait. I think I'd like everybody to move. Pick up your belongings, please. And hurry. We don't have time to waste. Let's get moving."

I clap my hands, then stand with my hands on my hips looking expectant. A few cooperative souls always stand up and gather their briefcases, binders, book bags, and backpacks; but most of the teachers sit and glare back at me. Clearly, this wasn't what they expected. Seeing how disappointed they are, I am tempted to give up the game, but to make sure I've made my point, I press on.

"These materials cost a lot of money to reproduce, so we aren't going to have any food or drinks in this room because we don't want to risk any spills or messes. If you brought coffee or soda in here with you, drink up or ditch it."

At the mention of discarding their precious caffeine-laden drinks, the group prepares to revolt. Before they begin throwing things, I raise both my hands and say, "Don't shoot. I was just kidding. Please, sit down. Relax."

Reluctantly, people take their seats, but clearly they would rather leave. Many sit with their arms crossed over their chests, using body language to send the signal that they have tuned me out. They have closed their minds and their notebooks, and they have put away their pens. They are no longer interested in taking notes from somebody who treats them the way I just did. They don't believe I have anything useful to teach them.

"So how do you feel right now?" I ask. "Feeling cooperative? Can't wait to hear what I have to say? Or are you checking your watch to see how long you have to put up with me? Some of you probably already sent yourself messages on your cell phones so that you could pretend somebody called you and you have to leave immediately."

People start to relax. A few even smile tentatively.

"It doesn't feel very nice, does it, when somebody treats you that way?" I ask. They shake their heads. It certainly doesn't. But how many times have we seen teachers treat students that way? In fact, most of us have been guilty of that kind of dictatorial behavior ourselves (once in a great, great while, of course). And then we wonder why students rebel against our rules or refuse to cooperate with us.

If you mention the word *discipline* to most children, they immediately think of punishment, because they have been taught only one facet of that multidimensional word. In the military services, however, *discipline* has a more positive connotation, because military personnel understand that discipline allows them to function as an efficient team. They know that discipline will help them develop self-control and strength of character.

Classroom teachers can use the principles of military discipline to teach their students how to develop self-discipline and respect for others. Of course, I'm not suggesting that you conduct your classes like a military boot camp, ordering kids to hit the deck and give you fifty push-ups when they step out of line, but I do believe that children need and want strong adult guidance and leadership. The world can be a scary place for children, and they want adults to establish boundaries for behavior and set limits for them, so that they can relax and learn without having to be responsible for more than they can handle.

Adults don't want to live in a chaotic world either. We want reasonable laws that allow us the maximum amount of freedom and the minimum amount of danger. Children are no different from us. In spite of the books and newspaper articles and TV programs that tell us that today's children are apathetic, learning impaired, developmentally delayed, unwilling or unable to pay attention, impossible to discipline or teach, I don't believe those things for a minute because I have taught too many of those "unteachable" children. Children are naturally curious and eager to learn, but when they go to school, unfortunately, their natural curiosity and enthusiasm are replaced by fears: that they will fail their classes, they will be unpopular and lonely, they will be assaulted by bullies, they won't be able to get good jobs even if they go to college, their parents will get divorced, they will die from AIDS or a random drive-by shooting or a drug-crazed mugger on the streets outside their school.

We can't address all of children's fears, but if we can create an oasis of calm and order in our classrooms, where students feel safe and protected, where they know what we expect of them and know that we will not permit other students to hurt or torment them, their curiosity and enthusiasm for learning will resurface; and they will apply themselves to the lessons we offer. Positive discipline is the key to creating that classroom oasis.

DEFINE YOUR PHILOSOPHY

Perhaps you have observed those "lucky" teachers who don't seem to have the discipline problems. Luck does play a part, but preparation has a lot more to do with classroom management. You can prevent many discipline problems if you lay the groundwork. I like to think of classroom rules as scaffolding for children. Our rules provide support and keep children from falling and seriously injuring themselves. As children grow older, we can relax or remove the rules one at a time until the children stand alone, making their own decisions, taking as much risk as their confidence and abilities allow. If we make reasonable rules, enforce them fairly, and adjust them to meet children's changing needs, we teach children that, instead of restrictions designed to spoil all their fun, rules actually can create more freedom for them.

As you design your discipline policy, keep in mind your purpose. Do you want to punish students who misbehave? Do you want to scare students and teach them a lesson? Do you want to help students learn to accept responsibility for their behavior and make better choices in the future?

Punitive discipline techniques are designed to punish, embarrass, frighten, or pay back a student for some transgression. Punitive methods may temporarily change student behavior, but they do not encourage students to take responsibility for their actions or motivate them to cooperate with adults. Far too often punitive disciplines such as spanking, making a student stand in the corner, sending a student to detention or suspension result in a cycle of misbehavior and punishment that escalates, causing more classroom disruptions and declining grades. Look at the high number of high school students who are repeatedly sent to detention. Many of these students end up in dropout prevention programs because they miss too many critical classroom lessons. They blame their teachers or parents or schools for their problems, and become less and less motivated to achieve with each punishment.

Positive discipline techniques, on the other hand, are designed to make students think about their behavior, accept responsibility for their actions, make amends when possible, understand the effects of their behavior on others, solve problems, and learn how to make better choices. Instead of relying on humiliation or threats, positive discipline provides an opportunity for students to discuss the reasons for their behavior and helps them learn new ways to behave. Instead of blaming teachers or parents for their own misbehavior, students realize that they can control their behavior and affect the way they are treated in school and in the world.

We tend to teach the way we were taught, unless we make a conscious effort to do otherwise. If you can recall your own childhood, perhaps you will remember that standing in the corner or sitting in detention did not inspire you to turn over a new leaf but rather to be sneakier in the future—and perhaps you spent the time plotting revenge against the teacher who doled out the punishment. Perhaps you can also recall a teacher who insisted that you accept responsibility for your own behavior and who rewarded your sincere efforts with a handshake, a pat on the back, a hug, a complimentary note in the margin of a paper, a note or phone call to your parents. And you may recall wanting that teacher to like and respect you, so you cooperated even when you didn't necessarily agree with all of his or her rules. On the other hand, perhaps you made a serious error and received serious punishment and stern lectures that actually caused you to change your attitude.

Your own experiences have shaped your attitude toward discipline, and you already have some basic beliefs about behavior, consequences, punishments, and rewards. Your classroom management techniques will be much more effective if you can distill your philosophy of discipline into one or two sentences. For example: "My goal in disciplining any student is to help that student be more successful in school, which will help him or her be successful in life. All consequences should address the specific behavior, with the goal of helping the student learn to make better choices in the future." Here's another example: "My goal is to make sure students take responsibility for their behavior and understand that they can choose to follow rules or break them. When they break rules, they will face consequences."

WHAT GOES AROUND REALLY DOES COME AROUND

If you use humiliation as a tool for embarrassing students, don't be surprised if they follow your example and try to humiliate each other. In my opinion, humiliation is not only unprofessional, unethical, and unfair; I believe it is psychologically abusive for adults to use humiliation to control children. Perhaps you can't remember how you felt as a child when an adult intentionally embarrassed you. Or perhaps you are one of the fortunate few who were never subjected to humiliation. You may be better able to empathize with your students if you imagine yourself in the following scenario.

Your principal has forwarded an important fifty-page report to all teachers. You find a copy in your mailbox on Friday with a note from the secretary saying that the principal expects all teachers to read the report before the staff meeting on Monday. You put the report in your bag and take it home, but between chaperoning your son's birthday party, doing the laundry, driving your daughter to a soccer match, visiting your mother in the hospital, and trying to squeeze in a few minutes for your spouse, you don't get a chance to read the report. You do glance through it, though.

At the staff meeting on Monday morning, the principal asks how many people read the report. You raise your hand because, technically, you did read a bit of it. Imagine that the principal then looks directly at you and asks you to stand. She says, "Please summarize the main points from the report." Clearly, she thinks you are lying. She senses that you haven't read the report, and she is going to make you do one of two things: try to fake your way through this experience or admit in public that you lied when you said that you had read the report. You now have the choice of discussing details of your home life in front of your peers or looking like a liar. The principal's only point in asking you to summarize the report is to embarrass and humiliate you. Perhaps she believes this tactic will make you want to read her next report in order to avoid being embarrassed, but it's far more likely that you will skip the next staff meeting or call in sick that day. There are better ways to supervise and motivate people—and far better ways to teach.

COWBOY PHILOSOPHY

One year, at the Southwestern New Mexico State Fair, I had the unforgettable experience of watching Craig Cameron, "the cowboy professor," in action. I was struck by the similarity between breaking wild horses and taming wild students. Cameron worked with two wild horses that afternoon—one that had never been ridden at all and one that had resisted being forcibly saddle broken. In both instances Cameron was able to mount and ride the horses within an hour, without raising his voice or using any force whatsoever. As I watched Cameron tame those horses and listened to him explain his actions, I realized that I was in the presence of a master teacher. I took copious notes.

"Many people set out to break the spirit of a horse," Cameron told the crowd who had gathered outside the round pen where he worked the horses. "The last thing I want to do is break down the spirit of any horse: I'm out to build it up so that I can utilize it. I want to relate to the horse on his own level and on his time schedule. If you want a horse to have a good attitude, you can't force things on him. You have to give him time to decipher what it is you want him to do."

As he spoke, Cameron picked up a saddle blanket and took a step toward the horse he was breaking. The horse took one look at the blanket and started running in the opposite direction (just as our students try to escape from difficult lessons). Instead of chasing the horse or trying to corner it so that he could place the blanket on its back, Cameron stood still and waited until the horse stopped running and, overcome by curiosity, approached the unfamiliar blanket to investigate. Cameron allowed the horse to sniff and nibble the blanket, then he brushed it gently over the horse's legs and belly before placing it on the horse's back. Immediately the horse bucked the blanket off and ran away. Cameron picked up the blanket and waited until the horse returned to inspect it again. Satisfied that it posed no danger, the horse finally stood still and accepted the blanket. Cameron could have saved time by hobbling the horse and tying the blanket to its back, as many people do, but he would have faced the same struggle every time he wanted to saddle the horse.

"People bring me all sorts of 'problem' horses," Cameron said, as he placed a saddle on top of the blanket and let the horse run off until it realized that the saddle wasn't going to hurt it.

"Usually the problem is the way the horse was taught in the beginning," Cameron explained. "Somebody tried to force a lesson on him, or he was punished harshly for not doing right. If he doesn't do the right thing, he knows you're going to jerk harder or spur harder or get a bigger mouth bit. So now he's nervous, scared, and defensive. He is just flat-out turned off to learning."

Again, the horse circled the pen several times, then slowed down and walked to Cameron and allowed him to tighten the cinch on the saddle.

Students, like horses, resist having their spirits broken or being forced into performing uncomfortable or unfamiliar actions. If we give them time to get used to us and time to understand what we want from them, they are much more apt to cooperate. We can beat children, scare, or bore them with endless repetitions when they don't cooperate. Children, like horses, may cooperate temporarily out of fear, pain, or exhaustion; but unless we gain their trust, we're going to have to fight the same battles over and over again.

One comment that Cameron made during his training session struck me as particularly applicable to classroom teachers who must deal with students who resist accepting authority. "Horses naturally understand a pecking order," Cameron explained. "Your horse can accept the fact that you are the leader of the herd and he is the follower. That doesn't mean that a horse won't test you from time to time. He's going to test you. But you can establish that you are the leader, number one in the pecking order, without causing your horse pain or fear. The way you do that is to control your horse's mind instead of his body."

If you back a student against the wall and demand respect or obedience, you are not apt to receive either one. Children's natural instinct is to escape when they feel frightened or threatened or to fight if escape is impossible. If you make clear from the start that you are the leader in your classroom and that your leadership is necessary in order for you to teach and for your students to learn, you allow students to accept your authority without feeling any loss of dignity. Instead of demanding cooperation, effective teachers make it a choice.

After seeing him work, I bought Cameron's videos, *Gentle Horse-Breaking and Training,* and *Dark into Light,* to watch at home. The longer I watched, the more I became convinced that teacher-training programs should assign his videos as required curriculum. If you'd like to read about Craig Cameron, you can find articles about him in many equestrian magazines such as *Western Horseman* or the *Quarter Horse Journal.* For information about his videos, contact

Craig Cameron Horsemanship
P.O. Box 50
Bluff Dale, TX 76433-0050
1-800-274-0077   1-817-728-3082

RULES VS. PROCEDURES

Rules and procedures are two very different things. Rules are rigid and inflexible; procedures can be adapted as needed. Rules are not made to be broken. Like laws, rules make no allowance for individual differences or circumstances. If you establish a list of rigid rules for your classroom, you may regret it later. For example, you may make a rule that you will not accept late work or that one missing homework assignment will preclude a student from earning an A in your class. What if a student cannot complete an assignment because of a true emergency, such as a serious illness, accident, or death in the family? You have two choices: stick to your rule or bend it. Either option has disadvantages.

If you adamantly stick to your rule, innocent students will suffer and you may earn a reputation as a harsh and heartless person. If you bend your rules for one student, other students will quickly line up to ask for special consideration because they too have emergencies (some of which may seem trivial to you but very important to someone young). No matter where you draw the line, some students will feel that you have wronged them, that you dislike them, that you play favorites. That's why I suggest making rules only about things that you will never tolerate, things that cannot happen by accident—swearing, hitting, racial insults, sexual harassment, for example.

Procedures, on the other hand, don't legislate behavior; they provide guidelines for completing specific activities, such as using the restroom, completing makeup work, requesting permission to miss class, requesting admittance to your class when tardy. Establishing procedures for your classroom provides clear guidelines for student behavior while leaving you more options. If special circumstances arise, you will be able to make changes without causing a lot of complaints or confusion. You will be able to make decisions based on individual circumstances. If students complain that you treat them differently from each other, respond by pointing out that you treat them individually because they are individuals. "One size fits all" does not apply to education because each student has unique talents, abilities, goals, challenges, and circumstances.

You can reduce the amount of disorder in your classroom if, early on, you establish a procedure for distributing and collecting papers, grading papers in class, turning in homework, collecting makeup work, dismissing class, issuing hall and library passes, allowing visits to other teachers, and so on. Instead of reviewing all your procedures during the first few days of class, when students are often too excited or overwhelmed to remember, review each procedure as it arises. Remember that many students learn by seeing or doing, so don't just talk. Show them what you want them to do, then practice each procedure until your students know the routine, especially with young children. You may opt to give students a copy in writing. You may feel like you are wasting time at first if you spend five minutes at the end of each class for two weeks discussing the procedure for leaving the room after the dismissal bell, but you will save yourself a lot of time and heartache later. Kids know that if they can get you to ignore their behavior once or twice, they can ignore your procedure.

Don't create procedures unless you think they are important; and if you make them, make sure your students understand and follow them. For example, high school students love to jump up during the last minutes of class and huddle near the door, waiting for the bell. If you allow that to happen once, it is much more likely to become an ongoing battle. So, before the bell rings, explain that jumping out of seats and huddling near the door will result in additional homework, having to sit and wait for thirty seconds after the bell rings before leaving the room, or some other unsavory activity.

RULES FOR CREATING RULES

You may have to experiment to find the best discipline methods to fit your unique personality and your students, but you are much more likely to succeed if you focus on three key concepts as you create your classroom rules:

- Limit the number of rules.
- State rules positively.
- Consider the consequences.

Be wary of making too many rules. The more you create, the more time you must spend enforcing them, the more complicated your list of consequences, and the more likely students are to misbehave out of defiance. Long lists of rules box in everyone, stifling creativity and hindering your efforts to develop a strong rapport and an environment of mutual respect.

My preference, after testing many methods, is to create one overarching rule for my classroom: Respect yourself and everybody in this room.

This simple rule covers any situation that may occur. For example, it is not respectful to chomp loudly on gum, stick chewed gum or candy on desks or books, hit or insult people, carve obscene words onto a desktop, arrive late to class, throw litter on the floor, interrupt other students who are trying to work, disrupt the teacher's efforts to teach a lesson, and so on. When a student acts disrespectfully, you may ask, "Do you believe your present behavior shows self-respect and respect for others?" At this point a student who persists in misbehaving is fully aware that any negative consequences will be self-inflicted. The student will be more inclined to choose a different behavior in the future and will not feel a need to exact revenge on you, the innocent teacher, for meting out punishment.

State your rules positively whenever possible. Remember that old joke that instructs, "Don't think of an elephant"? The same idea applies to rules. Don't give kids more ideas than they already have. Negatively stated rules (no gum chewing, no shouting, no running with scissors) provide a list of suggested misbehaviors for students who crave your attention, any attention, negative or positive. Negative rules also provide a challenge for students who want to distract you from teaching a boring or difficult lesson or who simply want to push your buttons. And finally, negative rules can inspire further negative behaviors. For example, if you make a rule that no gum chewing is permitted in your classroom, then some students are going to forget they have gum in their mouths or they may risk breaking your rule because they really like gum. When those students believe they are in danger of getting caught breaking your no-gum rule, they may hide their sticky wads under their desks, on your bookshelves, or in their textbooks. If, on the other hand, you have a positive rule in your classroom, "Dispose of all gum properly," then you leave it up to the students to choose their own behavior; and they are far more likely to cooperate.

Sometimes you won't be able to state a rule positively. Or you may have to add an addendum using negative words in order to avoid creating a mouthful of gobbledygook. My own one-rule policy, for example, includes a list of prohibitions for those students who require specific information. The addendum specifies: no put-downs of other people based on their race, religion, ethnic background, skin color, native language, gender, sexual preference, intelligence, body shape, or body size. But because I state the main rule positively, the overall rule doesn't have a negative connotation and students don't feel compelled to break the rule just to show that they can.

Consider the consequences of your rules on everybody, including you. Doling out demerits, for example, requires that you keep records of student offenses and spend time assigning punishments and consequences. Assigning lunch or after-school detention may seem like a good idea, but it punishes you as well as the student because you have to spend your time supervising your detainees unless you want their detention time to become a social hour. Making students write essays or reports is a popular punishment, but using writing as a punitive tool may backfire on everybody—you, the student, and the other teachers at your school—by teaching students to hate writing. Sending students to the principal, another popular tactic, may remove the student from your room but sends a clear message to students that you feel incapable of handling the situation alone.

CHARACTERISTICS OF SUCCESSFUL DISCIPLINE POLICIES

You can find any number of training courses, books, workshops, and journal articles that offer keys to effective classroom management. Much of that advice may be contradictory and confusing. Experts disagree vehemently about whether rewards have positive or negative effects on long-term behavior and motivation, for example. Some experts insist that assigning consequences is the key to molding behavior; others believe that consequences equal punishment and that we should view misbehavior as a problem for which we must brainstorm solutions. Every classroom-management program offers examples and testimonials to its effectiveness, and so many different approaches exist that you may be tempted to throw up your hands and wing it or just pick a policy and hope it works. I would like to suggest that you select or create a program that incorporates the following common characteristics of effective, successful discipline techniques:

- Model the behavior you expect from students.
- Separate the child from the behavior.

- Make the student accept responsibility.

- Allow the student to back down gracefully.

- Seek solutions instead of merely assigning consequences.

- Assign consequences that address specific behaviors.

- Clearly state your expectations for future behavior.

- Provide positive feedback when behavior improves.

- Wipe the student's slate clean.

- Identify the reason for repeated misbehavior.

- Focus on rewarding good behavior.

- Send students to the principal as a last resort.

Model the Behavior You Expect from Students

No matter how brilliant your plan, it won't work if you don't set the example. You cannot mandate respect, for example. If you want students to treat each other with respect, you must show them how it's done (and in some cases, show them and show them and show them, because this will be a new experience for them). If you want students to use a logical approach to solving problems, you must demonstrate the techniques for them by modeling the behavior when you encounter problems during the school day and explaining how you work through each step. Yes, modeling behaviors takes time, but spending that time at the start of the school year will save you hours of time later: your students will cooperate with you, and you won't have to waste so much time on discipline.

Note: do not let other adult staff members disrespect your students. Often adults will insist that they are "just kidding" when they insult or intentionally embarrass students, but because teachers hold a position of power, students may be afraid to protest that the teasing is offensive or insulting. Even when students do protest, some adults persist. Of course, you can't dictate adults' behavior, and it's hard to criticize them without stepping on their toes in front of students. You can't say, "Please stop abusing your authority," but you can call the adult aside and say, "Please help me out here. We have had a problem with teasing in my classroom, so we don't engage in that behavior at all. Sometimes students don't understand when teasing crosses the line, so we just don't do it. And it's important for us adults to set the example."

Separate the Child from the Behavior

Sometimes a child will intentionally misbehave just to irritate a teacher, but most misbehavior is a result of immaturity, impatience, frustration, or the desire to fulfill some imagined or real need. Children act like children because they *are* children; as human beings, albeit small ones, they are prone to making mistakes. Don't take your students' behavior personally unless it is clearly a personal attack on you—and even then you may simply represent authority. When teachers take children's behavior personally, we limit our ability to assess a situation objectively and choose the best response; but if we can separate the child from the behavior, we can follow the excellent advice, "Hate the behavior, love the child." This attitude helps us focus on solving problems and helping students learn to make better choices, instead of simply punishing the student or assigning meaningless consequences.

Make the Student Accept Responsibility

When teachers assign consequences and dictate behavior, we take control of and responsibility for a given situation. If we place the responsibility squarely on the student's shoulders, where it belongs, we experience a completely different response. For example, if a student disrupts your class and you immediately reprimand him or her and assign a consequence, you focus everybody's attention on you; and some people will automatically sympathize with the culprit just because he is in the less powerful position. If you ask the student to stop and think about his behavior and decide whether he wants to continue or make a change, the focus shifts to the student, who now controls the outcome of the conflict. He cannot blame you for his behavior or for any resulting consequences. Many teachers find that asking a student to step outside for a chat, fill out a form describing the unacceptable behavior, or sign a contract in which the student agrees not to repeat the behavior are more effective than assigning punishments.

Allow the Student to Back Down Gracefully

When students have the opportunity to back down gracefully, many of them will decide to cooperate with you. But when you back them up against the wall, most students will become stubborn and defiant; and many will lash out. This holds true even for very young children, who often have a stronger sense of dignity than many adults give them credit for having. When we allow a student to back down the first time he or she engages in a specific inappropriate behavior, we teach that student and any observers several lessons: we are responsible for choosing our own behavior; everybody makes mistakes; mistakes are not permanent; and a good leader exhibits compassion and respect. Our students imitate our behavior, whether or not they like us, so it behooves us to set a high standard and a good example.

Seek Solutions Instead of Merely Assigning Consequences

Sending a tardy student to detention does not address the problem of tardiness and will most likely result in a worse student-teacher relationship and possibly in academic problems. Assigning a student to spend ten minutes helping you clean your classroom would reduce the amount of effort and paperwork involved. Better yet, require the student to complete an exercise using a problem-solving model to brainstorm possible actions and implement a solution to his problem.

Assign Consequences That Address Specific Behaviors

Using detention or demerits to address every behavior is like using one kind of medicine to cure symptoms of a variety of diseases. This hit-or-miss approach often misses in a school setting. If you assign consequences, try to assign consequences that actually address the misbehavior you want to discourage. If a student draws a heart with black marker or scrawls obscenities on her desk, sending her to detention leaves you with a dirty desk. Making the student clean her desk—or all the desks in your classroom—would be more appropriate for a first offense. Likewise, sending a disrupter to detention doesn't teach him to be quiet and respectful. Asking him to stand outside your door until he feels able to control his behavior will give him an opportunity to practice self-control; if he makes an effort but fails, he may succeed if you provide a few more chances to practice. If he refuses to make the effort, then you may opt to assign consequences that directly apply to defiance and disrespect.

Clearly State Your Expectations for Future Behavior

One year I had a student who repeatedly interrupted my lessons by standing up, loudly clearing his sinus cavities, and walking across the room to spit in the trash can. Because he was a well-behaved student otherwise, I opted to warn him to be more polite instead of assigning punishments. Finally, I called the student aside and asked him why he continued to act so disrespectfully.

He said, "I'm not being disrespectful."

I asked, "Do you think walking across the room and spitting in the trash is respectful when I am trying to talk to the class?"

"Yeah," he said, earnestly "because I'm not spitting on the floor."

That conversation taught me to be more specific in my instructions to students. My warnings no longer leave any room for misunderstanding:

Keep your hands on your own desk. Throw things only in appropriate places, such as the gym.

Sleepy students may stand in the back of the room if they can't stay awake, but sleeping is never permitted.

Provide Positive Feedback When Behavior Improves

Everybody responds to positive feedback, and students are especially responsive. They are also especially sensitive to teachers' attitudes toward them. Often a child believes that the teacher no longer likes him or her after a confrontation, even a minor incident. After any incident that results in a private conference, consequences, or punishment, watch for an opportunity to praise the student who misbehaved. When she behaves appropriately, let her know you noticed and appreciate the improvement. Some children would prefer not to be recognized publicly, but they will not object to a phone call to say thanks, a quick note, a handshake, or a comment on the margin of a paper.

Wipe the Student's Slate Clean

In addition to providing positive feedback, make sure your students understand that a mistake is not a permanent condition. Just as we release criminals who have served their time, we must allow students a second chance. Of course, the more serious the offense, the longer it will take for a student to regain your complete trust; but if you make clear that you don't hold any grudges, the student will be much more likely to cooperate in the future.

Identify the Reason for Repeated Misbehavior

If you keep assigning the same consequences for the same misbehavior, nobody is gaining anything from the experience and everybody is losing valuable time. When a problem recurs repeatedly in your classroom, the student is sending a clear signal that he or she needs help in some specific area. Identifying the reason for a behavior may take some time and effort, but the time will be well spent if a casual conversation, a brief nonpunitive conference, an exchange of comments in a journal, a phone call, a confidential chat with close friends, or some other method can help you figure out why a student is behaving in a certain way. Often students misbehave repeatedly because they want the teacher to send them to talk to a counselor or psychologist or they want you to inquire about their home situation. If you can't communicate with the student, ask other staff members if they have any suggestions. Most students have one favorite teacher, coach, secretary, bus driver, security guard, school police officer, custodian, or counselor.

Focus on Rewarding Good Behavior

When you focus on rewarding good behavior instead of punishing bad behavior, you create a different dynamic in your classroom. Rewarding students is not the same as bribing them. A bribe is intended to entice somebody to do something for the sole purpose of earning a reward. Of course, we don't want to teach children that they will receive a reward every time they cooperate or work—because they won't. That's not the way the world operates. But they certainly will be rewarded for behaving responsibly as citizens and workers. We all respond to positive feedback, which may come in the form of verbal praise, high marks on our assignments, promotions, monetary raises, certificates, or other acknowledgment.

Send Students to the Principal as a Last Resort

A hundred years ago when I was young, being sent to the principal's office was a very big deal. The principal would paddle you; your parents would paddle you; and your siblings would shun your for embarrassing the family. If you send a student to the principal's office today, there is a good chance that the student will refuse to leave your room or that he will leave campus entirely. Even if he cooperates, he may spend an amusing hour trading jokes with other students in a waiting area or sit in a detention room reading comic books, doing word search puzzles, or staring at the walls.

When your wayward student arrives at the principal's office, the result may be very different from what you intended. Principals don't always support their teachers. Students don't always care whether they pass your class or graduate. Parents don't always accept reality or the responsibility for raising their children. And in the worst cases, students or their families may raise legal issues—valid or not—to avoid the real issues of personal responsibility.

In addition to the obvious reasons, my primary reason for not sending students to the office is that I don't like the cycle of behavior that usually results. What we hope will happen rarely does: the student accepts responsibility for his or her actions, learns from this mistake, and resolves to cooperate with the teacher in the future. What usually happens is more like this: the student misbehaves; you send the student to the office; the student becomes angry or embarrassed and blames you for causing those feelings; the student also blames you for whatever punishment the principal metes out; the student misses hours or days of valuable lessons in your class and other subjects; the student returns to your class still angry or ashamed or eager for revenge; and you're back to the beginning of the cycle, ready for another round.

With compassion and creativity, you can break this destructive cycle and offer alternative solutions. Being kind and compassionate doesn't necessarily equal being weak. Students understand this, but some adults have trouble accepting it. Again I'd suggest sitting for a moment in your students' seats. Imagine how you would feel if your supervisor at work objected to your behavior and, instead of explaining the objection, discussing the problem, and giving you a chance to change your behavior, the supervisor marched you past your coworkers to the company president's office for a reprimand? That may sound silly, but an office isn't so different from a classroom. You're the company president, and your students are your employees, whose job is to learn their lessons and complete their assignments in exchange for credits toward an academic promotion or a diploma. When they make mistakes or become ineffective workers, your task is to correct them quickly and without damaging their dignity any more than is necessary. (Of course, you will deal with serious offenses differently than everyday problems such as tardiness, inefficiency, forgetfulness, and general bad attitudes.)

TEN STEPS TO BETTER DISCIPLINE

"Theories are great, but I need practical advice," one young teacher told me during a workshop. "Could you tell me exactly what to do and say to my students?" Here is my ten-step response to her question. I have experienced good success using these techniques with a wide array of students, from troublesome teens to overachieving college-bound scholars. These steps are listed in order of power—beginning with the most subtle and least forceful responses from you. After you gain some experience, you may want to add your own variations, but this list is a good starting point. It will give you a solid basis and will provide opportunities for you to practice and evaluate different techniques.

1. Ignore the Offender

Often students act out just to gauge the teacher's response. If you are easily upset, flustered, or angered, they will take advantage of your short fuse. On the other hand, if you ignore mild misbehavior, it will often go away.

A student may whisper the F-word under her breath, for example, just to see if she can make you blush or yell. If you pointedly ignore the behavior, the student may get the message. If she does not, then you have many options, depending on the student. This approach sends a new, stronger message: this is my classroom, and I will decide when and how I respond to student behavior.

2. Send Nonverbal Messages

We all respond to body language. In fact, most students of human behavior agree that 80 percent of our communications are nonverbal. Take advantage of this powerful tool by using eye contact, changes in your voice and posture, and gestures and movements to alert students that they are approaching a danger zone. Above all, keep moving. Teachers who rove around their rooms experience far fewer behavior problems because students automatically react to the distance between them and the teacher. If this distance changes at random, students are much more likely to monitor their own behavior.

3. Drop a Behavior Card

Because so many students are visual or kinesthetic learners, they may not respond to verbal requests. Or they may forget a few seconds after you have reminded them to be quiet or sit down. Using colorful index cards that you can easily locate and retrieve in class, create some behavior cards.

For young students, write this message:

> Stop and think.
> You need to be more polite.
> I will talk to you about this later.

For older students, write this message:

> Your present behavior is not acceptable.
> Please be more polite.
> Return this card to me—in person—after class.

When a student begins to disrupt your class, walk past and drop a card on his or her desk. In most cases the student will stop the current behavior. Leaving the card on the desk serves as a visual reminder for students who tend to forget. Collect the cards after class if you teach multiple subjects or at the end of an activity with younger children. When you collect the cards, thank the students for choosing to behave and cooperate. (If you drop a card and the student ignores it or throws it on the floor, see the next step.)

4. Have a Quick Chat

If nonverbal signals and behavior cards fail to motivate your student, ask him or her to step outside the room. Don't worry about the other students. They will be interested in seeing what happens, and although they may make a little noise while you are in the hallway, they will be quiet when you return. (If a student becomes nosey and asks questions, invite that student to step outside. He may decline the invitation, but if he does step outside, out of curiosity or belligerence, treat him the same as your original disrupter.)

Ask your student if there is a reason for his or her disruptive, defiant, or disrespectful behavior. If there is and it's reasonable, figure out a way to address it. If the student can't offer a reason, ask the student if you have somehow offended or insulted him or her. If you have, apologize and offer to shake hands. If you haven't, tell the student that it is time to think. Here's the warning speech I make (you may choose to change the wording for younger students, but the gist of the message should be the same):

> You have the right to fail my class. If you truly want to fail, then I would like you to put that desire into writing and sign it so that I can keep it in my file to show you and your parents in the future if you question your grade. If you don't like the activity I have assigned, I'm sorry; but I am the teacher, and I chose that assignment because I believe it will teach important information and skills. You don't have to

do the assignment. You have the right to sit and quietly vegetate if you truly don't want to do the work, but you do *not* have the right to interrupt my teaching, stop anybody else from learning, or waste everybody's time with obnoxious disruptive behavior.

Ask the student if he or she feels ready to come back to class and cooperate. If so, shake hands and get back to business. If not, it's time for the next step.

5. Take a Time-Out

Leave the student standing outside your door (or in the back of your room, if you have small children or a strict policy that would prohibit having a student stand in the hall temporarily). Ask the student to consider his present behavior and whether or not he wants to continue. Go quietly back into your room and give the student time to think about his behavior. Occasionally step outside to see whether the student is ready to talk to you. If not, leave him there. If necessary, leave him there until the end of the class period or school day. Tell him you are trying to help him be a more successful student and person. Remind him that if he runs off, you will have to refer him to the office as being truant and then the matter is out of your hands. If he doesn't run off and doesn't talk to you, let the matter drop and see what happens the following day. Often students will pretend the entire incident never happened. You can then do the same.

6. Call the Culprit

One evening after a particularly trying day, I called the father of a student who had tried to drive me crazy by whistling softly at a very high and annoying pitch for ninety minutes in my classroom. Father wasn't home, and junior answered the phone.

"You know who this is?" I asked.

"Yes," he whispered.

"I was very disappointed in your behavior today," I said. "I like you, but I don't like the way you acted. It was very annoying, and it disrupted my teaching. It's important to me to be a good teacher. I don't want you to do that again. All right?"

"All right," he said.

He never whistled again, and I began calling students directly to discuss their behavior. In most cases those phone calls were much more effective than calls to parents, because the students were entirely responsible for their behavior. Often when the student behavior improved, I did call the parents—to tell them how much I enjoyed having their child in my class.

7. Sign a Contract

Just as behavior cards serve as an effective visual reminder to students who forget verbal instructions, student contracts serve as effective written reminders to students who have promised to cooperate. Your contract doesn't have to be elaborate, and it doesn't have to be a form. Some teachers use a form on school letterhead to make the contract look official; all they have to do is fill in the blanks. Other teachers ask the student to write out an agreement about what behaviors will improve and what consequences the student will suffer if he or she breaks the contract.

Just as positive reinforcement produces quicker and more lasting results in behavior, positively stated contracts result in quicker cooperation and a better relationship between student and teacher. Instead of listing things the student won't do, list things the student will do. And if possible, incorporate some reward—not a bribe— but something such as, if the student does not break this contract for thirty (or sixty) days, the student will earn ten points for good conduct and this contract becomes null and void. Think about how much more responsive you would be if a traffic officer gave you thirty days to prove you could drive safely instead of issuing you a ticket.

8. Send for Reinforcements

Sometimes even the best teacher meets an immovable student. If the first seven steps fail, and the student still causes major disruptions, don't waste time blaming yourself. Clearly, the problem is bigger than a simple personality clash or routine misbehavior. Send for reinforcements. Call security to escort the stubborn student to the principal's office. Meet with your principal and ask for suggestions and support. Call parents and request a conference. If parents or guardians are unhelpful or a key element in the student's problem, see if you can find an adult relative, such as an aunt or uncle. Check with the bus driver and your school security personnel to see if they have managed to create a good relationship with the student. Talk to your school counselors and psychologists and ask them to talk to the student and suggest alternative approaches for you to try. Ask a coach to counsel the student. If your community has a mentor program, see if the student has a mentor. If not, put in an emergency request. (And if your school doesn't have a mentor program, write a letter to the editor of your local newspaper and ask community organizations and businesses to sponsor a mentor program.)

9. Request a Transfer

If your school is large enough to have another teacher at the same level, see if that teacher would be willing to accept the student as a transfer into his or her class (of course, you and the other teacher can't make this transfer yourselves, but if both teachers agree, the office will be much more likely to cooperate with your request).

At small schools where a transfer is not an option, you may be able to find a fellow teacher who also has a problem student. Offer to switch students for a specified period of time each day, to give yourselves and students a break from each other.

10. Remove the Perpetrator

You may be stuck with an incorrigible student for any number of reasons: a small school with limited options, lack of administrative support, undue parental influence in the community, inflexible guidelines from your local school board. If you have exhausted every avenue and a student continues to disrupt your teaching and other students' learning, then you need to remove the student from your classroom—unofficially. I have used this method successfully myself, and I have recommended it to other desperate teachers, who report that it worked for them.

First, create an assignment folder for your troublesome student. Include the next two or three assignments that you intend to complete during class and a brief but complete description of any special activities or projects. Next, talk to your school librarian and ask whether you may send a student to do independent work as long as that student does not misbehave in the library. If the librarian agrees, explain that you will give the student a pass each day and that the student is to ask the librarian to sign the pass and indicate the time that the students enters and leaves the library. (In schools with no library or no cooperative librarian, find a counselor, coach, administrator, or teacher who can supervise the student and agree on a time period and location for this experiment. If no other location is available, place a desk outside your classroom door and have the student sit outside and do his work. If he leaves the desk and wanders off, he is now in violation of your school policy, and you must refer him to the appropriate office.)

Do not make any preface or provide any warning. Simply call your student aside, hand him the folder, and explain that he will be completing his work independently. Provide an instruction sheet that states your expectations about conduct in the library, the procedure for getting his passes signed, and his responsibility for returning the completed work to you at the end of the class period each day. Do not argue with the student. Hand him the folder, show him the door, shut the door, and teach the students who cooperate. If your troublesome student decides to take a vacation, simply fill out the proper reports and let the discipline system handle him. If he complies with your instructions, continue this policy for as long as necessary. Once I had to remove a student for an entire quarter, and I'd like to add that the day I reached the end of my patience and removed him from the class, several students stopped by individually to thank me for removing the troublemaker and making it possible for them to learn.

Of course, there is a chance that your administrators (or sadly, your fellow teachers) may object to your emergency independent-assignment procedure. If that happens, explain (and follow up with a letter summarizing your conversation to cover your back in case somebody decides to file a report at your district office) that you exhausted every legal option and the student still made it impossible for you to teach and other students to learn. Provide dates and times when you asked administrators for support or assistance, copies of disciplinary referrals, minutes from any conferences, and dates and times of phone calls or meetings with parents.

IF YOU MUST HAVE DETENTION, MAKE IT WORTHWHILE

Some schools insist on having a detention center, and many schools require that teachers take turns supervising detention. If that's the case in your school and you can't convince your administrators or fellow teachers to try a different approach, then do your best to make detention useful. Instead of simply enforcing a no-talking rule or overseeing time-wasting activities, find some interesting articles—interesting to young people, not necessarily to adults. For example, my students have responded enthusiastically to critical reviews of popular movies; feature articles about sports stars or musicians; essays about controversial subjects such as UFOs, tattoos, and body piercing; pop psychology quizzes; self-help articles on handwriting analysis, dating success, anger management, ways to stop bullies, and so on.

Don't make your reading assignments mandatory if you have a room full of little rebels. Just pass out the papers and say, "Here's something interesting we could read." Then give them a few minutes to look it over. Read a little bit out loud. Some students will follow along. If anybody seems interested, ask for volunteers to read. If nobody volunteers, read the entire article aloud yourself. Encourage the students to discuss the article, but if they prefer to remain mute, don't take it personally. Detention rooms may have some nasty bullies among the crowd, and many students prefer to keep a low profile. That doesn't mean they aren't interested, however. Hold your own discussion—with yourself. State your opinions. Collect the papers. Let the students go back to vegetating. Vegetating is boring, so some of them will think about what you just read. Some of them may even be inspired to think for several minutes in a row. That's a good start.

Beware: your efforts to stimulate thought may backfire. One teacher reported that when she began using short psychology lessons and discussions during her assigned detentions, students often complained when the bell rang to signal the end of the period. After a few weeks, some students began asking to be sent to her detention because they enjoyed the lessons so much!

KEEP RECORDS

Regardless of what behavior policy you choose, create a folder for discipline problems (in Chapter Three, I suggest making a Misbehavior folder). Keep track of your efforts to help students, with dates for each disciplinary action. You don't need to record quick chats and time-outs unless a student starts to show a pattern of serious misbehavior. If that happens, document everything—warnings, behavior cards, phone calls, notes to parents, referrals to the office (students can disappear en route or get lost in the shuffle), and requests for help from administrators and other teachers. This record will not only provide evidence in the unlikely event of a legal problem, it will also show you whether you have a pattern of becoming too stressed and short-tempered at the end of a grading period or the beginning of a new unit.

CONSULT THE EXPERTS, BUT FOLLOW YOUR HEART

Investigate resources and explore your options before you settle on a discipline program. Find a method that makes sense to you and that fits your own teaching style. Don't adopt somebody else's rules just because you think you should have rules. Children instinctively understand when adults are sincere, and heaven help you if they sense that you aren't. If you try to impose a behavior code that you don't really support, then nobody in your classroom—including you—will honor it.

After asking for advice from your professors and colleagues and conducting your own research, if you still find yourself at a loss for how to approach the discipline problem, you might start with a modern translation of the Golden Rule: treat people the way you would like them to treat you. Don't merely post the rule in your classroom. Follow the rule yourself. Treat your students the way you would like them to treat you. They may be a little slow at first, and some of them may need a short vacation (or two, or three) from your class; but if you sincerely respect them and maintain your own high standards of behavior, eventually they will come around. And eventually you will find an approach that works for both you and your students.

Should you encounter a plethora of die-hard, incorrigible little stinkers in your classroom who steadfastly refuse to appreciate you, hang in there. And hang a calendar in your bathroom where each night as you brush your teeth, you will have a visual reminder that you have survived one more day. Don't give up hope. Don't take the students' actions personally; they would torment another teacher just as they torment you. Do give up feeling guilty or unworthy. Most of us have had "one of those years."

EMERGENCY PLAN FOR TEACHER MELTDOWN

Occasionally several factors combine to drive a teacher past the point of his or her tolerance. Even the best teachers can crack under the right conditions. When students sense that the teacher is near the breaking point, a handful of sympathetic souls may behave themselves, but most students will become relentless in their efforts to break the teacher. This can happen even with students who are not vicious or unfeeling. It is a result of specific ingredients and group dynamics that are beyond your control.

I remember a dynamic young teacher with seven years of experience successfully teaching advanced-level classes at a California high school. Her students adored her, and graduates often came back to offer their thanks. One day a student in her class stood up without warning and started to criticize her teaching methods and curriculum. Caught by surprise, the teacher allowed the student to draw her into an argument, and before long the entire class of students polarized on the boy's side. A power struggle quickly turned into a shark feed. The teacher ended up running out of the room in tears, prepared to resign and give up teaching permanently. Fortunately, the principal refused to accept the teacher's resignation. He held a conference with the teacher, several students, and their parents. The parents supported the teacher and were able to apply enough pressure to force the students to stop attacking her. Within a few weeks, the students went back to adoring their teacher; but it took years before she regained her former confidence, and even then she admitted to having doubts.

When I observed that teacher's struggle, I felt sorry for her, but I didn't believe the same thing could ever happen to me. It didn't. Nobody ever stood up in my class, criticized my teaching, and stole my confidence. But just in case, I made an emergency meltdown plan and filed it away. A few years later, in New Mexico, I took over a class from a long-term substitute who didn't want to be replaced and had worked hard to turn the students against me. She took another sub position at the same school and devoted her energy to sabotaging my class. A few students responded favorably to me, but the ringleaders and the former sub were too strong for them to overcome. I won't go into details, but I will say that those regular students were far more vicious and stubborn than any of the so-called at-risk, incorrigible, or behavior-disordered students I have ever taught, including juveniles who have spent time behind bars. When I realized that I was in the midst of my own shark feed, I pulled out my plan.

1. Be professional. Make sure your lesson plans (or a rough outline) are in order for the next few weeks. Check to see that your sub folder (see Chapter Three) contains lesson plans, roll sheets, and emergency evacuation information.

2. Take a mental health break. This is an emergency. Don't feel compelled to provide specifics. Just call the office, say that you are seriously ill and will be in touch when you are feeling better. If you have a spouse or friend who can call for you, even better. Pay at least one visit to a doctor, therapist, counselor, chiropractor, masseuse, or other professional who can help you handle the stress; but don't make up a bogus medical condition. Stress is a serious problem all by itself. Give yourself at least three days. A week would be even better.

3. Do some serious thinking. Do you really want to teach? Or did you think you would enjoy teaching, only to find that you hate going to work? Do you struggle but find enough joy and satisfaction that you are willing to work on your teaching skills? Or do you have to admit that you just weren't cut out to teach, no matter how much you would like to?

4. If you realize you don't want to teach, figure out how soon you can quit. Do you have any other options for earning a living? Can you afford to quit right now? If you can't quit right now, create a plan for updating your résumé and conducting a job search. Contact professional colleagues and ask them for general letters of recommendation. Don't whine about your job; just say that you are thinking of making a career change in the future. Focus on creating the life you want instead

of hating the life you have. Just changing your focus will make it easier for you to teach until you can afford to leave. Knowing that you aren't stuck forever, that you have choices, will make a big difference. You may even find that once you've decided to stop teaching, you relax and enjoy yourself so much that you decide to stay.

5. If you decide you do want to teach (or you have to teach until you can afford to quit), then prepare yourself to make some serious changes in your classroom when you return. Plan to change everything in your classroom—from the decor to the furniture arrangement, student seating, even the rules and procedures. Also plan to change your attitude, your approach, your posture, even your tone of voice. Buy a suit or some other clothing that shouts "Power!" Check your local library or bookstore for books on power dressing; a black suit with a white shirt is the ultimate power outfit.

It may sound frivolous, but check your footwear. You may have to give up comfort for a little while. Find a pair of leather-soled shoes (boots are even better) that make an authoritative clunk when you walk, as opposed to the dainty click of high heels or the squish of tennis shoes. If your classroom is carpeted, make sure you leave the room once or twice during each class period so that students can hear you walking sharply back toward the room. When you enter, shut the door firmly behind you—not a slam but a nice, hard close.

6. Change the look of your room. Design an alternate arrangement of furniture. How you arrange it isn't as important as creating a new look. You want students to see immediately that things are different. Put your desk in a different corner. Shuffle some file cabinets around. Hang some new posters or artwork.

7. Rearrange the student desks. If you've been using a semicircle or U shape, move the chairs back into rows. If you've been using rows, find a shape that will fit your room.

8. Create a seating chart. Using one of the copies of your roll sheets that you keep at home for planning, create a chart that separates the strongest students from each other. Put a major power player nearest to your home base. Put another near the door, where he or she will have less distance to travel when it's time to step outside. Place that handful of good, decent kids near each other for moral support.

9. Create a week's worth of extremely interesting and challenging lessons, lessons that require students to do the bulk of the work. Place the focus on them, not on you. Search online, read magazines and journals, check the library and bookstore for ideas. The www.teachers.net Web site has a lot of links and suggestions.

10. Call on a Friday morning and tell the school you will be back on Monday. Treat yourself to a movie or a special meal on Friday. Try to relax because you will be working on the weekend. Spend that weekend rearranging your room and getting things in order. On Sunday night, take a long walk or get some exercise to help you sleep better.

11. On Monday morning get up thirty minutes earlier than usual. Do some calisthenics or yoga, meditate or take a quick walk—anything that will get your blood flowing and your heart beating a little faster than usual. You're in training for an important contest, so eat breakfast. Put on your power clothes, grab your lesson plans, and get to school ahead of the early birds. Write the instructions for your first assignment on the board and station yourself in the doorway. Block the doorway so that only one student can enter at a time. When students begin to arrive, look each student in the eye, say, "Welcome to my new, improved classroom," and direct the student to his or her new seat. Don't discuss the seating arrangements. If students ask questions, say, "We'll discuss it in a minute. Right now I'm busy."

12. When everybody is seated, tell them why you were absent. Tell them you didn't like what was happening in your classroom, so you have done some serious thinking and made some serious changes. If you have decided to stop teaching, just tell them that you are still considering different options for your future and that you have a lot of options because you are a college graduate. You haven't made any decisions about your career yet, but you have made some decisions about your classroom. You are going to conduct things differently. If anybody disrupts this speech, call security and have them escorted to the office immediately. If this is a completely hopeless situation and you end up sending the entire class, then send them. Let the administration be responsible for supporting you, which is their job. If your students are beyond help and your entire school is out of control, consider applying for a job at another school, working as a sub in your district or a nearby district, or taking a sabbatical. As one old rancher I know used to say, "Don't blame yourself if you can't put out a forest fire by peeing on it."

On the other hand, if you have decided you want to continue teaching, tell your students that's what you have decided. Tell them why you want to be a teacher. They probably don't have any idea how dedicated most teachers are. Explain that you want to help them be successful people and that you have made some changes in order to make that possible. Tell them everybody is starting with a clean slate but that you expect them to conduct themselves with self-control and self-respect. Then start your first lesson.

Good luck to you. Teaching is difficult work, but if you make up your mind that you truly want to teach, your determination and sincerity will lead you in the right direction.

One final note about discipline. Many teachers find it difficult to pinpoint the bullies in their classrooms, so I'd like to share my method for detecting them. Tell your students that you would like their input as you plan group activities. Ask them to write their own names at the top of a sheet of paper, and then list the names of three or four students they would especially like to work with. Finally, ask them to list the names of two or three students they never want to work with—no explanations or details, just names. Don't read the lists in front of the students. When you do read them, look for students whose names repeatedly appear on the "never want to work with" lists. Those are your bullies or your outcasts; both need your attention and help.

Motivation and Morale Boosters

Sometimes, even though you have energy, enthusiasm, and a student-centered approach to teaching, your students slump in their seats and yawn at you. Even though you've spent hours creating interesting lessons, they aren't interested. Even though you are well educated and passionate about your subject, your students don't appear to care one fig. They sigh and watch the clock. They daydream and tune you out. They roll their eyes at each other and shake their heads.

These students are doing their best to convince you that they hate learning, that they don't care about school, that they are just too cool to be bothered. I maintain that if they come to school, they do care, but that past teachers have squeezed or lectured or graded the creativity, imagination, and sense of play out of them. You can reintroduce your students to the joy of learning. In the words of my mentor, Al Black, "All you have to do is get their attention."

Here are twenty-eight suggestions that may help you get your students' attention. I have used every one of these techniques in my classroom, and they work. And I'd like to add that my teaching experience is not limited to at-risk, disenchanted teens.

I have taught a wide variety of students, from non-English-speaking high school freshmen to university graduate students. Regardless of their age, intellectual ability, and academic background, my students have all responded to these approaches.

HELP STUDENTS BELIEVE SUCCESS IS POSSIBLE

Brains, like engines, don't operate at peak efficiency if they are low on fuel, clogged by dirty oil, or missing small but critical parts. If your students are all well fed, adequately parented, emotionally well-adjusted, and well educated, you probably won't face any serious problems when you try to motivate them to learn. But if they are hungry, tired, suffering from emotional stress, or poorly educated, you have a challenge on your hands. Don't despair. What you bring to your students is just as important as what your students bring to your classroom.

We have all heard the statistics, and we have learned from our own experiences that the teacher's attitude toward his or her students is the primary factor in student success. When we believe that students can succeed, they succeed. But your belief is only half of the solution to the problem of poor performance. Your belief alone isn't enough; you must help your students believe that success is possible. When students believe they can succeed, they try and they learn. But if they don't believe success is possible, it doesn't matter how intelligent the student or how easy the material, they will not try. When you honestly believe that all students can learn (they can) and when you convince your students that success is possible, you hold the key that unlocks the door to learning.

How do you convince students that success is possible? Some people suggest that you provide an exercise or activity that guarantees success for every student. I disagree with that approach. Usually such success experiences are far too easy and therefore defeat their own purpose. Instead of convincing students that they are capable of achieving, easy assignments and esteem-boosting activities send the message that students aren't capable of handling truly difficult challenges. In other words, you gave them an easy assignment because you believe they are dumb. So instead of creating an easy task, assign a truly difficult task and then help your students complete it. When you introduce the task, explain that it is difficult and that you don't expect anybody to do it perfectly—including yourself. Tell them you are going to tackle this project because you believe they are intelligent and that you know they can learn because you see evidence of many things they have already learned: they can read and dress themselves; they know their own addresses and phone numbers; they can play musical instruments and a hundred different games; they know the words to a lot of songs; they can fix meals; they know how to operate machines and kitchen gadgets and computers and VCRs.

Where do you find the challenging assignment? One good place to look is at your own school. If you teach second grade, for example, ask a fourth-grade teacher for a sample vocabulary lesson. Tell your students that they are going to do an assignment that kids two whole grades ahead of them are doing, just to see what those kids are learning. And if they do a good job, they will earn extra credit. If you teach middle school or high school, find a college textbook that has an interesting essay. Tell your students that they are going to read something that college students read; show them the textbook so that they can see that you are telling the truth. Explain that their brains work just as well as the brains of college students, but they don't challenge them the way college kids do. Assure them that if they don't know all of the words in the essay, you will help them because that is your job. Then read the essay aloud in class, discuss it, and ask your students to write their responses to the reading. When they finish this project, some student will very likely say, "That wasn't so hard." And this is your cue to respond, "Of course it isn't, because everybody in this class knows how to think, and thinking is the key to learning. We have good brains in this room, so let's use them."

ASSESS THE ATTITUDES IN YOUR CLASSROOM

Find out how your students feel about school, themselves, and your subject. You could ask your students how they feel. Some of them will be eager to tell you, but most students opt to observe instead of participate in class discussions; they don't want to talk about school. They don't want to write essays or paragraphs about school either. But most of them will be willing to give you a few comments, if you insist. Go ahead and insist, because you want maximum input from them on this topic. Distribute index cards and ask your students to write down their thoughts about school in general and your subject(s) in particular.

Tell your students that they earn credit for cooperating and that everybody who fills out a card will earn the maximum grade. Make sure that they understand that names are optional, so that they can freely state their opinions without fear of offending you or feeling vulnerable. (If you walk down the rows and collect the cards in order, putting each one on the bottom of the stack, you will be able to figure out which students said what, just in case you find any extreme comments that need your attention.)

Some groups will go to town on this project, but others will require a little prompting. For your visual learners, write these questions on the board:

- What do you like most about school?

- What do you like least?

- What are your favorite/least favorite subjects?

- Do you like to read? Why or why not?

This next step is optional, depending on your students. If they are reasonably well-behaved and paying attention, you might consider reading a few comments from the cards, after you have collected enough that students won't be able to identify the author. Read comments that you think might elicit a response from others: "I hate writing because I always run out of stuff to say," for example, may prompt a discussion and alert you to the need for a lesson on prewriting and developing ideas.

Whether you discuss the cards or not, thank your students for taking the time to let you know their opinions. Take the cards home and read them carefully. Look at the spelling, sentence structure, vocabulary, and handwriting for clues to student personalities and areas of difficulty. Look for areas of common concern and specific problems that you can address in the future. Make a note of any special interests or hobbies, and incorporate those into your lessons whenever possible. You may be surprised by the positive student response to even a simple comment, such as "Learning to identify an adjective is easier than tying a fishing fly," or "This is a great vocabulary word for rappers because it is onomatopoeic and rhymes with so many other words."

ADJUST THE ATTITUDES

If you haven't already done the "I have to" and "I can't" exercise from Chapter Four, this is a good time to do the exercise and discuss the power of choice. This exercise usually has a remarkable effect on students' perceptions of school attendance. At the end of the exercise, they have to admit that they choose to come to school and that they can choose to succeed or fail.

Also discuss Maslow's hierarchy of needs, if you haven't already done that (see Chapter Four for a brief outline). If you have discussed this theory, remind your students that they must fulfill their need to be accepted and respected by a group so that they won't become targets for people who will be a bad influence on them. Tell them that you want to help them be successful students and successful people and that this is one way they can help themselves. If you spend a little time on activities whose sole purpose is to help your students be successful, they get the message that you truly care about them; and it's hard to hate somebody who likes you and tries to help you in spite of your negative attitude.

After you have adjusted your students' attitudes, it's time to adjust your own. You may think your attitude is just fine, but if you are having a problem with discipline, motivation, or participation, then you may be part of the problem. Perhaps you aren't prepared when class begins, so students follow your disorganized example. Or maybe you believe you are treating your students with respect, but you have a hidden agenda that you are going to save them from themselves—and they have detected your patronizing attitude.

How much do you listen, really listen, to your students? And how do you respond to their comments? Do you always have the last word? Do you correct their grammar when they are talking passionately about something? Do you imply that your values and standards and lifestyle are superior to theirs? Do you belittle their ideas or brush off their concerns as trivial? Do you use a dismissive tone of voice? Even if you think you are always courteous and respectful, try setting up a tape recorder near your desk and taping your class for thirty minutes. You may be surprised to hear the tone of your voice or the way you speak differently to different students. (I have tried this myself and was unpleasantly surprised the first time.)

Many teachers have trouble getting students to talk to them. The same students who talk each other's ears off may suddenly become tongue-tied if you ask them to talk to you. Or you may have one or two students who dominate every class discussion. In order to involve everybody in your class, I would suggest that you try beginning each class period by asking, "Who has a question? You can ask me anything about anything. If I don't know the answer, I will find out where we can locate the information."

Students don't automatically respond to this approach. It make take several days or weeks of asking this before somebody finally responds. Once somebody responds, others will follow. But you may have to do a lot of prompting to get that first response. You might find that if you ask your own question and answer it out loud, students may respond. You might say, "I was thinking about reality TV shows last night. And I wonder if those shows could really be called reality because the people know they are being filmed, so they probably don't act like they would if they weren't being filmed. Some of them act like they are just picking fights with each other because they know they will get attention and more people will see them." If nobody comments, just say, "Well, that's what I was thinking." Then start your lessons.

The next day you might say, "Who has a question? Anybody? Let's wait a minute to see if anybody has one." Wait a full minute to see if anybody can think of one. Watch the clock for a full minute. If nobody speaks, say, "Well, I was just wondering what happens to change our society so drastically. When I was a kid, the only people who had tattoos were bikers and ex-convicts and people who wanted to make a statement. Today tattoos are like jewelry. I wonder what happened to change that." Then wait a second to see if anybody responds. Choose a student who seems to be considering your comments and ask if he or she has a comment. If not, start your lesson.

Continue each day asking your own question for two or three weeks, even a month if you can think of enough comments. If nobody ever responds, then you might want to consider trying a different approach. But don't give up easily. And don't think your students aren't interested. They will be listening even if they pretend they aren't.

Although this technique works very well for me, it wasn't originally my idea. A few years ago, I attended an awards ceremony for a student who had won an essay contest. He wrote about his teacher: "Our teacher used to come in every morning and say, 'What do you want to know?'" The boy told me, "Nobody ever answered him, but he kept asking. Finally, after a really long time, I asked him a question. The next day I asked another one. Pretty soon other kids were asking questions, and we started talking about all kinds of stuff. And after a while, we got to like school again. That teacher showed us that we had forgotten how to dream. He gave that back to us. That's why I wrote my essay about him."

After meeting that student, I tried his teacher's approach. It worked so well that I have continued to use it in every class, regardless of my students' age or academic background. One of my former students, a young man who was in my class in 1993, recently sent me an e-mail in response to my request for advice to teachers who want to connect with students. Alex wrote:

I liked when you took time to have class discussions at the beginning of class for a few minutes. Sometimes you would focus on one student, and the rest of the class was paying attention because they knew they might be next. I did not feel pressure when you asked me a question because at the end, no matter what our response was, you always made us feel good for responding. You listened to us. After that warm welcome to class, it did not matter what kind of hard work you gave us. We tried our best to do the work.

One more tweak to your attitude may be in order. If you earned consistently high grades in school or if you haven't been to school for a while, try taking a very difficult class, one that you will have to struggle to pass. If you are creative, for example, enroll in statistics or advanced mathematics. If you are scientific-minded, try an art class. Your goal is not to earn an A but to remember (or find out for the first time) how it feels to be intelligent yet unable to easily grasp a new concept. Some teachers find that an academic adjustment enables them to better empathize with their students. If you share your own struggles with your students, even better. They may be surprised at first to learn that you can't ace everything. In fact, they may not believe you. You may have to bring in an assignment or exam with a low grade to provide proof. This won't diminish you in their eyes, and they won't lose respect for you either. They will realize that you are human, and they may begin treating you more like a human being.

ADD SOME RIGHT-BRAIN AND KINESTHETIC ACTIVITIES

Unless you teach art, music, or some other creative class, you may tend to focus all your lessons on left-brain (logical) activities. Although making generalizations can be dangerous, I believe it would be safe to suggest that the majority of teachers are left-brain thinkers. Left-brainers like school because their natural learning style coincides with the most common teaching styles. Unfortunately, the majority of students are not left-brain thinkers. For the sake of argument, let's assume that half the students in a given class are right-brain (creative) thinkers. They think differently from their left-brain teachers, and they often become discouraged or uninterested in school because they are made to feel unintelligent by virtue of their learning styles.

You can change the dynamics in your classroom by adding some right-brain activities and educational games. Word games that do not involve definitions or spelling are good choices. Exhibit 6.1 contains a word puzzle that I like to use to identify my right-brain students. Don't read the answers immediately. Instead, read the directions and try to solve each puzzle. If you are a left-brainer, this may be very frustrating for you.

If you do this exercise with your students, you may find that the students who enjoy it most are those who do not have the highest grades in your class. The scholars sometimes become very upset because they are used to being smarter and faster than their classmates. Your right-brain students will enjoy being the "smart kids" for a change. (Be prepared: some right-brainer may figure out alternative answers that aren't on the answer list but are equally correct.)

After you do your right-brain activity, tell your students that you would like to help them identify their own learning styles (be sure to write the three primary

---

Exhibit 6.1. Right-Brain Word Puzzle.

Directions: Each group of words shares a common trait (*not* definitions). Only one answer shares that same trait. Figure out the common trait and select the correct answer.

#1	#2	#3	#4	#5
sexes	golden	tea	modem	youth
level	tallow	eye	willow	usher
redder	clamp	sea	domed	item
a. dined	a. trace	a. wee	a. clash	a. water
b. mom	b. crawl	b. ate	b. winter	b. there
c. start	c. oven	c. you	c. tablet	c. hero

Answers:
#1. mom: the word spells the same forward and backward
#2. trace: remove the first letter to form a new word
#3. you: sounds like a letter when you say it (tea, eye)
#4. tablet: the word begins and ends with the same letter
#5. hero: the word begins with a pronoun

styles on the board for your visual learners): auditory (listeners), visual (lookers), kinesthetic (movers). Then ask your students to think about how they approach a new game. Do they like to have somebody explain the game and the rules and give them verbal instructions? Do they like to watch other people play for a while and then jump in themselves? Or would they prefer to just get into the game and learn as they go along?

Another example that helps students identify their learning styles is to give them directions. For example, tell them to imagine that they have asked you how to get to the post office. First, say, "You exit the school and turn right. Go two blocks and take the next left turn. Go up the hill and around a curve, then take the second right. After the second stop sign, turn left and then make an immediate right into the parking lot." Ask how many students feel confident that they can get to the post office after listening to your instructions. Those who raise their hands are your auditory learners (probably a small percentage of students).

Next, draw a map on the board or distribute copies of a map you have drawn. Use the same instructions that you gave verbally. Now ask how many students feel confident that they can get to the post office. Probably more than half your class will raise their hands; these are your visual learners.

Watch for students who are frowning at the map or turning it sideways. Perhaps they are tilting their heads. Ask, "If I drove you to the post office right now, how many of you would be able to retrace that same route, even if we drove it only once?" Those frowning students (your kinesthetic learners) will shoot their hands into the air, relieved to learn that there is a third alternative.

Now go over the three styles and teach your students how to ask for help from their teachers, tutors, or parents. Students who become confused often say, "I don't get it." And teachers repeat what they have said, either more loudly or more slowly. But that response will help only auditory learners. Auditory learners do need to say, "Could you please repeat that?" or "Could you please explain that to me again, a little more slowly?" Visual learners need to say, "I can't quite picture that. If I could see a drawing or a graph or video or something, I think I could understand it better. Maybe an example would help me." And your kinesthetic learners need to say, "I learn by doing things. Could you walk me through a couple of examples, step-by-step, so that I can practice doing them and get the hang of it?"

And of course, teachers need to remember that different students learn in different ways, so we need to vary our methods of instruction to incorporate visuals and movement, as well as listening activities. When you discuss a new concept, for example, be sure to provide some kind of visual to accompany your verbal introduction. And make sure that you walk students through several examples. Your kinesthetic learners need to do the examples themselves, however. Copying your work from the board isn't enough for them; they need to do the work themselves with your guidance.

In subjects such as math, this is especially important. If you simply present the lesson and then instruct students to complete an assignment, some students will get about half the answers right and it may appear that they understand. But those correct answers may be accidental or the result of faulty logic. Correcting faulty logic is important for long-term student success. My eight-year-old nephew, for example, looked as though he understood the concept of carrying numbers to another column when adding three-digit numbers. He got about sixty percent of his math problems correct. Because he did get sixty percent correct, his teacher and his parents thought Anthony was simply being lazy or trying to work too fast. When he did his math homework at my house one night, I asked Anthony to explain each step he made. When he carried a number, it was often incorrect, because as he explained, "If the number is ten or higher, you write a number up here and keep going." When I showed Anthony how to correctly carry a number, he was thrilled and his math grades immediately began to improve.

Regardless of your subject, it's important to check thoroughly for student understanding. After you look at examples of a new concept in the textbook and work out a few on the board, some students still will not be able to do the assignment on their own. Watching you complete an example isn't enough. Hearing repeated instruction is not enough. Students need to do a few examples themselves, with your guidance, until the new concept "clicks" for them.

REQUEST FREQUENT STUDENT FEEDBACK

Students are far more likely to cooperate when they have the opportunity to provide feedback to their instructors about the level of difficulty, specific or optional requirements, and the time allowed for completing their assignments. Of course, it's important to remind students that you, the teacher, make the decisions about what and how you teach but that you would appreciate their input and will not retaliate if they provide honest, constructive criticism. Some students may need a reminder that constructive criticism offers a thoughtful suggestion for improving something. (If you get some ridiculous or mean-spirited comments, don't reward the students who wrote those comments by responding to them; file their worthless feedback in the trash can during a private moment.) Thank the students who provide honest feedback and tell them you will consider their comments as you plan future assignments. Depending on your students' age, maturity, and personalities, you may decide to allow them to provide anonymous feedback. I usually make names optional (and most students do include their names because they want me to know that they gave a thoughtful response).

Monthly feedback works for some teachers; others like to wait until the end of a unit or the end of a quarter or grading period. I prefer frequent feedback because in my experience, students' morale improves when they know I care about their feelings.

Whether you allow students to comment on your teaching style or methods is up to you. Some teachers prefer to stick to lesson content and format, activities and projects, quizzes and tests. Here are two different groups of feedback questions that I have found useful. If you ask open-ended questions, such as those in Exhibit 6.2, be sure to allow ample space. Students tend to write very brief answers when the spaces are small.

For younger students, immature students, or groups that insist they are allergic to writing, I use a simpler form, such as the one in Exhibit 6.3.

REVIEW MASLOW'S HIERARCHY

If you haven't already done so, you might consider discussing Maslow's hierarchy of needs with your students. Of course, you may have to simplify the wording for younger children, but even little ones understand the importance of belonging and feeling accepted by others. Aside from helping students better understand themselves and their own behavior, discussing this theory shows your students that you truly care about them and are trying to help them be successful people. A teacher who doesn't care about his or her students isn't going to spend time trying to help them feel emotionally stable.

TEACH PROBLEM-SOLVING SKILLS

Students who misbehave often have poor problem-solving skills. Instead of thinking through a situation, they react and do the first thing that comes to mind. Until they can deal effectively with their personal problems, students won't

Exhibit 6.2. Informal Course Evaluation.

Instructions: Give it to me straight; I can take it! You don't have to include your name, but I would appreciate your thoughts.

1. Do you honestly feel prepared to do library research and write a paper? (Circle one.)   Yes   No

    If not, what could we have done in this class to better prepare you?

    _____

    _____

2. What are your thoughts on journal writing?

    _____

    _____

3. How did the peer critique groups affect your writing?

    _____

    _____

4. What did you like best about this class during this quarter and why?

    _____

    _____

5. What did you like least about this class during this quarter and why?

    _____

    _____

6. Which would you prefer (check as many as you like):
    ❏ Grammar instruction in class
    ❏ Self-paced grammar assignments and then a test
    ❏ Regular homework and quizzes on grammar

7. In reference to group activities, please check all that apply:
    ❏ I like changing groups for each activity.
    ❏ I want to keep the same groups every time.
    ❏ I want the teacher to assign groups.
    ❏ I want students to choose their own groups.
    ❏ I think group activities should count for grades.
    ❏ I don't think group assignments should count heavily for grades because some people don't work.

Thank you ever so much for completing this evaluation. I will read all your comments, and I will consider making changes to help you be more successful and happy in my class. Thanks.

Exhibit 6.3. Handy Dandy Student Feedback Form.

Instructions: Feel free to include your name, but you don't have to.

Please check the box that most closely states your feelings about each topic.

Topic	Forget It! Yuck!	Cut It Back	Just Right	Add a Little	Give Me More!
Grammar instruction					
Peer critiques					
Les Brown videos					
Journal writing					
Class discussions					
One-minute speeches					

Comments (optional): _____

_____

_____

_____

Thank you ever so much for completing this evaluation. I will read all your comments, and I will consider making changes to help you be more successful and happy in my class. Thanks.

be able to concentrate on your lessons, so it is to your benefit to teach them problem-solving skills. The model I use in my classes is a combination of models I learned during military training and later at corporate seminars. Basically, problem solving is a cycle, much like goal setting. We can teach children how to solve problems logically by showing them the steps involved in the cycle and providing a chance for them to practice. Some teachers like to present a problem that their students face: gang violence, peer pressure to use drugs, bullies, or ways to deal with parents' divorce. You may elect to use something less personal and more universal during your introduction to problem solving so that your students have a chance to practice the model without erupting into arguments over personal issues. I like to use these sample problems: (1) my friends always want to copy my homework; or (2) a few students disrupt the class and make it hard for everybody to learn.

Brainstorming is often students' favorite step in the process, but often they forget that the key to successful brainstorming is to make no judgments about others' suggestions during the brainstorming session, no matter how outlandish or silly the suggestions may sound. A silly suggestion may spark a truly innovative and effective solution to a problem, but the spark will never ignite if people laugh at each other's ideas. You may have to make the first crazy suggestions in order to encourage your students to think creatively. Another thing to keep in mind is that brainstorming in a large group tends to disintegrate into a series of smaller conversations, leaving one or two people working with the group leader. Smaller groups, with three to five people, are more effective for brainstorming.

Because children tend to act first and think later, the next step, analyzing the possible solutions, is the most important for them to practice. Students also need frequent reminders that simply choosing a solution doesn't mean they have solved a problem. They must implement the solution, evaluate its effectiveness, and select an alternative if the first choice isn't successful. At first they may complain that this process is too detailed or time-consuming, but with practice it becomes a quick and easy habit and one that will help them effectively handle problems that arise in school as well as their future careers and personal lives.

Exhibit 6.4 provides a brief outline of the problem-solving process, and Exhibit 6.5 gives some sample problems that my students suggested. Undoubtedly, your students will be able to suggest additional problems. Again you may need to simplify the instructions, but young children are excellent at brainstorming and making suggestions. When you solve a problem involving your own students, ask them to focus on solving the problem and not on assigning punishments.

After we teach the model and solve some sample problems, we are not finished with this topic. We need to refer back to the model frequently and demonstrate our own problem-solving skills during the school year as we encounter problems in our classroom. Some classroom problems can become class projects, but you may choose to keep others as a "teacher problem." If a student plagiarizes a term paper, for example, you would not be likely to publicize the incident. Even when you don't allow students to participate in solving a problem in your classroom, however, you can emphasize the importance of logical problem solving, by explaining to your students how you brainstormed, selected, and implemented a solution and how you evaluated the effectiveness of your solution.

After you have done the problem-solving activity, you will be able to refer back to it when students misbehave. Instead of assigning consequences or punishments,

---

Exhibit 6.4. Problem-Solving Model.

---

1. **Identify the problem.** Often several issues surround one central problem. Pinpoint the primary problem. For example, perhaps you fight all the time with one of your brothers or sisters, and your parents ground both of you. The problem isn't being grounded; it's the constant fighting between you and your sibling.

   Focus on one problem at a time.

2. **Brainstorm possible solutions.** Don't edit yourself or stop to criticize. Just shout out solutions or write them down as fast as you can. Be creative. Often a silly idea will lead to a truly ingenious idea that you might never have considered if you hadn't come up with the silly idea first. Take ten minutes to write down every solution that comes to mind.

3. **Select the three best solutions.** Consider the possible effects of each solution. Choose the one that seems most likely to be successful and make a plan to enact it.

4. **Implement your plan.** Put your best solution into action, making adjustments as necessary.

5. **Evaluate the effectiveness of your solution.** If your solution worked—good! If not, make some changes to your chosen plan and try it again. If changes aren't possible or just won't work, go back to your brainstorming list and choose a different solution. Repeat steps four and five until you find a solution that works. Even if you don't solve the problem completely, you can make it a much smaller problem.

ask them to step outside or sit at their desks and see if they can think of a way to solve a particular behavior problem. A solution-seeking approach will change the dynamic between you and your students. Instead of you taking responsibility for what happens to them, you are placing the responsibility for their behavior on their own shoulders, where it belongs. Further, many students actually enjoy learning how to monitor, assess, and alter their behavior.

TEACH STUDENTS HOW TO ARGUE EFFECTIVELY

Unfortunately, many students (and even more unfortunately, many of their parents) believe that an argument is a fight, with a winner and a loser. They have learned their arguing skills from watching talk shows and undignified TV courtroom dramas and

Exhibit 6.5. Problem-Solving Activity.

Instructions: In a small group, brainstorm for 10 to 15 minutes, then discuss possible solutions and choose the best one. Draft a plan to put your solution into action.

Problem A: It seems as if everybody has friends except you. You are too shy to introduce yourself to kids you don't know. You never know what to say. You're tired of feeling lonely.

Problem B: One of your teachers doesn't like you. It isn't your imagination; your friends have noticed it too. This teacher is giving you bad grades on assignments.

Problem C: Some older boys at your school grab kids in the hallway and steal their backpacks and belongings. Lately, those boys are after you.

Problem D: Every time you go out with one of your friends, he shoplifts small items such as candy bars or sodas. You really like this person and don't want to lose him as a friend. But you don't want to get arrested for shoplifting.

Problem E: One of your best friends always asks if she can copy your homework. When you say no, she gets really mad. You have been friends for a long time, and you don't want to lose her friendship. But the teacher has warned your class that if two papers are identical, both students will get Fs.

Problem F: Your stepfather is mean. No matter what you do, he finds reasons to fight with you. When you try to talk to your mother about the problem, she defends him and says to give him time.

Problem G: Every week you decide you are going to start getting your homework done on time and not be late to class, but after two days you slide back to your old habits. You feel out of control.

Problem H: Two or three kids constantly disrupt your math class. Your teacher gets mad and punishes the entire class by assigning extra homework or pop quizzes. You and your friends are tired of this.

comedies. Reminding them to be polite, considerate, or respectful isn't enough for most students, because they honestly don't know how to maintain a respectful attitude while arguing with somebody else.

After reading a number of articles about effective arguing, I designed some handouts for my students that describes successful and unsuccessful behaviors during arguments. Before I distribute the handouts, I ask students to think about the last time they witnessed or were involved in an argument. I don't ask them to discuss their personal lives, but I ask them if they can describe some of the behaviors they saw, including their own. They usually list all the unsuccessful behaviors on my handout, although they may use different terminology. Next, I ask, "What is an argument?" Nearly always several people say, "It's a fight." I ask if they can think of another definition. Usually they can't. If you encounter a group who can, you have the foundation for a good group discussion.

After we talk about arguments, I write this on the board: "An argument involves two or more people, each person expressing an opinion with the hope of changing the other people's minds about a particular subject. The point of an argument is to exchange ideas and opinions—*not* to win or lose. At the end of an argument, we have several possibilities: (1) all of the people involved change their minds and accept another person's ideas; (2) some people change their minds while others stick to their original opinions; or (3) nobody changes his or her mind."

I ask students to think about what happens when somebody "loses" an argument. They respond with a variety of answers, all basically stating the same thing: people who lose arguments want to regain their dignity, seek revenge, or get even. Losers are determined to win the next round. Sometimes a loser will start another argument just to see whether he or she can win. And this cycle goes around and around and around, but nobody ever really wins. Instead of an argument, the people become involved in a power struggle.

Then I give students the handouts (Exhibits 6.6 and 6.7).

TEACH STUDENTS HOW TO TALK TO TEACHERS AND OTHER ADULTS

Once you have taught your students how to argue, it's time to teach them how to argue with—and simply talk to—teachers. Few students know how to talk to any adult, but even fewer know how to hold an effective conversation with a teacher.

Exhibit 6.6. An Argument Is Not a Fight:
There Is No Winner or Loser.

An argument is successful when everybody involved respectfully expresses his or her opinions, respectfully listens to the other people's opinions, and takes the time to consider the other viewpoints. When an argument escalates into name calling, insults, threats, or violence, it's no longer an argument; now it's a fight. Civilized and educated people prefer to argue to solve their differences. Uncivilized and uneducated people prefer to fight.

In our classroom we will try to follow the example of civilized and educated people. We will try to use successful arguing behaviors.

Poor and Unsuccessful Arguing Techniques

Shutting Down: Turning up the TV or stereo to drown out the other person, stomping out the door in an angry huff, slamming doors, shutting yourself in your room

Physical Force: Hitting, throwing things, breaking things, threatening to hurt people or animals

Ignoring the Obvious: Insisting that the issue isn't important. Refusing to face the problem.

Placing Blame: Claiming that the situation is entirely somebody else's fault, trying to place blame instead of sharing opinions and feelings

Tantrums: Crying, screaming, shouting to shut the other person up or drown them out

Manipulation: Making jokes, acting sexy, tickling somebody, doing anything to distract the other person and stop him or her from expressing opinions

Nuking: Listing everything you can think of that the other person has done wrong, even far in the past, in order to make excuses for your own behavior or avoid talking about the current situation

Rejection: Withholding love, affection, conversation, or sex unless the other person gives in; giving somebody the silent treatment or saying that you no longer love them

Successful and Intelligent Arguing Skills

Be fair. Don't kick somebody when they are down. Don't say cruel things just to hurt somebody else. Try to be open-minded.

Stick to the Topic. Focus on the current situation. Don't bring up old problems. Save them for another time.

Ask Questions. Ask why the other person behaved as he or she did. Don't assume you know why.

Listen. Listen to the other person. Make eye contact. Don't watch TV or listen to the stereo while somebody is trying to talk to you.

Cool Down. If you need to take a walk or sit quietly in your room, say so. Don't just leave.

Be Responsible. Own up to your behavior. If you did something inconsiderate or wrong, admit it. You can explain why you did what you did, but that doesn't necessarily excuse the behavior.

State Your Feelings. Try to keep your comments real. Don't try to tell the other person how he or she feels. Say, "I feel bad when you tease me," or "I feel disrespected when you keep me waiting." Don't say, "You don't care how I feel," or "You're selfish." Stick to stating how *you* feel.

Smile. If you think it's appropriate and will relieve the tension, make a joke. But don't make fun of the other person's feelings or comments.

Offer a Truce. If things come to a standstill, offer a truce so that you can both think things over. Agree to treat each other kindly until you have time for further discussion.

Shake Hands. Don't go away mad. You may agree to disagree, but don't carry a grudge. If you need to have another discussion, have it later. But don't go to bed angry. You may not wake up in the morning, and you don't want your last words to be cruel ones.

Exhibit 6.7. Two Argument Scenarios.

Instructions: Here are two scenarios. See if you can spot the unsuccessful arguing techniques. How could these people argue more effectively?

Scenario 1

Ty has been waiting an hour for Tiffany to arrive at the restaurant. Tiffany rushes in and tries to kiss Ty. He turns his head and gives her a cold look.

Tiffany: Sorry, sweetie. I forgot my purse and had to go back and get it. Then I hit rush hour traffic.

Ty: You're always late. What else is new?

Tiffany: I got here as soon as I could. Aren't you glad to see me, you gorgeous hunk? *(She pinches his cheek and smiles sweetly.)*

Ty: You always have a good excuse, but you don't care how long I have to sit around and wait.

Tiffany: Well, at least I don't flirt with other men right in front of you.

Ty: What's that supposed to mean?

Tiffany: Duh! Everywhere we go, we run into an old girlfriend of yours. Or else you stare at the waitresses and drool.

Ty: And I suppose you never dated anybody else. And I've seen you checking out the waiters.

As you know, this argument can go on forever and nobody ever wins. What's the real problem here?

Scenario 2

Monique comes home three hours after curfew. Mom and Dad are waiting.

Dad: Well, young lady. I hope you have a good excuse for making your mother and me worry ourselves sick.

Monique: As a matter of fact, I do.

Mom: Do you have any idea what you put us through?

Dad: Do you care?

Monique: I'm seventeen years old, but you treat me like a baby.

Dad: You act a baby.. You know the rule: if you're late, you call.

Monique: I tried to call, but the phone was busy. You must have been on the Internet.

Dad: I checked my e-mail twice—I wasn't online for more than fifteen minutes.

Monique: More like an hour, I'd say.

Dad: What's the difference? You should have tried again later.

Monique: I tried at least ten times.

Mom: Don't exaggerate, dear.

Dad: You could have called the neighbors. You know they'd give us the message.

Monique: Whatever.

Dad: You're grounded for a month.

Monique: But the prom is next week.

Dad: You should have thought of that when you were acting so irresponsibly.

Monique: But I bought my dress and shoes, and Brett rented a tux and a limo and everything.

Mom: Maybe we should let her go. After all, the arrangements have been made . . .

Dad: Go ahead. Spoil her. No wonder she acts like a baby. You baby her. And I guess I don't count around here.

Monique: Can I go to bed now while you two fight?

Dad: You'd better watch that smart mouth of yours—or else!

Monique: Or else what? You gonna give me a knuckle sandwich?

Dad: You're grounded. Period. End of discussion.

Dad sputters and stomps out of the room and upstairs, where he slams the door to the bedroom.

Mom: So what happened? You're not going to bed until you tell me.

Monique: Brett got a flat tire and his cell phone died, so I had to walk to a pay phone to call. I kept going back to help him. I was holding the flashlight so that he could see. And the phone was pretty far away.

Mom: Well, why didn't you tell your father that in the first place? He would have understood.

Monique: He doesn't understand anything. He never listens to me. He's a jerk. I hate him.

What could this family, especially the daughter, have done differently to make this argument more effective?

Some children can't seem to talk to any adult without getting into an argument that makes both parties want to scream. In those cases I don't think the kids are trying to be irritating. They don't possess a shred of tact, and they don't know how to discuss or argue without putting people on the defensive. Therefore, they think adults are ill-tempered and unreasonable.

Bad timing is the primary cause of student-staff communication problems. The worst time to argue about grades or request help is exactly when most students demand attention—just before or after class. Teachers have a hundred little tasks to perform during those three or four minutes, and student demands may irritate or exasperate them. Tell your students that if they want to talk to you or another staff member, approaching just before class begins or just after it ends is fine but only to ask when it would be convenient to have a longer talk. Be specific. Teach them to say, "I would like to talk to you. When would be a good time?"

When the teacher names a date or time, the student needs to write that time down to confirm the appointment and as a reminder. Making the appointment is the first step; the second step is gathering information. If a student wants to discuss her grade on an exam or report card, she needs to bring the exam or report card to the meeting. If the student wants to request help on a difficult lesson, he needs to bring the textbook or worksheet with him and be able to pinpoint the place where he is having trouble.

The third step is the most important. Students need to use tact in their discussions with teachers. Instead of insulting or demanding action from a teacher, students need to request information. We must explain to students that stomping into a teacher's room and announcing, "You made a mistake on my grade," is not likely to inspire a warm welcome. The teacher isn't going to say, "Why, certainly, Johnny, let me just grab my grade book and change that D to an A."

Students often think that they have license to be rude when a teacher makes a mistake in grading. But we must make students understand that nobody likes to look foolish, and teachers are in a particularly vulnerable position because they have to safeguard their authority in order to be effective in the classroom. When a student accuses a teacher of making a mistake in grading, he or she is very likely to say, "I gave you the grade you earned."

Role playing is a good way for students to practice these new skills. Have your students approach you with a real or practice problem. Here are several suggested conversation starters:

"I really want to earn a good grade in your class. Could you tell me what I can do to bring up my grade?"

"I really studied for this test, and I don't understand some of the answers. Could you go over them with me and explain where I got confused?"

"At home I've been trying to keep track of all my grades in my classes, and I must have made a mistake because I thought I had an A [or a B or C] in your class. Could you go over my grades with me and show me where I went wrong?"

"I thought I did a really good job on this assignment, but I got a low grade. Could you tell me what I could have done to improve it, so that I can do better on the next assignment?"

Explain to your students that these new, polite approaches give the teacher an opportunity to correct an error without losing face. The teacher's grade book may contain a mistake; the teacher may realize that a test question was confusing or that the student turned in work that the teacher failed to record in the grade book.

If the teacher responds graciously, the student should say thank-you and be proud of acting like a responsible and polite young person. If the teacher responds in a grouchy, rude, or unhelpful manner, the student needs to ask a parent or the principal for help.

The same conversational rules apply to other adults. We must teach our students to begin the conversation by asking for assistance or information. Write some negative comments on the board, such as, "Miss Jones is a crabby old fart," or "Mr. Smith is jerking me around with my grade." Then, ask students to come up with comments that will demonstrate their tactfulness and good manners. You might have to suggest something to get them started. "I have a problem, and I wondered if you could help me," is a good beginning.

Students need to learn one more thing about communicating with teachers: how to ask teachers for help. Students usually say, "I don't get it," or "I can't do this." Then they expect the teacher to help them. This is especially true in math classes where the teacher then repeats the instructions, and the student repeats his or her complaint. The teacher thinks the student would understand if he or she did the homework and solved the problems in class, but the student insists that he can't do the homework or problems because the teacher hasn't properly explained how to do them. If you find yourself involved in one of these conversational cycles, this is a heads-up that you need to teach, or remind, your students how to ask for help.

Students must learn to articulate their needs. We can teach them to do this by teaching them how to backtrack in their textbooks, workbooks, or notes to pinpoint the exact place where they got lost. We must insist that they show us the point from which they can't continue, so that we can see what the student needs to understand (one prealgebra student who asked me for help didn't understand what a negative number was; another didn't understand a number line).

When you are certain that your students know how to ask for help, you can identify serious problems more easily. If a student can't do even the first problems or questions in an assignment after repeated discussions with you, the student needs a comprehensive review session, remedial classes, a tutor, or perhaps a visit to the school nurse for a hearing and vision exam (even if he or she has already been tested because an illness can affect vision or hearing after the student has been tested).

PROVIDE FREQUENT PROGRESS REPORTS

Ironically, the students who claim to care the least about school are the same ones who complain the most about the bad grades they earn. During my first year of teaching, I had one class of accelerated and one class of remedial English students. The college-bound students accepted their first-quarter grades with a few sighs and moans, but the self-proclaimed too-cool-for-school remedial students spent an entire class period arguing about their grades. Some begged; others demanded an audit of my grade book or questioned my sanity.

After the deluge of complaints after report cards went out, I tried holding individual conferences to keep students informed of their progress. Next, I tried giving students periodic written progress reports. Twice each month, while they were busy working, I would circulate through the room and hand them slips of paper showing their current grade. I would stop by the student's desk and place the paper facedown.

"Good work," I'd write, or "You're moving up. Hang in there." To failing students I'd write, "Your grade is not passing right now, but if you want some help, let me know. You are a bright young man [or woman], and I'm glad you are in my class." Regardless of the grade, I shook the student's hand. Some kids preferred not to shake, because they didn't want to give the impression that they cared about school. To them I'd give a quick and silent thumbs-up. When semester report cards arrived, moans and groans were down by about half, but clearly the other half of my students believed that I had somehow robbed them of their due.

The first day of the second semester, I offered my students a deal. Everybody who came to class every single day (no unexcused absences), earned at least a C on every classroom and homework assignment without copying, cooperated with me and participated in every lesson, and earned a C or higher on every quiz would earn a passing grade, even if they flunked their final exam.

"What are you trying to do, psych us out?" one boy asked. Ryan was one of the brightest, least motivated young people I've ever had the pleasure of trying to teach. He earned an A on every assignment he did, but he did only half the assignments, so he ended up with 50 percent and an F on his report card. Ryan wasn't the only underachiever in his class. Failing grades, missing credits, truancy, and bad attitudes were much more common than good attitudes and high grades.

"Absolutely," I told Ryan. "I am trying to psych you out. I don't believe it's possible to come to class every single day, honestly try to learn, complete all your assignments by yourself with a passing grade, and still fail to learn what I'm teaching. Anybody who does all those things and who has a functioning brain will pass. You all have functioning brains, so that's the deal I'm offering you. Why not try it? You have nothing to lose, and you might find out that you're a lot smarter than you think you are."

Ryan took me up on my offer and started doing all the assignments. His grades were at the top of the class, but he couldn't believe he was passing. Every day he'd ask to see his grade in my grade book. It didn't matter that I told him every day that he was passing. He had to see it for himself, in writing, on the page. Soon other students started joining Ryan, clamoring to see their own grades. As a self-defense tactic, I created a wall chart for Ryan's class that turned out to be an excellent motivator, even for my most unmotivated students.

On a large sheet of poster board (I could have used a blank page from my grade book, but back then I didn't think to make a copy of the book before entering grades), I printed the names of the students in Ryan's class down the left-hand side of the sheet and divided the rest of the sheet into small squares. I made sure to leave enough squares to list each assignment, including homework, quizzes, exams, and special projects. Above each square, I wrote the name of the assignment, using abbreviations such as *w/s* for worksheet and *T* for test (*Sp T-1*, for example, meant spelling test number one). If a student completed an assignment with a passing grade, he or she earned an X in the square for that assignment. I drew a green box around the square for students who failed or were absent. If the student made up the assignment before the deadline (which I wrote just below the name of the assignment so that there would be no doubt about due dates), then I placed an X in the box to show that the student had completed the assignment with a passing grade. I put a big red zero in the box for any assignment that was incomplete or failed without any attempt to bring the failed grade up to par.

The chart didn't contain any grades, because I don't think it's a good idea to humiliate students or try to create competition for grades as a motivator. Some people simply can't spell, for example; and although spelling doesn't indicate intelligence, poor spellers who are constantly compared to others feel like failures. I wanted my students to compete with themselves, to make sure there was an X in every box.

"If you have all Xs, there is no way that you can fail my class," I assured them. "The quality of your work will determine whether you earn an A or a D, but if you do the work, you're going to pass this class."

Even my most unmotivated, apathetic students couldn't ignore the string of red zeros placed beside their names. They didn't rush into my room and run to check the chart as most students did; they shuffled in, yawned, sidled a few steps until they could check the chart while pretending to glance casually over their shoulders at something more compelling. During the first report period that I posted the chart, the students in my lowest-achieving class complained that it wasn't fair that they couldn't make up all those missed assignments. I made a super-duper, incredible, onetime offer: a three-week grace period during which students could make up any missing or failed work. After that, deadlines would be nonnegotiable.

It worked. A few red zeros remained on the chart when the next report cards came out, but every single student passed my class.

When my other classes saw the progress chart for Ryan's class, they demanded similar charts for their classes. Even the good students, who routinely took home report cards filled with As and Bs, wanted tangible proof of their progress and of the demands I would make of them. That's when I realized that many unsuccessful students give up because they can't visualize themselves making real progress toward the end of a quarter or semester. To them school is an endless journey that is made more difficult by mountains of paperwork. When they see visual proof that they are succeeding, they stop pretending that they don't care. They may not become scholars, but they begin to believe that they may actually survive school and eventually graduate.

If you are a visual learner, you might prefer to see a sample of my wall chart (Figure 6.1).

TEACH STUDENTS HOW TO READ TRANSCRIPTS

A good way to demonstrate to students that you want to help them succeed, which in turn motivates them to try, is to teach them to read their transcripts. In spite of all the guidance that counselors give, many students blunder their way through

Figure 6.1. Progress Wall Chart Report.

deadline =	9/6	9/15	9/20	9/25	10/3												
X = done / □ = missing / ⊠ = made up / ⊠ = no credit	Journal #1	Spelling #1	Vocab Worksheet #1	Vocab quiz #1	Literature worksheet #1	Journal #2	Spelling #2	Speech #1	Vocab w/s avg	Vocab quiz #2	Journal #3					
Aguilar, M.	X	X	⊠	⊡	X	X	X	X	X	X	X					
Bailey, T.	X	X	X	X	X	X	⊡	⊠	X	X	X					
Chavez, L.	⊡	⊠	⊠	⊠	X	X	X	X	X	X	X					
Cohen, N.	X	X	X	⊠	X	X	X	⊠	X	X	X					
Dexter, P.	X	X	X	X	X	X	X	X	X	X	X					
Farley, S.	X	X	X	X	X	X	⊠	X	X	X	X					
Hong, K.	X	X	X	⊠	X	X	X	X	X	X	⊡					
Holly, M.	⊡	X	X	⊡	X	X	⊠	X	X	X	X					
Jones, J.	X	X	X	X	X	X	X	X	X	X	X					
Langley, M.	X	X	X	X	X	X	X	X	X	X	X					
Newton, R.	X	X	⊠	X	X	X	X	X	X	X	X					
Ponter, J.	X	X	X	X	X	⊡	X	X	X	⊠	X					
Quintera, A.	X	X	X	X	⊠	X	X	⊠	X	X	X					
Steiner, R.	X	X	X	X	X	X	⊠	X	X	X	X					

2nd Period – English II

school without knowing how to read their own transcripts; and a surprisingly high number don't know their school district's requirements for graduation. Even those students who do understand how to read their transcripts are often at a loss when it comes to correcting errors in their records.

I realized that my own students knew very little about their own records when one of my seniors arrived on my doorstep in tears one day because a counselor had just informed her that she couldn't graduate with her class. She was missing one-half of a credit for math. I was as upset as Stacey was because the counselors had visited my classroom at the start of the semester and distributed official transcripts to all the seniors. When the counselors collected the transcripts after their presentation, they asked whether anybody had questions. Nobody had questions. I assumed that my students had followed the counselor's instructions to review their records and would report any mistakes or missing information to the office immediately. Stacey not only failed to read her transcript, she forgot that she was missing one quarter of credit from a course she had failed during the second semester of her freshman year. She forgot, and nobody in the office noticed the missing half-credit until it was too late to make up the work. Fortunately for Stacey, one of the math teachers agreed to create an independent study course for her and administer the necessary exams. Thanks to that teacher, Stacey was able to wear her cap and gown and graduate with her class.

When her classmates learned of Stacey's dilemma, several of them admitted that they hadn't read their transcripts either or hadn't understood what they had read, in spite of the counselors' offers of assistance. So when the counselors scheduled their presentation at the start of the following school year, I asked them if I might make copies of all my students' transcripts so that we could keep them in our classroom and update them each quarter. They agreed, and I created a form on my word processor that listed the specific graduation requirements for our district. After I made a copy of the graduation checklist for each student, we spent a class period learning how to read the transcripts, comparing them to the checklist, and marking every requirement that students had successfully completed. If there was an incorrect or missing grade, I showed students how to write a memo to the guidance office and track the memo until guidance staff made the correction.

Guidance office personnel are among the most overworked people in any school system, so I don't blame them for making an occasional error. As I explained to my students, "It may be the counselor's job to make sure you have the right classes, but they are people and they can make mistakes. They want you to graduate, but it's your responsibility to make sure that you do. If your transcript isn't accurate or you don't have all the credits you need, the counselors will say they are sorry, but no one will be as sorry as you when you don't graduate with your class. Don't expect somebody else to be responsible for your success in life."

I gave each student a file folder to label, and we filed their transcripts in a file cabinet near my desk. After each report card, we spent a few minutes recording the new credits on the graduation checklists. With the transcript reviews, the graduation checklists, and the progress charts posted on my classroom's walls, many students who had once shrugged and ignored their disastrous report cards became convinced that they could graduate—and most of them did. Seeing visible proof of their progress gave those students the hope they needed in order to believe in themselves.

SHOW STUDENTS HOW TO SET GOALS

Unsuccessful students are rarely good goal setters. They blame their failures on other people, circumstances, or luck. One of the most valuable lessons you can teach your students is how to set realistic long-term goals, divide those goals into a series of short-term goals, and make a list of steps that they can take immediately to get started. Goal setting doesn't have to be a separate lesson. Regardless of your subject, you can incorporate goal setting into your curriculum by asking students at the start of any grading period to set a goal for their grade in your class. Ask them to write down their goal for the grading period and then list three things they can do that day to get started. Collect your students' goal sheets and file them in a handy location. At regular intervals (I'd suggest weekly to keep them on track), take out the goal sheets, ask students to evaluate their progress, make notes, and revise their short-term goals if necessary. Don't worry about the handful of students who will refuse to set goals. Focus on those students who appreciate that you are teaching them a valuable life skill.

If you have the time and inclination, you might expand this exercise to include personal goals, such as setting a target weight for bench press, losing fifteen pounds, finding a job, improving a relationship with a family member, becoming a published writer, performing as a dancer or singer in public. For students who seem lost and unable to think of a single goal they'd like to achieve, you might consider researching John Goddard, author of *Kayaks down the Nile* (Brigham Young University Press, 1979). At age fifteen Goddard made a list of 127 goals that he wanted to accomplish in his lifetime. A voracious reader, he listed many unusual adventures in exotic locales, including mountain climbing in Peru and New Zealand and studying primitive cultures in Borneo and Brazil. His list also included less taxing feats such as typing fifty words per minute, owning an ocelot, building a telescope, learning to play polo, and lighting a match with a shot fired from a .22 rifle.

Goddard's story and his list of goals make an attention-getting introduction to goal setting. After reading his list, students who couldn't think of a thing they wanted to do often create long lists of goals for themselves. Your own list of life goals might be just as intriguing and inspiring to your students, especially if you check off the ones you have completed. How you approach the topic isn't as important as providing a model for students to follow. Children who have no experience in setting goals often throw their hands into the air and give up when they face new and challenging concepts or school subjects. After you teach them how to break a long-term goal down into manageable parts, they no longer feel so unable to cope. For example, several of my students admitted that they feared they would flunk geometry after the first day of class because the textbook looked "really hard."

"I'll never be able to learn all this stuff," one boy said in a trembling voice.

"You aren't going to learn all that stuff in one week or even in one month," I said. "Let's open the book and take a look."

Everybody who had the class pulled out their textbooks. We looked through the table of contents and read some of the chapter titles. Then we counted the number of chapters and divided that number by the number of weeks in the semester. The result was about one chapter per week. So we looked through the first chapter and read the examples.

"Maybe it isn't that hard," the boy said.

"Don't you think you could learn this in one week, if you have a teacher to explain everything to you?" I asked.

The boy and his classmates agreed that they just might be able to. So we pulled out their goal-setting sheets and wrote, "Read and understand Chapter One in the geometry book." By the time they reached Chapter Three, they insisted that they didn't need to write down each chapter as they finished it. After all, they explained, anybody could do one chapter if they had a whole week.

CREATE A CHALLENGE

Instead of dumbing down the curriculum when you work with unmotivated or underachieving students, try smartening it up instead. When you assign easy work, students receive a clear message: you don't consider them smart enough to do harder work. For elementary school students, use the GED spelling list in place of, or in addition to, your standard spelling list. Use the standard list for grades and the GED list for special credit. For older children, use the SAT vocabulary lists. Yes, those words are hard, but many vocabulary books are too easy; if your students know three out of ten new words on each list, the words are too easy. Again you can use the SAT list as special credit or bonus questions on your own vocabulary tests. Or write one word on the board each day and see if anybody can figure out what it means without any hints. Then try a hint or use the word in a sentence.

If you teach students who expect to attend college after graduation, give their egos and their preparedness a boost by teaching them how to write response papers and the various essays required in freshman composition classes (narrative, explanatory, persuasive). Your local community college or university will have a writing center or an online Web site on which you can find instructional materials for your students.

Regardless of your students' age, introduce them to analogies. Lower-level students are rarely exposed to analogies (which may be one of the reasons they are such poor thinkers and struggle so much with algebra), yet most standardized tests, such as the SAT and GRE exams, consist primarily of analogies.

MAKE MISTAKES ACCEPTABLE

We often tell children that mistakes are OK because everybody makes them, but we then turn around and punish students academically for being less than perfect. Imagine that your supervisor expected you to perform eight out of every ten tasks perfectly. Few salespeople can boast of a 70 percent success rate; most would be happy with 50 percent or even lower. Baseball players are considered top-notch if they can hit more than 30 percent of the pitches thrown at them. Yet we expect children to perform with 70 percent accuracy when they are working with unfamiliar material and learning new skills. How unreasonable can we get?

Of course, we have to have tests, exams, and other measures to assess how well students are learning; but if we want children to be interested in learning, we must allow them to make mistakes without embarrassing or penalizing them. For example, instead of grading a regular classroom assignment as soon as students finish it, why not let them keep their papers while you go over each item and discuss the correct answers, possible answers, and common mistakes? Let students explain how they arrived at their answers, both wrong and right, and then allow them to redo the assignment before they turn it in. Their comprehension will improve, and they will be much more likely to remember the information if you correct any misconceptions immediately than if they have to wait a day or two (or six) to see how well they did. In the meantime that misinformation percolates in their brains and may work its way into their long-term memories.

Celebrate mistakes, even yours. When you make a mistake, ask the students to give you a round of applause for demonstrating that although you are an educated and undoubtedly intelligent teacher, you are also a human being. Don't worry that students will lose respect for you when they learn that you aren't perfect. On the contrary, they will respect you more for admitting your mistakes and helping them learn from theirs.

During class discussions, when a student offers an incorrect answer or idea, instead of simply saying, "Wrong" or asking another student, try saying, "That's an interesting idea. How did you arrive at that conclusion?" or "I hadn't thought of that. Could you explain your thinking?" Not only does this teach students that mistakes are acceptable, but you may identify misinformation before it solidifies in a student's mind. For example, if a student identifies $2/3$ as an improper fraction, that student may not understand the basic principles of fractions. If you ask how she arrived at that answer, you may be able to adjust her thinking and set her back on the right track.

I have to admit that I have been guilty of hiding my mistakes. During my first years as a teacher, when one of my wonderful activities bombed in class, I would collect the papers and throw them away after students left the room. Usually the students forgot about the fiasco, but if anybody asked, I'd say, "Oh, I haven't had a chance to grade those papers yet." Eventually they would forget about the exercises that didn't work, but I didn't. After one of our discussions about mistakes, I realized how hypocritical it was for me to encourage my students to make mistakes and then hide my own. The next time an exercise failed miserably, I stopped the students and told them what I had hoped the activity would teach them. Then I asked them to form small groups and discuss the assignment. They could either fix the assignment so that it would work or decide it wasn't worth saving. In every case the students came up with a more challenging and complex assignment than I had. And in addition to the academic lessons, they learned that teachers aren't perfect and that mistakes really can be stepping stones to improvement. After more than a decade of teaching, my lesson designs have improved, and I don't have many flops; but when I do, I share them with students. Surprisingly, revealing my mistakes doesn't diminish students' respect for me; their respect actually increases.

MODEL ACCEPTABLE BEHAVIOR AND EXCELLENCE

Modeling is one of the most effective ways to teach new skills. The less accomplished the students, the more they stand to gain from watching you perform the tasks you are trying to teach them. But even good students can benefit from observing your approach. When I assign journal writing, for example, I always sit down in the middle of the class with my own journal and do the assignment. If reluctant writers are watching, I touch the tip of my pencil to my lips for a second and look at the ceiling to show that I am trying to think of something to write. Then I pause periodically and frown at my paper. Perhaps I cross out a word and write in a different word, then nod my head to agree with myself that I have improved my writing. Occasionally I scratch my head, stare out the window, close my eyes, or make some other gesture to show that writing well can take some time and effort. At first students snicker and make comments, but I ignore them. If their comments are loud, I whisper, "Shh. I'm trying to think." I don't look at them. I keep concentrating on my writing. Eventually they follow my example.

In a class with more scholarly students, I may not add the gestures, but I still pause occasionally to reread what I have written, make simple revisions, and perhaps circle a paragraph and draw a line to another location where I think that paragraph would more logically fit. I want them to see that first drafts don't have to be beautiful or perfect.

And always I ask for a volunteer to read my journal. Although I don't grade journals on grammar and spelling, I do grade them on content. So I ask my students to grade my ideas, looking for logical development, details to support my main ideas, and so on.

In addition to modeling behavior, I like to provide models for students so that they know what I consider adequate, good, and excellent work. If we want students to produce excellent work, we need to show them what excellent work looks like. Some capable but underperforming students spend their entire school careers unaware of the kind of work other students are doing. After a journal-writing exercise, I read out a few of the most thought-provoking entries, without revealing the authors' names (students who want recognition always find a way to take credit for their writing). After students complete a literature worksheet in which they write short essay responses to questions, I delete the names and post samples of student work. I label a paper that answers the questions with minimal information and some grammar errors "Adequate." A paper that demonstrates more student effort, with more complex and sophisticated answers will earn a "Good" rating. An "Excellent" paper will have complete answers, complex sentences, logical development of ideas with details to support the ideas, and few grammar or spelling errors.

LOOK FOR OPPORTUNITIES TO PRAISE

Children crave attention. If they can't catch our attention by behaving well, they will misbehave because they know that we won't ignore them when they do wrong. And we teachers know we should focus on the positive, but we still tend to accentuate the negative in school. We remember having to ask a student to sit down or be quiet, but we forget how many times that same student participated and cooperated and acted like a decent human being. With practice and persistence, we can learn to notice when children are behaving. There are many more opportunities to catch them being good than there are to catch them being bad. If we want children to be kind, considerate, compassionate, generous, and honorable, we need to notice and thank them when they do act in those ways. We don't have to give them candy or points, but we do need to give them praise.

One way I remind myself to catch students being wonderful is to take three blank index cards to class every day with the names of three students written on them. During that day I make sure I notice when those students do something kind or admirable—lending somebody a pen, offering to collect papers, picking up litter from the floor and placing it in the trash, erasing the board without my asking, helping another student complete an assignment. The act isn't important as long as it was honestly spontaneous. I take a minute to write notes that I hand to students at the end of class. The notes aren't long: "Thanks for helping to keep our classroom clean today. I appreciate you" is enough. Don't be surprised if a student confides that yours was the first positive note any teacher ever wrote about him or her. It's enough to make a grown woman cry.

REACH OUT TO PARENTS AND GUARDIANS

Parents and guardians are used to receiving phone calls from school staff and teachers complaining about unexcused absences, tardiness, missed assignments, bad attitudes, and disrespectful behavior. Often they become defensive because they believe teachers are blaming them (and sometimes we are) for their children's misdeeds. But they are equally responsible when their children behave respectfully and decently. So we need to call and let them know that we appreciate their efforts.

When a student in your class behaves especially well, call the parent or guardian and say, "I just wanted to thank you for doing such a good job of raising your son [daughter]. I know that kids don't behave well by accident. They were taught by their parents. I wish all my students were as well behaved as yours. Thank you for making my job easier."

Likewise, when a student who isn't always cooperative does behave or completes an assigned task well, I'm quick to call parents and let them know. The student receives positive attention from parents and comes back to my class with a desire to repeat that pleasant experience. In addition to creating a good relationship with parents and improving student performance, good-news phone calls let the students know that you and their parents are working together. Sometimes children try to play their teachers and parents against each other, but if you make the first contact a positive experience, you won't be a victim to that scam. And if you should ever need to call those same parents or guardians because of a behavior problem, you will find them much more receptive than they might have been otherwise.

CHANGE STUDENTS' PERCEPTIONS OF THEMSELVES

In a passing conversation, I once asked a high school junior what he planned to do after graduation.

"I'll probably go to prison," Julio said.

Surprised, I asked him if he was in trouble with the law.

"No," he said.

"Then why would you go to prison?"

"Because that's where all the men in my family go."

"Well, you don't have to go to prison. You're going to graduate, and you already have a job waiting for you."

"You don't understand," he said. "The men in my family always end up in prison."

"You don't understand," I said. "You don't have to go to prison."

Neither of us understood. Of course, I was upset by this conversation and determined to change the student's mind. I never could. And he did eventually go to prison after graduation. But a couple of years later, one of his friends called me and said, "Julio is out on parole, and he has a good job, and he just wanted you to know he's doing all right."

From that experience I learned that I needed to change my approach. Instead of trying to bulldoze students into accepting my perception of them, I needed to find a way to help them change their perceptions of themselves as hopeless losers or powerless pawns—a subtle but powerful difference. I began by asking the group general questions when I felt they were in a comfortable and talkative mood.

"How many people plan to go to college?" (Some hands waved.)

"How many would like to go, but you don't think you can do it?" (More hands.)

"How many people here think they will end up on welfare someday?"

"How many people think they will travel all over the world?"

"How many people see themselves having pretty good jobs?"

"How many think they will probably go to prison?"

"How many people think they will be married and have a family in ten years?"

"How many people think there's a good chance they will be dead before they are thirty years old?"

I don't respond individually to students during this quick survey, but I do make notes of the students who raise their hands in response to the negative questions. Then, during the normal course of a school day, I find opportunities to tell those students how I see them and the possibilities for their future. For example, I might say, "Do you know how much artistic talent you have? I see you as an architect or a graphic artist someday." To kids who are especially interested in computers, I say, "You have such a good imagination, I bet you'd make a great video game designer. I could also see you working as a systems analyst, helping people figure out what kind of computer system they need for their business."

I persist in telling students how I see them, every chance I get. And it works. Eventually they begin to see themselves as people with talents and skills. Sometimes I even ask them to humor me and try a visualization experiment. I ask them to close their eyes and imagine themselves getting up in the morning, getting dressed, grabbing their briefcase and a cup of coffee, and driving to work in a spiffy car. Then they enter the reception area of a big company, greet the receptionist, and head for their office, where they turn on the computer and check their mail.

Another day I might ask them to imagine that they get up very early, eat a hearty breakfast, and grab their toolboxes. They jump into their pickup trucks and head off to a construction site where they will install kitchen cabinets in a new housing development.

These scenarios are very helpful because most students have no real idea of what any occupation involves. They may hear about jobs from the counselors and see people portraying different occupational roles in movies, but they don't really know what those people actually do on the job. I encourage them to think of themselves in a variety of situations until they find one that feels right for them.

Another way I try to change students' perceptions of themselves is to ask experts to tell them for me. I have invited handwriting experts to analyze my students' handwriting and focus on their positive traits (this was a huge hit). Local businesspeople will come to your classroom and conduct mock interviews with your students—and give positive feedback and constructive criticism about their interviewing skills. Parents or other teachers who have experience in creative arts or business are often willing to come in and teach a skill in order to tap into untested talent among your students. A sculptor or painter may inspire a student simply by noting his or her eye for color.

This may seem like hocus-pocus and New Age karma crap, but it isn't. When you say to a student, "I see you as an intelligent, talented person," that student can no longer think of himself as a stupid or untalented mess. He won't change his perception immediately, but we do know that once you introduce a new idea to a brain, it can't go back to its former state. The seed of that new idea will grow, even if it isn't watered.

PACE THOSE TORTOISES AND HARES

Be prepared to help students who fall behind or race ahead of the pack. When lessons are too hard or too easy, students tend to tune out and give up or to seek ways to entertain themselves, often at their classmates' and teachers' expense. Aside from making it easier to manage your classroom, your young tortoises and hares will receive a better education if you spend a little time preparing lessons that meet their needs. You don't have to create a separate curriculum, just do a little tweaking. For severely dyslexic students, skip the spelling test grades and replace them with worksheets with spelling strategies and practice exercises (you can find plenty of examples online, in textbooks at your own school, or in bookstores). During group or team exercises, pair your slow students with compassionate students or assign yourself to their group.

Most teachers are prepared with extra assignments, enrichment activities, peer tutoring, or other interventions for the laggards in their classes; but many teachers fail to consider students who are ahead of the game. And many teachers fail to recognize that their loudmouths and stand-up comics may be looking for ways to entertain themselves because they are bored by lessons that are too easy for them. Sadly, some teachers even feel threatened by brilliant students, instead of delighted to have the opportunity to encourage and guide them.

When you suspect that a student may be misbehaving from boredom, call the student aside and tell him what you suspect. Give him some assignments or a diagnostic exam that will allow you to assess his skill and knowledge level accurately. If he does score high, then offer to recommend him for transfer to a gifted or advanced placement class. If transfer is not an option or the student prefers to remain in your class, then negotiate a contract and have him sign it, agreeing to cooperate with you in order to be permitted to remain in your class. Make it clear that you will expect the student to take the same quizzes and exams as the other students but may excuse him from doing routine assignments as long as his grades remain high. Then design a series of independent projects for your exceptional student. Don't make more work for yourself. Simply outline the projects. For example, younger students may enjoy working on the computer, doing basic research in the library, creating a science project, enrolling in an online course, or acting as your classroom aide. Older students who plan to attend college can benefit from doing SAT preparation exercises (there are plenty of books available) or learning how to research and write thesis papers or response papers such as those they will be assigned during college composition or literature classes.

When assigning independent work, emphasize learning and progress over grades, so that students have the opportunity to learn for learning's sake—one of the best lessons you can teach a child. Also be prepared to drop the independent work if the student starts to cooperate and do the regular activities. Sometimes students just need your acknowledgment of their superiority or their struggle to stay with the class. One rambunctious young man actually wrote me a note that said, "Thanks for showing me that I'm smart and I don't have to be the loudest person in the room. I'm sorry I caused you so much extra work, but now I feel a lot better." He folded his note into a tiny square and handed it to me before he ran out of the room on the last day of school before Christmas vacation. When he returned in the new year, he didn't need the extra assignments. He joined the class and earned the A he should have had in the first place.

SEPARATE STUDENTS FROM GRADES

I remember clearly when one of my students said, "I know you like Isabel better than you like me because she earns better grades than I do." His remark prompted a class discussion, and nearly every student agreed that teachers like their A students better than they like the others. I explained that teachers appreciate hard workers and are delighted when students earn high grades but that we don't dislike students who earn poor grades. We may dislike the behavior of students with poor grades. We wish they would do homework, behave themselves, pay attention, try harder, participate in class, and accept our help; but we don't dislike them for making mistakes or for struggling to learn (and if we do, we shouldn't be teachers).

Of course, we need to be honest. We need to draw a distinction between students who struggle to learn and students who intentionally disrupt the class out of boredom or spite. Nobody likes it when a person creates unnecessary stress or extra work. But again it is the behavior we don't like, not necessarily the person.

Remind your students frequently that an A person with poor grades can work to improve his or her grades but an F person with high grades still has a rotten personality—and that is a sad, sad thing to have.

CREATE PEER SUPPORT GROUPS

Many schools have peer-tutoring programs, and usually those programs are popular and successful. Unfortunately, not all schools can offer peer tutoring. You can give your students the same benefits of a peer-tutoring program by forming work teams at the start of the year and providing opportunities for those students to work together on difficult assignments. Instead of requiring students to sit quietly at their desks and work individually, give them time and encouragement to work together—which, by the way, is much more like the way they will work at college or at their jobs in the future. Few people work solo all the time. Your room won't be as quiet, but the increased morale and improved performance may help you ignore the noise.

Don't pit your teams against each other; pit all the teams against the curriculum. Instead of making the goal be to beat each other, set a goal for the class to complete a unit by a certain deadline or for everybody to earn a minimum grade on a test. Encourage students to exchange phone numbers so that they can call each other nights and weekends to study together or provide advice and encouragement over the phone.

If your administrators are cooperative, ask them to schedule the students in your work teams in classes with each other the following year. Even better, ask to keep the same students (or some of them) for two or three years. Recent studies show that pairing teachers and students for two or three years pays off. Students develop very strong bonds when they work together, and they respond very positively (so do their grades) when schools permit their teams to stay together for two or three years. Students are far less likely to get into trouble or drop out of school when they have a peer support group.

ASSIGN WORKABLE GROUPS

Every group of students has a unique dynamic and will interact differently. You cannot judge ahead of time how students will respond to each other, but you can save a lot of stress and time by planning how you will handle situations in which students need to work together. Before you assign working pairs or groups, pay attention to the way your students interact. If you haven't already identified your outcasts and bullies, and rival gang members (see Chapter Five), find out who they are before you expect students to work together.

In a class that seems to have a lot of rivalry, you might elect to select groups yourself. Otherwise, you can give students a chance to form their own groups; or you can use a deck of cards, different candies, or some other identifier to randomly assign groups. With older, well-behaved students, I simply place chairs in small groups and allow students to self-select, although I retain the right to change groups if misbehavior interferes with the activity.

Be prepared for students who refuse to work with anybody else at all. Either assign those students to their own "groups," put them with your most mature and outgoing students, or work with them yourself.

Any time you assign group work, be sure to include self-evaluation forms and a rubric so that students can evaluate their group's progress and each member's contributions. Keep in mind that some kids will gang up on each other, so make sure that you observe them during their class-time work periods to determine whether they are way off track in their evaluations. Including a grade for participation and cooperation, as well as a grade for completing the goals of the exercise, will go a long way toward motivating students to work together.

PERSONALIZE YOUR LESSONS

Take home a copy of your roll sheet for each class. As you design worksheets and quizzes, include your students' names. They will be delighted when they find their names in a grammar worksheet or in a math problem. Be sure to check off the names as you use them, and use every student's name at least once to avoid hurting feelings.

If you have a sense of humor, use it. Add a note at the top of the worksheet that says, "This excellent worksheet was brought to you by your teacher, Miss Smith." Or at the end of a difficult test, add a disclaimer: "Mr. Brown regrets that he had to give you such a hard test, but he is truly proud of your efforts." At the end of my own tests, I always include this note: "This test was brought to you by Miss Johnson—your teacher who loves you."

You can use those index cards you filled out on the first day of class to make another good morale booster. I keep the cards arranged by students' birthdays instead of alphabetical order. Each weekend I go through the cards and select the ones whose birthdays fall in the coming week. On the student's birthday, I give him or her a bright sparkly pencil and say, "This is a magic birthday pencil, and it only gets good grades." Even totally cool and awesome ruthless gangsters laugh and use the pencils.

LET STUDENTS SHINE

Many of your students have amazing talents that, unfortunately, they never have an opportunity to display during school. I remember one stocky boy in my sophomore class, a boy I thought of as a little slow. Ira earned good grades, but he appeared to put much more effort into his grades than most students did. Ira worked diligently but slowly and methodically, and he didn't mind working alone. He would work with a group if I asked him to, but other kids often teased him for being so serious and stodgy. He never responded to their taunts, however, and they left him alone for the most part. Occasionally another boy would try to taunt Ira into fighting, but Ira would tilt his head down and look quietly at the boy over the tops of his eyeglasses until the boy gave up and walked away, shaking his head.

One day I decided to let students design their own projects to present to the class. The only limitations were that projects could not involve nudity, obscenities, pornography, racism, fire, reptiles, poisonous insects, or extremely loud noises. Each student had to sign a contract stating whether he or she was working alone or with partners, briefly describe the project, and agree to complete the project by the deadline in order to receive credit. When I read Ira's contract, I was a bit doubtful. He wrote that he intended to give a martial arts demonstration.

Ira volunteered to go last, which didn't surprise me. Other students clamored to present their projects first. We had demonstrations of hair dyeing, cookie-dough mixing, model-airplane flying, dancing, singing, rapping, lip-synching, as well as TV game show satires, movie reviewers, videotaped comedy routines and commercials, and a model low-rider car that bumped and hopped across the floor. Then it was time for Ira. He asked his classmates to push all the chairs against the walls to clear the center of the room. Students shoved the chairs quickly, eager to see Ira's demonstration. From the expressions on their faces, I could see that many students expected to get a good laugh at Ira's expense.

Ira took off his street clothes to reveal a white *gi* with a black cloth belt cinching his waist. He knelt in one corner of the room and placed his forehead on the floor. Then he stood, exhaled slowly, and began an incredible display of strength, control, and concentration. This "slow" boy could move his hands and feet so fast that they became a blur. Now we knew why he never accepted an invitation to fight. He didn't need to beat anybody up. He knew he was a champion, and he didn't need to prove it to anybody else.

Those student projects took one week out of the school year, but they paid off enormously in motivation, morale, and attendance. Students who had never had a chance to be the star had their turn. Individual projects became a standard in my curriculum. I highly recommend adding them to yours, regardless of your subject. I would offer these suggestions if you do choose to use projects:

- Allow shy or introverted students to prepare a report or other nonverbal presentation, so that they won't be forced to speak in front of a group.

- Don't require projects to be about your class's subject. Encourage creativity.

- Give every student who completes a project full credit. Instead of giving letter grades, ask three or four students to provide a peer critique (to avoid negative responses and crushed feelings, you might provide forms on which students check off positive aspects).

- If students agree, invite parents or other teachers to observe. And if you have a video camera, tape the performances. (I wish I had caught Ira on tape, but video cameras then weighed twenty pounds and required a tripod.)

USE PRIVATE JOURNALS AS A TOOL

If you use journals and your students aren't writing very much, there is a reason. I could suggest a few possibilities, based on my own students' comments about journal writing: you don't read the journals; you grade entries on spelling and grammar, which inhibits expression; you don't allow enough time, so they feel rushed and unable to think; you allow too much time, so they procrastinate and lack focus; or your prompts are not inspiring.

Inspiring prompts are a must if you expect journal writing to produce results. Prompts such as "Write a letter to Abraham Lincoln" or "Write your own obituary" may sound interesting to adults and may appeal to more scholarly students, but they won't work for students who aren't excited about school or are frightened by death. If you want students to write a letter to somebody, choose a person they would actually consider talking to in the first place. Most children wouldn't be inclined to talk to a dead president or a historical figure. They would, however, talk to their parents, relatives, teachers, principals, and friends. If you use letter writing as a prompt, assure your students that you will not send their letters off and that students can destroy them as soon as you have recorded their grade for completing the writing assignment.

Letter writing can be a great catharsis for students who are distracted by emotional stress or too keyed up to focus on school. You can use journal writing to teach students that writing down their feelings, especially when they are angry, helps dissipate pent-up energy and may help them calm down.

For teachers who haven't used journals or haven't used them successfully, my high school students created the following list of dos and don'ts:

1. Read them. If you aren't going to read them, don't ask us to write in them.

2. Make at least one comment on every page.

3. Don't mark every spelling and grammar error. You can circle some of them.

4. Give good prompts. Make them interesting for kids.

5. Show us samples of good journals that other kids have written.

6. Read some journal samples out loud, anonymously.

7. Let us know when we write something especially good or original.

8. Let us use our journals as rough drafts for essays and literary critiques.

9. Make journal writing a regular activity, at least once a week.

10. Let us write swear words sometimes if we are really mad.

11. Give some choices that we can write about, not just one thing.

If you have a problem coming up with good prompts, do an online search for journal writing. There are a number of good sites on which teachers share their own prompts for various age levels. In the meantime here are a few of my most popular prompts:

- Boys have life easier than girls do—what are your thoughts on this matter?
- What do you think is the biggest problem in the world today?
- What is the best invention ever created by human beings?
- Tell about a time you made a big mistake and what you learned from it.
- Tell about a time you accomplished something really difficult.
- Write a letter to your parents; tell them what a good or bad job they are doing.
- Write a letter to your best or worst teacher from the past.
- Describe your best or worst teacher. What does he or she look, sound, and smell like?
- Describe your favorite place in the world and explain why you like it.
- What are the three most important things in your life and why?
- If you could change one thing about your life, what would you change and why?

Unless I am using the journal-writing exercise to help students think of comments on a story we have read in class, I always include this as the final prompt: "Tell me what's on your mind (something real—don't tell me what you're going to have for lunch)."

Note: recently a teacher contacted me by e-mail to say that she had decided to use journal writing as the starter activity for the first ten minutes of every class but that her students balked at the assignment. I advised her to continue with the journals so that her students wouldn't think that they could make her give up any activity they didn't feel like doing. I also suggested that she require journals for two or three weeks and then stop for a few days. A few weeks later, she sent me an e-mail that said, "I did it. Now my students are complaining that they never get to write in their journals. They like having that quiet activity to help them calm down and focus."

INTRODUCE ETHICS TO YOUR STUDENTS

Children have an innate sense of justice, but they also tend to view themselves as the center of the universe, which can cause problems because they are unaware of the effects that their actions have on other people. By introducing students to sociology and psychology, you can help them see the bigger picture and realize that they each play a small but important role in a large society. Our goal as teachers is not to impose our own values and ethics but to encourage students to explore, form, and articulate their own.

I first introduced an ethics exercise to a class in which negative peer pressure was causing a lot of stress and behavior problems. I wanted my students to realize that each person has an individual code of ethics, even if he or she isn't aware of it. I thought that if they could articulate their values and morals, they would be less likely to succumb to negative pressures. For the first experiment, I used something relatively impersonal but universal—money. I asked students to select their best answers to the questions in Exhibit 6.8 in their journals.

After students wrote their answers, I took a quick survey and tallied their responses to question one on the board for each category: yes, no, and maybe. Then we had a class discussion about the topic for ten minutes. Next, students formed groups of three to five people and discussed the questions for another ten minutes. After their small-group discussions, students returned to their desks and wrote down their thoughts about the discussions, particularly if they changed their minds. I asked those who had changed their minds to write the reasons. Finally, we took another quick vote to see if people had changed their views. Many more students had joined the "no" group, those who would return the money. Students enjoyed seeing where they fell along the ethics spectrum, and many of them expressed admiration for the students who originally said that no, they would never keep the money. Those students were steadfast in their refusal to compromise their ethics.

You can slant ethics exercises to fit your subject. In a social studies class, for example, after conducting the exercise about whether to keep money that doesn't belong to you, the teacher could assign the project of researching crime statistics for ten, twenty, and thirty years ago and have students chart the trends. Math students could figure the percentage of people who would keep or return the money and the percentage of people whose votes changed after the discussions. Computer classes could generate charts or tables to display voting results. Art students could make drawings or posters expressing their feelings about money and greed. English composition students could write essays about their thoughts on ethics in general or stealing in particular.

With a bit of practice, you will be able to design ethics and sociology activities that are appropriate and effective for your students, but Exhibit 6.9 contains a few exercises to get you started. (In each case I suggest beginning with journal writing so that students can think about their own values instead of being influenced by others.)

Exhibit 6.9. More Ethics Exercises.

Values Clarification

List the five most important things in your life.

(After students write individual lists and participate in class and group discussions, request volunteers to share their lists. See if there is a difference between group lists and individual lists.)

Friendship

What qualities or behavior are important in a friend?

Code of Conduct

Describe the code of conduct that guides your own behavior. (This is difficult and may require more time or instructor assistance.)

Kidney-Donor Dilemma

You are a famous surgeon. Mr. and Mrs. Jones are seeking your help. They have twin sons who are fourteen years old, Jim and Jerry. Jim is in serious need of a kidney transplant. If he doesn't get a new kidney, he will definitely die. Mr. and Mrs. Jones want Jerry to give his brother a kidney because his would be the perfect match. Jerry refuses to give Jim a kidney; he says he hates Jim and wishes he would die. Jerry also claims that his parents care only about Jim. They spend all their time talking about Jim and bragging about his accomplishments. They ignore Jerry. They don't attend any of his sports games. They don't even notice that he's there most of the time. Jerry says that if you take his kidney, you will have to knock him out and operate against his will. Mr. and Mrs. Jones have the legal right to authorize this operation, but they don't know if they should. They want you to decide. If you agree to do the operation, they will sign the papers. If you say no, they will not argue with you. They will try to find another donor and accept the fact that their son may die before they can find one. Will you operate or not? Why?

(This exercise is based on an article I read about an ethics question posed to students at Harvard Medical School. Some of the details may differ from the original case, but the basic situation and outcome are real.)

The kidney-donor dilemma is very intriguing to students, and their reactions range from scientific to highly emotional. Some will argue that family is family and that a brother should be willing to die for a brother. Others argue that nobody has a right to operate on you without your consent. After the votes and discussions, I reveal the answer: the doctor refused to operate. The doctor reminded Mr. and Mrs. Jones that any operation runs the risk of death and that both sons might die. He said they should love both their sons and give them equal attention. Also, he said that the entire family needed to go to counseling and address the issue of Jerry's unhappiness. He believed that the parents had caused Jerry psychological and emotional distress by treating him like a second-class citizen. After counseling, if Jerry changed his mind, then the doctor would agree to operate. But he would not operate on a child against his or her will. (Be prepared for an additional heated discussion after you reveal the doctor's decision.)

MAKE TESTS A TRUE TOOL

Exams are supposed to measure learning, not serve as barriers to advancement, hoops to jump through, methods of gathering statistical proof, or attempts to qualify for federal or state funding. Therefore, I believe we teachers should use tests primarily as measurements of our effectiveness as instructors. Exams are checkpoints for me to see whether my students are ready to move on or whether we need to back up and cover some ground again, but students' daily work provides a much better record of their achievement and progress than any test can.

Tests that are designed to be graded quickly and easily by a person or a machine are rarely good indicators of true learning, skills, or ability. Such tests measure students' ability to memorize and regurgitate. I believe tests should focus on higher-level thinking skills, even with young children. To test children's knowledge and skills accurately, we need to ask children to write out answers to questions, provide examples to support their ideas, predict future outcomes and draw conclusions based on information provided, read aloud to us privately (and individually), and summarize what they have read. Good tests don't have to include hundreds of questions, and the best tests do not include matching or multiple choice (unless they are for young children who haven't yet progressed to higher-level thinking).

Teachers can't control the testing machine that threatens to clog our school systems until they stop functioning, but we can do our small part to support intelligent testing by learning how to design worksheets, quizzes, and exams that truly measure student skills, knowledge, and progress.

We can make sure we don't include ambiguous or trick questions, which serve no purpose other than to confuse or embarrass students.

We can allow students to complete practice exams and reserve those scores so that students who honestly suffer from test anxiety can keep the practice scores if they freeze during the real exams.

We can respond to cheaters by waiting to assign consequences until we have asked ourselves: *Why did this student feel he or she needed to cheat to pass this exam? Did I teach the material poorly? Was this student absent frequently during the unit? Is there a lot of parental pressure on this child? Does this child have a learning disability or low-level reading skills? Is this student just lazy?* Our response to the cheater should depend on the answers to those questions.

We can strive for quality instead of quantity on our quizzes and exams. Instead of offering one hundred multiple-choice questions, we can assign short essay questions and open-book exams similar to the ones that college professors use.

We can avoid using machine-scored forms that limit us to matching and multiple-choice answers.

We can provide immediate feedback whenever possible so that students don't leave our classrooms with misinformation in their minds. We can require students to complete their tests in pencil and then have them put the pencils aside and grade their own tests in green pen. Unless those are final exams, we can give credit for corrected answers.

And we can take our own tests before we give them to students. We can see how long it takes to complete our exams and check for ambiguous questions. We can make sure that we have provided enough space to write answers, because we know that if we provide a small space, we are going to get a short answer.

We can encourage excellence by teaching our students to answer short essay questions articulately and completely. We can provide samples of unacceptable (F), poor (D), acceptable (C), good (B), and excellent (A) answers so that students know exactly what we expect from them. I post samples on the walls of my classroom, something like the one in Exhibit 6.10.

Exhibit 6.10. Samples of Grades for Essay Question Responses.

Essay question: After reading *Of Mice and Men,* do you believe George made the right choice at the end of the story? Explain your answer.

F (unacceptable) answer: No. He made a dumb choice.

D (poor) answer: Yes, I think he made the right choice at the end of the story. He did what he had to do.

C (acceptable answer): No, I don't think he made the right choice. He could have tried to take Lennie someplace to hide. Or he could have got him a good lawyer or something. But he didn't even try to save him.

B (good answer): I don't think George should have killed Lennie, because he was supposed to be his friend. I know if George hadn't killed Lennie, Curley and his posse would have killed him or at least beat him up. Or else they would have locked him up in a mental institution. Curley had a grudge against Lennie from the fight and because Lennie killed his wife, so there is no way he would have let him go without hurting him. But still, George could have tried to think of some way to save him.

A (excellent answer): George faced a terrible dilemma at the conclusion of the story: should he kill his friend, or let Curley and his posse hang him? Even if Curley didn't kill him, Lennie would have been sent to jail or put into a mental institution for the rest of his life because he killed Curley's wife. Lennie didn't mean to kill her. It was an accident, but the courts would say that Lennie was dangerous to other people. Lennie would have suffered a lot in jail or in a hospital because he wouldn't have George to take care of him and be his friend. So, George made the decision to kill Lennie to prevent him from suffering. I don't know if I could have done it myself, but I think George made the right choice.

TAP INTO CHILDREN'S LOVE AFFAIR WITH COMPUTERS

Children love computers and quite often are more adept at using them than we adults are. If you have computers in your classroom or your school library, encourage students to use them for something other than surfing the Internet and playing video games, where the sole purpose is to win points. Teach your students how to find online sources for study aids, spelling strategies, educational exercises, and games designed to teach and test everything from geography to spelling to science. Here are just a few of my favorite Web sites, with a brief description of each one.

www.eslcafe.com Dave's ESL Café is a great site for English as a second language (ESL) learners, but the grammar quizzes are just as useful for native English speakers. Most of the material is too advanced for elementary students, unless they are grammar whizzes, but the site has quizzes on a number of subjects, including geography and American idioms, as well as links to a wide variety of other online sites.

www.everydayspelling.com One of the most helpful Web sites I've found, this is hosted by publisher Scott Foresman. It contains word lists; frequently misspelled words; strategies for spellers (kids would need help from teachers to use most of the tips); cross-curricular lessons in social sciences, health, math, and reading; and a series of excellent spelling quizzes. Although the site lists lessons for first through eighth grades, I have found those for third grade and higher very helpful for adult ESL learners. Check this one out.

www.funbrain.com This fun, kid-centered site has some excellent educational games such as Grammar Gorillas and Spell Check, and a great selection of math games.

www.grammarbook.com This super site provides high-level grammar, punctuation, and composition instruction, along with online quizzes—appropriate for advanced middle school, high school, and college students. In addition, it contains links to software and books on writing.

The Three R's: Reading, Reading, Reading

Aside from one graduate-level course in reading instruction, I was not trained to teach reading; but I found that in my work with disenchanted teens, reading was the single most common obstacle to academic success. By trial and error, I learned how to motivate reluctant readers to open a book. And by voracious reading and research and a great deal of practical experience, I have learned a bit about the subject of reading. Here are some of the conclusions I have drawn.

OUR APPROACH TO READING INSTRUCTION IS ILLOGICAL AT BEST AND INHUMANE AT WORST

All children become naturally curious about reading at some point in their lives. Unfortunately, our system doesn't allow for natural development. We insist that all children must learn to read at the same age because it is more convenient for adults to divide children into groups by age and then move them forward at the same time, ready or not. And often we compound this error by insisting that all the children in a particular classroom learn to read at the same rate. (Let me note here that I am not blaming the elementary teachers. It isn't the teachers' fault that they have so many children in their classrooms that they can't provide individual attention and instruction.) Many children become so discouraged and frustrated by their inability to keep up with the group (or being made to slow down and wait) that they give up entirely. Some lose all confidence in their ability to learn; others lose interest in school out of boredom. Each year those reluctant readers fall farther behind, and many eventually end up having serious behavior problems; they misbehave because they would rather be sent out of the classroom than be humiliated or bored every day. At least nobody forces them to read books they don't want to read when they are sitting in the principal's office or the detention center or at home on an out-of-school suspension.

CHILDREN LEARN TO READ QUICKLY WHEN THEY ARE READY

After I read several articles about children who had taught themselves to read, the need to teach reading when a child shows a natural interest, and the tendency of children to resist reading if they are forced to read before they are ready, I decided to try an experiment with my six-year-old stepson. An intelligent, outgoing boy and the youngest of three children, Brian absolutely refused to read in school, reported his teacher; this didn't surprise us because he wouldn't read at home either. Both Brian's teacher and everybody in our family had done our best to convince him to try, but as the first semester concluded, Brian was still one of the only nonreaders in his class. His teacher feared that he would be left behind in the second grade the following year. We were perplexed. Brian's vision was fine, and the school counselors couldn't detect any signs of a learning disability. He loved having somebody read a book to him, but he insisted that he couldn't read. I concluded that Brian was refusing to read because he wasn't ready to give up being pampered. He still wanted the attention that he enjoyed as the baby of the family.

After a family powwow, we decided to see if we could make reading seem like so much fun that Brian wouldn't be able to resist. That weekend Brian's dad, brother, sister, and I all chose one of our favorite books and gathered in the living room to read on Saturday morning. As we read, we frequently laughed out loud and then shared the titillating tidbit with each other. Instead of reading the bits, we would show them to each other and laugh appreciatively. When Brian asked us to read to him, we'd say, "I'll read to you later. Right now I want to read this book. I love this book."

For about twenty minutes, Brian went from person to person, wriggling his bottom beside us on our chairs or climbing over the back of the sofa to get a peek at our books. We ignored him and continued reading. Finally Brian disappeared into his bedroom and came back with one of Shel Silverstein's poetry books. He opened it to a page and began reading silently, then laughed out loud, as we had been doing.

"What are you doing?" his brother, Sean, challenged. "You can't read."

"I can too," Brian insisted. "Listen." And he slowly worked his way through a short poem. "See? I told you."

"Wow!" Sean said. "Did you hear Brian read that poem, Brigit?"

"No, I didn't," Brigit fibbed. "Brian can't read."

"Yes, I can," Brian said. And he read the poem again to prove it.

"I read that poem to him a hundred times," Brigit said. "He memorized it. He can't read."

"Yes, I can!" Brian hollered. He turned the page and read another poem.

Although we can't use such blatant child psychology on people who aren't children (or on very precocious children), we can make reading an attractive and appealing activity for students of all ages. We can motivate nonreaders by demonstrating our own passion for books and actively participating in the reading programs we design for our students. When parents complain that their children won't read, we can suggest that they make reading a family activity and provide a list of interesting books for them to try. Many nonreaders come from nonreading families, in which parents don't read well themselves and may feel uncomfortable at the thought of entering a public library or bookstore. If we provide parents with a list of books that includes both easy and challenging titles, they are more likely to encourage reading at home.

CHILDREN WHO HATE READING HAVE BEEN TAUGHT TO HATE READING

Children don't automatically hate reading. When they are very small, they love books. They carry them around and look at the pictures over and over again. They gnaw on the edges of their favorites as though they would like to eat those beloved books. And it isn't unusual for a toddler to request to hear the same book read fifty or a hundred times as a bedtime story. So what happens to make those little book lovers such adamant book haters?

We adults are responsible—for making them read before they are ready, demanding that they read faster than they are able, embarrassing or shaming them for reading poorly, requiring them to read aloud when they don't feel confident, and forcing them to read books they don't enjoy. Although our intentions may be good (we want children to learn to read), our results are often very bad indeed. We take one of life's most enjoyable pastimes and most essential skills and turn it into a dreaded experience. Tragically, many people become lifetime nonreaders because of those dreadful childhood experiences.

OUR FIRST EXPERIENCE WITH READING INFLUENCES OUR PERCEPTION OF OURSELVES

If you ask adults, "Do you consider yourself above average, about average, or below average?" most of them have a clear picture of where they fall on the intelligence spectrum. But what I find most interesting is that when I ask those same adults how old they were when they formed their opinions of their own intelligence, nearly all agree that they decided how smart they were during the first few years of school, when they were learning to read. Call them bluebirds and sparrows, stars and stripes, bears and bobcats, children always know who are the fast readers (translate "smart kids") and who are the slow readers (translate "dumb kids"). They know exactly where they fall on the reading-speed spectrum, and they believe this correlates to intelligence. Most of them will believe for the rest of their lives that they are smart or dumb or average, depending on how quickly and well they learned to read.

Because so many people carry the imprint of their first experience with reading for so many years, I encourage elementary school teachers to group students randomly, instead of by reading ability or speed. Of course, in a perfect world, students would receive individual instruction in this crucial skill; but we must deal with our imperfect schools. Also I encourage teachers to allow students to read at their own pace, even if it means that those slower students don't cover as much ground as their quicker classmates. Parents repeatedly ask me to tutor young children whose teachers have claimed that a learning disability prevents the children from learning to read. Invariably, the real problem turns out to be speed. Those children simply can't read at the fast rate that their teachers demand. When they are allowed to read at their own individual pace, those children do learn to read. One young girl went from failing grades to straight As in less than two months after I convinced her to take her time and stop trying to race through her reading.

Children don't have many options when their teachers insist that they read at a rate that is too fast for them. They are unable to articulate their frustration, so they choose one of the two obvious behaviors that occur to them: they either try to blast through the reading, skipping any words that are unfamiliar or difficult to pronounce, or they quit trying altogether (and perhaps become behavior problems instead of problem readers). Some poor little people become victims of psychosomatic illnesses that literally make them sick when they have to face another day in the classroom. My youngest brother, who struggled very hard to learn to read, often vomited in the mornings before school because reading was such a traumatic experience for him. When my older sister and I finally identified his problem and worked together to help our brother learn to read, his illnesses immediately disappeared, and his grades shot up from failing to above average.

THE PROBLEM

People who hate reading don't read well. That makes sense. We don't like doing things we do poorly, especially when we have to do those things in public. But reading is so important that we teachers must discover why our students don't like reading if we expect them to be successful in school and in the workplace. Without good reading skills, school becomes a painful struggle; and students either flounder, fail, or drop out. Unfortunately, high intelligence can camouflage a reading problem for years. Just as a blind person's sense of hearing becomes more acute, a poor reader may develop much sharper skills to compensate. Poor readers are often expert memorizers and mimics. They become excellent readers of body language as well, taking their cues from the slightest change in a teacher's facial expression or posture. And poor readers are often able to mask their lack of reading comprehension until they become freshmen in high school, at which time the textbooks and concepts become too complex or abstract to memorize. They can't solve math problems if they can't read and understand the problems, regardless of their intelligence; and they can't memorize an entire biology text.

When I began teaching disenchanted students and remedial readers, I used to wonder how so many students arrived in my high school classroom unable to read and comprehend the simplest books. Many of them admitted that they had attended school for ten years but had never read a single book, aside from those that teachers force-fed to them. *What were their teachers thinking, passing these students on to the next level, when they clearly couldn't read?* I wondered. Then I started corresponding with those students in their journals and working with them individually, and I learned how good they were at hiding their poor reading skills.

I began conducting informal surveys in each new class on the first day of school, asking, "How many of you love reading?" A few always raise their hands. Then I ask, "How many hate reading?" Usually half the hands in the room wave wildly, churning up the air with their negativity. We usually spend twenty or thirty minutes discussing our feelings about reading and why those who hate reading feel the way they do. Following are the reasons that my antireading students (ages six to fifty-one) have repeatedly given to explain why they hate reading:

1. Reading gives them a headache or makes their eyes hurt.

2. They believe they are going to be embarrassed because teachers are going to force them to read out loud and other students are going to laugh at them. (Sadly, sometimes teachers laugh too.)

3. They expect to be required to read so much material of no interest to them.

4. They know they will be required to finish reading everything they start in class, no matter how long, how difficult, or how boring it may be.

5. They know they are going to be tested on what they read, which makes reading a chore instead of a means of gaining information, seeing new perspectives, or being entertained.

6. They get lost when they are reading because they lack basic comprehension skills.

7. They believe that catching up is hopeless. When they read below their grade level, they don't understand that increasing their skills to the next level won't take a full calendar year. A ninth grader whose test score places him at a fourth-grade level, for example, thinks he will run out of time before he can catch up with his peers.

8. They believe they are going to be asked to state their opinion of a book or story verbally or in writing but that they will earn a bad grade for telling the truth. They know that the teacher expects them to agree with his or her opinion of the material. If students say they don't like a book or story, the teacher will argue with them or make them feel stupid for not appreciating it.

THE SOLUTIONS

I would like to suggest the following solutions to the eight problems that those antireading students identified.

1. Discuss Scotopic Sensitivity Syndrome with Your Students

Recent research suggests that nearly half of people who are labeled as learning disabled actually suffer from scotopic sensitivity syndrome—a sensitivity to light. People with scotopic sensitivity find reading difficult and sometimes painful when the material is printed on glossy paper. Fluorescent lighting or other lights that cause glare on the page make reading even more difficult. High-contrast print, such as black letters on white paper, is the most difficult for people with scotopic sensitivity to read. Unfortunately, such high-contrast print is the most common format for texts and other school materials.

You may notice some students who lean over their desks and wrap one arm around their books and papers. Sometimes teacher assume those students are trying to protect or hide their books and papers; often those students are trying to create a shadow to make reading easier. Many students prefer to wear baseball caps with the brims low over their eyes for the same reason—not simply to rebel.

Perhaps after an extended period of reading, you may have the feeling that the page is making your eyes burn, or you find yourself rubbing your eyes to clear your vision. This will give you an idea of what reading feels like all the time to people with scotopic sensitivity. And sadly, the harder they try to focus and concentrate, the worse the irritation or pain becomes. I have even had students whose eyes turn red and teary after just a few minutes of reading. Even more sadly, many students who struggle with scotopic sensitivity find themselves placed in special education classes or programs for behavior-disordered children because they refuse to read in class or they misbehave in order to avoid having to read.

Quite often, scotopic readers love stories and enjoy hearing them read aloud. They participate in group reading assignments and may have excellent comprehension skills. When you ask those students to read on their own, however, their behavior changes dramatically. If you have students who are generally cooperative but start to wiggle and squirm as soon as you ask them to read independently, be alert for signs that reading is uncomfortable for them. They may squint, frown, rub their eyes, try to shade their books with their hands or bodies, hold their books far away or very near to their faces, blink rapidly, or lose their place repeatedly when reading. Often schools mislabel scotopic readers as dyslexic (they may or may not suffer from dyslexia, as well) and give them tutoring to provide strategies that don't work, because the glare and discomfort remain.

If you haven't heard of scotopic sensitivity, your best source of information is the Internet. Be sure to check the sponsors of any Web sites you visit to make sure that they are reputable. A number of universities and education organizations offer links and resources, as do independent consulting firms. Many Web sites will offer testimonials from people who have used transparent colored overlays or filters with great success.

In my own experience, about one-half of a given class of remedial readers showed signs of scotopic sensitivity and responded positively and immediately to using overlays to read. Other teachers have reported similar success. One teacher in Illinois sent me an e-mail to let me know the results of preliminary testing in her school district. With schools in six different towns and only one testing packet to use, it took some time for teachers to test all of the struggling readers, but the teacher wrote, "the results are astounding—about 50 percent of our students noticed a significant difference with the overlays. We used a self-test first that I found online, and it amazed me how many of the questions were checked yes for most of our students. . . . We just received our full-size sheets, so I'll be waiting for feedback from our teachers."

An educational consultant from Raleigh, North Carolina, told me about her experience testing students at a local high school. The principal asked her to test one of the students who used foul language, disrupted class, was in recovery for recreational drug use, and had been repeatedly suspended from school. Because the boy kept returning, the principal had given him multiple second chances.

"The boy was very responsive to my questions," the consultant told me. "After he was screened and tested and received his overlay, his grades went from failing to As in English after only three weeks. His principal called to tell me about the success that he has had, and they called me back to screen thirty more students. Twenty-eight were scotopic. One boy even seemed to have a tic, but he was just trying to following the swirling lights that he saw when he tried to read, jerking his head. Another boy said he saw red, green, gold, and blue sparkles on the page."

A number of good Internet sites for information exist, but you might start with www.nrsi.com or www.irlen.com or search for the scientific studies of Dr. Paul R. Whiting, who published the journal article, "How Difficult Can Reading Be?" when he was on the faculty at the University of Sydney.

Also, be alert for new research on what is being termed vision therapy, vision convergence problems, or developmental optometry. Having 20/20 visual acuity doesn't automatically mean that a student has no vision problems. An August 2004 news release from the College of Optometrists in Vision Development reports that because symptoms may be quite similar, visual disorders caused by faulty skill patterns may be "misdiagnosed as learning disability or ADHD." The article reports that students who fail to respond to ADHD medication can experience dramatic improvement with vision therapy. To read more about vision therapy for problem readers, visit www.covd.org.

2. Make Reading Aloud Purely Voluntary in Your Classroom

Attendance, punctuality, and morale will improve if you stop forcing students to read aloud. Let students volunteer if they choose. Urge them to try. Don't allow other kids to laugh at the ones who do read, and beware the sneaky snickers. If you ask students to read aloud in your classroom, you owe it to your readers to make sure that nobody shames or humiliates them for trying. And if you have shy or timid students who refuse to volunteer, listen to them individually until they develop the confidence to read aloud (some kids will never volunteer, but that doesn't mean they aren't learning; and at least you won't have made them dread reading).

Many teachers insist that all students must read aloud. My response to those teachers is, "Why? What do you gain from forcing students to read aloud that is so valuable it outweighs their embarrassment, their stomach aches, their sweaty palms, their heartaches, and their reluctance to enter your classroom?" I would also ask, "If your current method isn't working, why not try a different approach? You don't have to continue if the new approach doesn't work, but if it does work, your students are the winners."

Some teachers call on students to read aloud as a way of keeping them awake or alert in class, but you could call on a volunteer who is seated next to your drowsy or daydreaming student. When his classmate begins to read, the daydreamer will tune back in, without feeling embarrassment or hostility toward you.

And finally, if you require students to read out loud simply because your own teachers required you to read out loud, I urge you to find some of your classmates who hated reading and ask them how they felt. Most teachers enjoyed school. We enjoyed reading. We don't know how it feels to hate reading so much that we are willing to jeopardize our own grades—even drop out of school—in order to avoid reading out loud. We need to have more empathy if we truly want to help our struggling readers.

3. Offer Reading Materials That Are Truly Interesting and Relevant to Students' Lives

Scholars can be convinced to read anything in order to analyze and evaluate it; poor readers, struggling readers, and students who are still in the process of developing good critical thinking skills cannot be convinced. But those struggling readers will flourish if you give them material that is so interesting that they forget they are reading.

Find some compelling magazine articles, essays on controversial subjects, or exciting stories. Many boys hate fiction. They simply cannot or will not suspend their disbelief long enough to become engaged. But they will read nonfiction—about bugs, dinosaurs, race cars, computers, sports, space ships, inventors, dragons. If you allow those children who dislike fiction to read nonfiction until they become good readers, they will be better able and more inclined to read fiction when you ask them to. You will have taught them that books can be enjoyable but that sometimes we need to read something we aren't wild about in order to learn a new thinking skill.

Read your selections as a group, but instead of announcing that you are going to read something, simply distribute the story. Let your students look it over on their own. Some of them will begin immediately. Others will wait for your cue. If your quick starters begin making comments about the story, don't hush them up. Their comments will create interest and entice other students to read. Let them talk for a while, unless they begin shouting. Then ask them if they would mind backing up so that you can read the entire selection together as a class in order to discuss it afterward. (If some students ignore you and continue reading ahead on their own, let them go, as long as they are polite. They aren't holding anybody back, and they will probably reread the selection along with the class after they have finished it. It is very frustrating for fast readers to be held back. Many of them will shut down mentally or become disruptive out of boredom. So, if you can give up some of the desire to control and let them read ahead, you will be doing everybody a service, including yourself.)

Teach your students to analyze the reading selections and articulate their opinions about what they are reading. Explain that we need to be able to evaluate whatever we read and intelligently articulate our opinions in order to be successful in school. Even little children will have an opinion about whether a story is interesting, informative, or exciting; whether characters are good or bad; whether descriptions paint vivid pictures; and whether the ending satisfies the reader. Prompt your students. Ask questions: Why do they dislike certain stories and books? Is the vocabulary too hard? Can they give some examples of difficult vocabulary words? Are the sentences too long and complex or too short and choppy? Are the characters unlikable or unbelievable? Is the plot too unrealistic? Where does the plot become unbelievable? Is the pace of the story too slow or fast? Is there too little dialogue? Or is it hard to tell who is talking?

If your compelling reading selection is short, ask the students to read the entire selection and then respond verbally or write their critiques. If your selection is longer, consider allowing students to read just enough so that they can write a valid critique, and then allow them to stop reading and start writing. If, after you have taught your students to intelligently analyze and evaluate reading material, students complain that a book is boring or stupid, you can explain that *boring* and *stupid* are not acceptable adjectives to describe a book or story. Students must be able to explain exactly why they do not like a given selection. Validate their opinions, as long as they state those opinions in an intelligent, articulate manner.

When you first begin to work with a group of reluctant readers and you must use a required reading list, at the very least let your students vote on the order in which they will read the books so that they don't feel quite so powerless. If more than half of your class dislikes a book or story, find out why, and consider replacing that selection with another that is equally challenging but more interesting to them.

One activity that I've used with good success is the book exchange. I get a number of books from the public or school library on a wide array of topics, from spaceships to teen romance novels to horror stories. Then I place a book on each student's desk before class begins. Students read the books on their desks for five minutes, then give the book a rating of one to ten and jot down a few quick notes on an index card. They exchange books and read for another five minutes, then rate the book and take notes. They repeat this until they have read at least five books. If they like a particular book, they can keep the book. Students who don't like any of the books continue to exchange books until they find something they like. Some students may have to spend a class period (or two) in the library doing their own book exchange before they can locate something irresistible. It's worth your time and theirs to allow them this opportunity.

4. Allow Students to Decide Not to Finish Reading a Given Assignment

Instead of forcing reluctant readers to finish books and stories that they clearly dislike or materials that are far beyond their abilities, give them the option of stopping. A challenge is good, but an impossible task is not. Students cannot read simply for the sake of reading until they become good readers. Good readers will tackle anything because they know that although sometimes reading requires real effort, they will be rewarded by gaining a new perspective, acquiring new knowledge, encountering an exciting but unfamiliar idea, experiencing a brain tickle, entering a completely new world, or simply enjoying the satisfaction of having conquered a difficult mental challenge. Poor readers don't experience those rewards, so you cannot convince them that reading is enjoyable until they learn to read well enough to forget that they are reading.

One of the quickest ways to discourage poor readers from becoming good readers is to make them finish reading things that they hate. This suggestion may go against your teacherly grain, but I urge you to consider it: promise your students that you will expect them to read half of any article, novel, nonfiction book, essay, story, or dramatic play that you give to them. At the halfway point, you will take a vote by show of hands to see whether the majority of your class wants to finish the given selection. If more than half of the students vote against the reading material, put it away. Allow students to finish it on their own if they choose, but do not pursue the reading as a class. Ask students to write a brief critique of the selection, and then move on to the next activity (I'd suggest doing a nonreading activity next).

Let me explain why I make this suggestion. In one of my high school classes, students were reading the short story, "The Birds," by Daphne DeMaurier. When they saw the story listed in the table of contents in their literature textbooks, they were excited about reading it because it sounded scary and some of them had seen the movie or heard about it. They looked forward to reading the story, writing their critiques, and then watching the film. Halfway through the story, I noticed that several heads were drooping and more than a few students were sound asleep.

After rousing the sleepers, I said, "I thought you guys were looking forward to reading this story. What happened?" They didn't know, but they were clearly disappointed with the story. Nobody wanted to finish reading, so I put the students in small groups and asked them to figure out why they didn't like the story as well as they had expected. In their critiques they concluded that the story was written in an "old-fashioned style," with stilted language and far too little dialogue. Some students argued that what might have seemed thrilling and scary when the author wrote the story was no longer frightening to people who had seen so many horror movies with incredible special effects. They thought the sentence and paragraph structure was too complex and contributed to the story's slow feel.

"Fine," I said, after reading their critiques. "Let's stop reading this story and find something more interesting."

"For real?" several students asked.

"Yes, I'm serious," I said.

"You mean we don't have to finish this?"

"No," I said. "In real life, if you don't like something, you don't have to finish it. When you go to the library and check out ten books, you don't have to read them; you don't have to write a book report on them. You can read one chapter—or one page—from each book and then take them back. And you can keep doing that until you find some books you want to read. After a while you learn what styles of writing appeal to you and what subjects and ideas interest you. Those are the things you read."

"That's cool," one student said. "But do we get to watch the movie anyway?"

"No," I said. "If we don't finish reading something, we don't watch the movie version, if there is one. We don't have a test. We write our critiques, have a short discussion, and then go on to something else."

Those students responded so enthusiastically to the "something else" that I made "read half–take a vote" my standard policy for reading with any remedial class or any class in which I have several reluctant readers. Of course, when I announce the policy, students always grin and warn me that we aren't ever going to finish anything because they are going to vote it down. Especially Shakespeare, they say. We know we aren't going to vote to read that hard stuff. But I have never had a class, regardless of how much they hate reading, vote to discontinue reading *The Taming of the Shrew, Othello,* or *The Merchant of Venice.* (I will discuss my approach to teaching Shakespeare in detail later in this chapter.)

I believe that one of the reasons this approach is so successful is that it gives students the feeling that they have a choice in what they read. And once they know that they can vote to stop reading a story or novel, they will often continue reading because they don't feel compelled to rebel just for the sake of rebelling. (Note: once in a while, a group will start voting down everything, just to be obnoxious. In that case I assign a really long and difficult reading assignment, so that by the time they reach the halfway mark, they are more than willing to be more receptive to the next short selection I offer them.)

5. Read Some Things Without Having a Test Afterward

Occasionally ask what students think of what they've read, without testing them. Hold a brief discussion and thank them for their cooperation. Period. Show them that reading isn't a test; it's a skill, and we don't have to test our skill level each time we use a skill. We simply use it. Let them read some things just for the sake of reading them, so that they learn from their own experience that reading is not a chore but a means of gaining information, tickling our brains, or being entertained.

When you do test students, don't use the same format for every test. Instead of asking them to select the correct answer on a multiple-choice or matching quiz, try open-ended short essay questions. Ask why they think a particular character acted the way he or she did. Ask them to think of three good adjectives to describe a specific character and give examples of things those characters said or did to support the students' choice of adjectives. Ask them to rate the story's conclusion and explain why they would give it a thumbs-up or thumbs-down.

6. Teach Strategies for Improving Reading Comprehension

Some students get lost when they are reading. One boy described his experience: "It's like I'm reading one of those signs in front of the bank where the letters move. As soon as I read the words, they disappear."

You don't have to be a reading teacher to give students some basic pointers on reading comprehension. First, explain that when we read, we create a mental picture of what we are reading. As we add details, the picture becomes more clear or changes to adjust to new or different information. If you lose the picture when you are reading, you are starting to lose your comprehension. Back up until you can see the picture again, and continue reading. If you do this as a class, with a story or article, you can read a paragraph, ask students what they see, and discuss their different visions. This will help students who still don't get it to understand what you are talking about. Then read the next paragraph and stop again to ask students to describe their mental pictures. When I do this with a class, even with adults, they usually become very excited because they finally (some for the first time) understand what all the fuss is about and why some people enjoy reading. This exercise works far better than simply asking questions to check their comprehension after they have read a selection, because students with poor comprehension don't understand why they can't remember information and other students can.

Another option is to use books on tape, either commercial or homemade. I have made a number of tapes on which I read material for my classes. I play the tape in class, and the students follow along. This helps them learn pacing and phrasing, and it frees them to focus on maintaining a mental picture, instead of worrying about pronunciation. I ask them to listen to the entire selection once and then ask questions before we listen a second time. And of course, we know that students learn better when they teach what they have learned, so asking students to read something and then give a summary to another student who hasn't read that selection is also a good activity.

If you detect serious comprehension problems, or if a student asks for more help, find out if your school has a reading specialist on the staff or as a regular visitor. If not, check with your local library to see if it has a literacy program, and encourage your students to attend the free sessions. Also, look for good Web sites devoted to reading. Do an Internet search for "online reading instruction," and you will find a plethora of books, articles, exercises, games, and instructional materials.

7. Give Your Struggling Readers Hope

Give them a pep talk before and after any standardized reading exam. Discuss test-taking strategies, and provide sample questions for them to practice. And above all, emphasize that reading is a skill like any other skill; they must practice in order to improve. Although most intelligent people read well, reading is not an indication of intelligence. It is a skill that intelligent people have worked to master.

"Even NBA All-Stars have to practice," I remind my students. "You don't get good at anything without practice, even if you are born with talent. Tiger Woods practices all the time; so do professional musicians, singers, rappers, poets, writers, dancers, and race car drivers."

Explain that a grade level in reading doesn't correspond to a calendar year. It is just a measure of how well a student reads a specific level of complexity in vocabulary and sentence structure. Encourage them to learn how to derive the meaning of unfamiliar words from the context of a sentence and to practice reading every day in order to improve their reading rate. One method I have used successfully is to copy some generic magazine article or selection from a textbook that is one or two pages long. I distribute copies of the pages and ask students not to begin reading until my signal. When I say, "Begin," everybody starts reading. They read for one full minute until I say, "Stop." They circle the last word they read. Then I teach them how to count the words on a page without counting every single word. Count the number of words in four individual lines, then add the numbers and divide by four to get the average number of words per line. Then the students count how many lines they read, multiply that by the average, and get a word count for one minute. They write that number down in the margin, and I collect the papers. We put the reading-rate papers away for a month, but we work on our reading skills with other materials every single day.

At the end of the month, we read the same reading-rate selection again and see how many words we have read. Students will nearly always improve if they have been making an effort in class. This shows them that practice doesn't make perfect, but it certainly makes improvement. Give them verbal praise and put the papers away for another month. When the material starts to sound familiar, give them a new reading-rate page.

8. Respect Each Student's Right to His or Her Opinions

So many students—most with tears in their eyes—have told me about the same experience: a teacher asked them to write their opinion about a book or story. The students worked hard on their essays and expected high marks for effort and content. Their teachers either assigned a D or F with no explanation or wrote some insulting comment such as "Wrong!" or "This is ridiculous!" in red ink across the top of the paper. In addition to doling out low grades and making students doubt their own intelligence, those teachers sent a clear message to the students: your opinion is worthless. If you ask for an opinion, accept what you get and grade the writing on composition and content—not on whether the student agrees with your opinion. Certainly, you can appreciate the literary merit of *The Scarlet Letter, Great Expectations,* and *Julius Caesar;* but sometimes young people simply aren't able to appreciate things we think they should appreciate. Instead of belittling them or lowering their grades when they don't get it, reward their honest effort and encourage them to develop their ideas logically and completely. If you allow your students to maintain their dignity and self-respect, they will continue to try and continue to progress. With maturity and practice, their reading and writing skills will improve; and they will be better able to appreciate literature that demands a more sophisticated approach.

SHAKESPEARE FOR RELUCTANT READERS

Before I ever mention Shakespeare to my students, I make sure that they know I care about them and truly have their best interests at heart. I want them to trust me when I tell them that I am not going to give them the standard style of test: they won't have to memorize Shakespeare's birth date and birthplace, draw a picture of the Globe Theatre, or identify the speaker of random quotes from whatever play we have studied. (Later, after they have read some of his works, students tend to be interested in the historical details and I include them in our lessons and discussions, but not as test items.)

I promise my students that I will not make them hate Shakespeare. And I also promise that after we have read exactly half of the first play, we will take a class vote. If the majority of the students want to stop, we will close the books and move on to something else without any penalty, although I will ask for their reasons for not wanting to continue and we will not watch the movie version. (I have never had a class that opted to quit reading; students always want to know the ending because William tells a good tale.)

When a class seems ready to read Shakespeare, I tell them that I think it would be a good idea for us to read one of his plays just for fun (of course, they protest that it won't be fun). I explain that we won't read his work just because he is one of the "boring dead white guys" in the literary canon but because he was an intensely talented and prolific writer. Quotations from Shakespeare appear in so many aspects of world culture that being unfamiliar with his works puts students at a disadvantage in society (fickle men are often referred to as Romeos, for example; and people giving speeches sometimes begin by saying, "Friends, Romans, countrymen, lend me your ears"). In addition, every college student in the United States and Europe is expected to have read at least a few plays and sonnets at some time during high school.

Students usually protest that Shakespeare is too hard to read. I assure them that reading Shakespeare requires effort: some people spend four or more years in college just studying his work. But difficult doesn't mean impossible.

"There is nothing wrong with your brains," I explain. "Ideas don't have grade levels. You can think about things just as well as the next person, even the kids in advanced placement classes. Your reading skills may need some help, but that's why you have me. I will help you with the reading."

After I first mention Shakespeare to the class, I wait a week or so. Then one day I write several "backwards style" sentences on the board: "Where goest thou after class? He thinks to woo the fair maiden. 'Twere better, methinks, to run than to tarry." I ask my students to figure out the sentences and to try to write more of their own, to get them used to interpreting an entire phrase rather than word by word. Then I make a short glossary of words from the upcoming play, such as *marry, tarry, prithee, hence, 'tis, whence,* and so on. (Students always raise a delighted ruckus when we get to the word *Ho.*) We make a poster of the glossary and keep it on the wall for reference. We add another chart with brief definitions of literary terms such as *irony, foreshadowing,* and *motivation,* which we include in the class discussions.

The Art Part

Next comes the art part, to pull in the visual learners. On the board or on large paper, I sketch a scene to represent the play and the main characters. If we are reading *The Taming of the Shrew,* I draw the two sisters, one smiling and one frowning, and the suitors standing in the street (Figure 7.1). Petruchio is about to enter town on horseback from one direction, while Lucentio and Tranio enter from the opposite direction.

Before we begin reading *Romeo and Juliet,* I draw two walled estates with a road running in front of them. I draw Juliet looking out her window and Romeo looking out his, with hearts connecting them (Figure 7.2). I draw two of the other main characters, Mercutio and Tybalt, fighting in the street. The Capulets and Montagues are distinguished by their family colors, which usually prompts a discussion of the similarity between the two ancient families and modern-day gangs because of their fierce loyalty and willingness to die for the "family."

(Note to the artistically challenged: as you can see, I never learned how to draw in perspective. Bad art is good for the classroom because students love to improve on my drawings. Usually several students volunteer to correct my artwork or draw their own. Sometimes students discover new talents as they try to teach me to draw a horse or a castle or a fair maiden.)

The Ground Rules

Before we begin reading, we create a list of all the primary characters and hang the list on the wall near the glossary so that nobody will get lost during the reading. Then I explain exactly what I expect:

Figure 7.1. The Taming of the Shrew.

Rules for Reading Shakespeare

1. Nobody is required to read out loud.

2. Nobody has to participate in discussions.

3. Points will not be deducted for quiet listening. Points will be deducted for sleeping, laughing at people who volunteer to read, or disrupting the class during reading.

4. In order to earn a passing grade for the unit, students must remain seated upright, awake, books open to the page that we are currently reading. They must pay attention and ask questions if they become lost. And they must listen quietly even if they choose not to take notes when we discuss the play at the end of each act.

The Opening Curtain

We begin slowly. I explain the basic setup of the play. Then I read the first few lines and stop to paraphrase them. I read a scene, trying to add drama by using different voices for the characters. After a short while, I stop and ask for students to help me

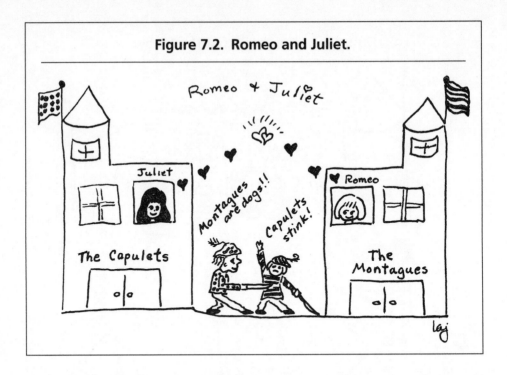

Figure 7.2. Romeo and Juliet.

out by reading a part. If nobody volunteers, I continue to read, stopping frequently to sum up the action. Occasionally I read an entire act by myself before students feel confident to try reading aloud.

In the beginning we do not spend the entire class period reading Shakespeare. We read one or two scenes, discuss them briefly, then go on to something different. After we finish reading one act, we make a set of class notes, using the board or overhead slides. I ask the class to state in one or two phrases the most important things that occurred in each scene. When we have finished reading the play, they have a complete outline of the plot, and I allow them to use their plot outlines during the test. (Those students who opt not to take notes are not permitted to copy other people's notes at the last minute. I don't force them to take notes, but I remind them that if they don't take notes, they won't have notes for the exam. By the time we have read the second act, the holdouts have usually joined the note takers.)

The Final Curtain

When we finish the play, we watch the movie version if one is available. Then each student takes the unit exam, writes a two-page essay about some aspect of the play (many choose to compare the movie and the print versions), and chooses one of three projects: illustrate a scene from the play, write a magazine-style review of the play, or make a display poster to advertise the play.

The unit exam counts for 50 percent of the unit grade; the essay and art project or review make up the other 50 percent. The exam does not include lower-level thinking skills such as matching. Instead, I ask short essay questions (five for younger students or ten for older teens) that require a basic understanding of the plot, character motivation, and setting. Here are some sample exam questions:

1. Give one possible reason to explain Kate's behavior. What might have caused her to act like a shrew?

2. If you had to marry one of the two sisters, Kate or Bianca, who would you marry and why?

3. What kind of person is Romeo? Give examples of his behavior to support your opinion.

4. Give an example of foreshadowing that occurs in *Romeo and Juliet*. (Be sure to include a description of the event that was foreshadowed in your answer.)

5. How do you think you would respond if your newlywed spouse treated you the way Petruchio treats Kate?

6. At the end of the play, do you think Kate is really tamed or just pretending? Explain your answer.

Students can't cheat or fake their way through this exam. In order to answer the questions, they must know the story. But instead of simply recalling information, they must analyze and evaluate what they have read. Invariably, after we finish the first play, students ask if we can read more Shakespeare.

Reading Shakespeare this way takes more time, at least the first few times, but the payoff is huge. Students learn that Shakespeare is accessible, that the quality of his writing makes the effort worthwhile; most important of all, they learn that they are not stupid and can indeed read what "the smart kids" read. It's not unusual, after reading the first play, to hear students trying to use "old Shakespeare talk" in their conversations. "Yo, Tony, goes thou to lunchest?" or "Check out Tyrone—he be wooing and courting the fair Tyeisha." Because my tests focus primarily on understanding the characters and their motivation, along with student evaluation and analysis, students finish each project feeling that they have reviewed the play rather than been tested on it; methinks that difference be a huge one.

USE MUSIC TO INTRODUCE POETRY

Because so many of my students hated reading or had described their negative experiences with English classes, I knew that if I announced that we would be reading poetry, I would lose them before we began. So I decided to sneak in the back door with a little rhythm and rhyme. In the movie *Dangerous Minds,* the producers took some liberties when they portrayed my approach. Yes, I did use song lyrics, but not Bob Dylan's "Tambourine Man." Instead, I typed out the words to the Public Enemy rap song "911 Is a Joke," Smokey Robinson's "Tears of a Clown," an English translation of the Hispanic folk song "Guantanamera," and the Garth Brooks hit "We Shall Be Free." When my students walked into class, I distributed the lyrics without saying anything.

"What's this?" they asked.

"Something I think is interesting," I said. After a few minutes, one of the kids said, "Hey, I know this song." Several private conversations sprang up around the room. Finally, somebody said, "Hey, Miss J, how come you gave us these songs?"

"I wanted to know if you think they are poetry," I said. (I love it when the kids play right along with my script.)

"Poetry?" a few kids mumbled. They shrugged and looked at each other. "Is this poetry?"

"You tell me," I insisted. "You know what a poem is, don't you?"

"Yeah," they said. "Poems rhyme."

"Is that all poems have? Just rhymes? Do all poems rhyme?"

"They got rhythm too," somebody else interjected.

"Right. Poems have rhythm or rhyme and sometimes both," I said. I held up the lyrics sheet. "So is this poetry?"

"You're the teacher," one girl said. "You tell us if it's poetry."

"You're the student," I said. "You tell me. Take your time. Think about it. Feel free to discuss it among yourselves. I'll wait." And I sat down with a very patient look on my face.

After a few minutes, one of the boys ventured a tentative, "I think they're poems. They all have music, and music has rhythm. And most of them rhyme."

"I agree," I said. "I think many song lyrics are poetic, and the best songs are very good poetry. And I'm going to give you the opportunity to bring in your favorite song lyrics to share with the class." Several students applauded. Some cheered. Nobody protested.

"What if we don't have the words?" one girl asked.

"If the CD or cassette doesn't provide lyrics, you can check the Internet to see if you can find the words. Or you can listen to the song several times and write them down. I'll type them for you."

Those students were ready. Some of them opened their notebooks and began singing to themselves, jotting down song lyrics.

"But there is one condition," I added. "You will need to explain to the class why you admire your particular song choice as good poetry."

"That's it?" a boy asked. "We just have to say why it's a good poem?"

"Yes," I said. "That's it. One little condition. So who's interested?" Nearly every student raised his or her hand. "Good. But in order to explain why your song is good poetry, you're going to have to learn the language of poetry. If you'll bear with me for a week or so, I'll teach you how to talk about poems."

A few kids frowned, but before they could voice the suggestion that they had been had once again, I launched into my introductory lesson on onomatopoeia. Slam! Bam! Pow! Ping! Before they knew what had hit them, those students were reading poetry.

I'd like to share with you the results of that first poetry experiment with those antireading students. Everybody in that class, including me, expressed very distinct preferences for music. Before we started that project, I dismissed the idea that any student could find a poetic heavy metal song, but somebody did. Very few of those students had been introduced to jazz, and many of them became big fans. And students who claimed they hated rap or country found themselves responding to the lyrics of songs when we read them without hearing the music. We discovered that it was often the beat we disliked, not the song itself. Students from very disparate backgrounds realized that they shared common emotions and dreams. Also I learned that filthy, disgusting racist, sexist, or violence-promoting songs can't be passed off as good poetry. One young man (an angry young man who usually sat with his arms crossed and his mouth clamped shut during our class discussions) brought in a rap song filled with profanity and obscene language. Instead of dismissing his song choice, I asked him to tell me what he admired about that particular song as poetry.

"I like the beat," he said.

"We aren't looking just for good beats," I said. "We're looking for really fine words in this project. Which words in this song do you really admire as good poetry? Can you show me some internal rhyme or a metaphor? Maybe a simile? Some alliteration?"

He frowned at the lyrics he had scribbled on a sheet of notebook paper. "Well, I don't really like the words that much," he admitted. "But it has a really good beat."

"Then you need to find another song with words that you do admire," I said. The following day he brought another song. It wasn't exactly the kind of song parents would appreciate, but it wasn't vulgar and obscene; because he was prepared to participate in his own learning for the first time, I accepted his contribution.

Two amazing things occurred after we completed that poetry project. First, my students didn't protest when I announced that we would be moving on to our textbooks to analyze and discuss classic poetry, including Shakespearean sonnets. Clearly, because they had analyzed and evaluated so many songs and original poems, they felt confident of their ability to tackle any poetry they might meet.

The second amazing thing was that my belligerent, pugnacious, disenchanted students unanimously elected "We Shall Be Free" as the best poetry of all the songs we read, which made me realize that instead of being amoral, apathetic young rebels, they were idealistic and hopeful children desperately in need of good adult leadership. For those who are unfamiliar with the song, here are the phrases that my students voted as best poetry:

> *When the last child cries for a crust of bread*
> *When the last man dies for just words that he said*
> *When the last thing we notice is the color of skin*
> *and the first thing we look for is the beauty within. . . .*
> *. . . then we shall be free.*

A five-senses poem may work better as an introduction to poetry for teachers who work with young children or older students who may not be good candidates for a lyrics project. This poetry form does not require a complicated introduction, and it always elicits a response because it's fun to read and write. Begin by asking your class, "What does love smell like?" Some students will frown or become confused, but others will shout out answers. Acknowledge all answers and thank the students who suggested them.

Now, write the word *Love* on the board, indicating that it is the title of the poem. Below the title, you write each of the five senses:

Smells like

Looks like

Sounds like

Feels like

Tastes like

Ask students for suggestions and choose interesting responses to complete each line. You will end up with a poem. Here's one that a class of high school freshmen wrote:

LOVE

Smells like banana bread
Looks like a little baby
Sounds like a song
Feels like a hug
Tastes like ice cream

Repeat this exercise with another word: *hate, school,* and *friends* are popular and all students can think of responses very easily. Be sure to encourage both literal and wildly imaginative answers, so students get the message that poetry is an art form and does not have a "right" answer. For example, one student might describe school as smelling like dry erase markers while another may describe it as smelling like dirty socks.

Next have students write two or three sense poems on their own, using words of their own choice. Ask for volunteers to read their poems aloud, and let the most enthusiastic poets write their poems on the board. At the end of this exercise, ask your students to give themselves a round of applause. Tell them, "Who knew you were such good poets?" You won't be lying, because they will surprise you with creative and thought-provoking examples.

I like to build on this exercise by encouraging students to copy out their poems on sheets of plain white or pastel paper, adding illustrations, and then tack their poetic artwork to the walls around the room. If you have the time and facilities, you might consider compiling them into a booklet that students can take home.

If you use this as your introduction to poetry, you have just demonstrated imagery and sensory detail. Now you will need to incorporate an overview of other poetic terms and techniques (appropriate for your grade level) into your subsequent lessons before you assign a portfolio assignment.

POETRY PORTFOLIOS

After my first successful song lyric or poetry writing experiment, I design a poetry portfolio project for students to complete prior to sharing songs. The portfolio is a two-week project that includes teacher demonstrations and short lectures, guided practice, and individual activities. On the first day of the project, I go over the definitions of poetic techniques with the class, giving examples of each technique so that students can take notes to refer to during their individual work. Each day I introduce a different kind of poem (haiku, limerick, diamond poem, five-senses poem); after we read several samples, I ask the class to write a few examples with me and then complete some worksheets (Exhibits 7.1 and 7.2). Then they are free to work on their own portfolios (Exhibit 7.3). (If you have concerns about grading or monitoring portfolio assignments, see Chapter Ten.)

SOURCES FOR COMPELLING READING MATERIALS

Until your students learn to enjoy reading, you may need to find materials to supplement their textbooks. I sometimes make copies of a short selection that is in their textbook because many students feel such antipathy toward anything in a textbook. If they notice later on, I pretend to be surprised to find such an interesting selection in their very own text. Here are just a few of the many sources I have used to find reading materials so interesting that students forget they are reading.

www.bbc.co.uk/learning This is my number-one pick of Internet sources. This Web site covers an incredible array of topics for every level of student from preschool to college. The phonics, reading, and spelling games for children (also great for ESL students) are first-rate. The fact sheets, online activities, and quizzes for high school students are interesting and challenging (check out the graphics and games under biology and physics, for example). And the free online courses cover such a huge selection of topics that you could literally spend months at home studying each evening without exhausting the list.

www. bbc.com For social studies classes, this site provides an alternate view of news headlines. Students enjoy comparing U.S. newspaper reports of topics to those by British reporters. It helps them see how others view the United States.

Exhibit 7.1. Poetry Worksheet 1.

Your Name: _____

1. Write a simile: _____
   _____

2. Write a metaphor: _____
   _____

3. Write a short poem with the rhyme scheme AABB:
   _____
   _____
   _____
   _____

4. Write a line that contains internal rhyme: _____
   _____

5. Write an example of a person's name that uses alliteration:
   _____

6. Give three examples of onomatopoetic words:
   _____

7. Find a poem in your textbook that uses a metaphor.
   Author: _____
   Title of poem: _____
   Metaphor: _____
   Is this metaphor effective? Why or why not? _____
   _____
   _____
   _____

8. Write a haiku. (It doesn't have to be great; just follow the format.)
   _____
   _____
   _____
   _____

Exhibit 7.2. Poetry Worksheet 2.

Your Name: _____

Directions: On the blank line(s), write the poetic technique, form, or device that is shown in the example. The possibilities are **alliteration, free verse, haiku, end rhyme, metaphor, simile, personification, internal rhyme,** or **onomatopoeia.** You'll use some terms more than once, and some items will need two terms—not to trick you but because some poetry is complex. One line can contain internal rhyme and alliteration, for example.

1. My puppy whirls through the house like a little black tornado.
   _____

2. I love great big gooey chewy chunky chocolate chip cookies.
   _____   _____

3. The tiny purple flowers danced and tossed their heads.
   _____

4. On my way home from school
   I was laughing like a fool
   Then I began to drool
   which was totally uncool
   _____

5. Sometimes in the night, I wake and think of you
   You are right there beside me
   I can hear the beating of your heart
   I can feel you kiss my cheek
   _____

6. Rat-a-tat-a-tat went the machine gun.
   _____

7. Winter sneaked up on us when we weren't expecting her.
   _____

8. Snowflakes fall softly
   Thousands of tiny white stars
   Shining in the night
   _____

9. Kenny is a lean mean dancing machine.
   _____   _____

10. Homework is like a toothache: you can't ignore it.
    _____

Exhibit 7.3. Poetry Portfolio Instructions.

For your grade on the poetry unit, you will be required to turn in a poetry portfolio. You may use any binder or folder you choose. If you are artistic, you may choose to draw a picture or otherwise illustrate the outside of your portfolio, but a plain cover is just fine.

During the next two weeks, we will read various poems in order to study and recognize poetic devices such as alliteration and onomatopoeia. In addition, we will analyze poetry, and you will write one literary essay, either interpreting a poem or comparing two poems. (Don't worry, we'll write the rough draft of each different kind of poem and drafts of your essays or interpretations in class, so that I can help you if you have problems!)

Your portfolio should contain the following items for a total of five hundred (500) points:

Poetry overview worksheet with definitions and examples	50
Roses are red poems or diamond poems	25
Five-senses poems	50
Word poems (that is, Brother, Sister)	25
Haiku or limericks	50
An illustrated poem (if you can't draw, use illustrations from a magazine)	50
"Your page" for English B (see Langston Hughes's poem)	50
Analysis of a Shakespearean sonnet or "Richard Cory"	100
Your literary essay about poetry	100

The items listed above are the minimum requirements for a passing grade. You may include additional original poetry in your portfolio.

Portfolios are due on _____

Late work will lose one letter grade per day (four days late = zero credit).

www.commondreams.org This site provides an assortment of newspaper articles and editorials from around the world, giving a global perspective on current issues.

www.ipl.org/div/kidspace/storyhour This wonderful Web site connects to the Internet Public Library, sponsored by the University of Michigan. The Reading Zone contains the full text of many popular books, and the links connect you to a number of useful sites for teachers at any grade level.

www.thelyrics.com This is just one of many online sources for song lyrics to find some examples when you introduce a poetry project that involves music and songs.

www.thereadinglady.com Hosted by a primary school teacher, this site has a wealth of reading activities, exercises, lesson plans, and reading selections. I especially like the poetry and reader's theater materials.

www.utne.com This magazine presents articles not commonly available in mainstream commercial magazines, and many are one page or shorter. The colorful graphic format evokes interest; and the articles often contain information about science, technology, ecology, health, and personal growth.

Teachers Talk: Q&A

When I give a keynote presentation or conduct a workshop, teachers often call me aside to discuss their particular classroom problems. They hesitate to discuss these situations with teachers or administrators at their own schools because they don't want to jeopardize their jobs or betray their students' confidence. Because so many teachers face variations of the same problems, I thought it might be helpful to share some of their concerns and questions. I hope these letters will spark discussions among teachers and between teachers and administrators, because I believe that a problem is halfway solved once we shine the light of discovery on it. Even a seemingly impossible situation feels less hopeless and overwhelming when we have sympathetic souls to help us share the burden.

Some of these questions arrived by e-mail, some by letters, and a few by telephone. In every case I have included the city and state (or country) so that teachers can see that their concerns are universal, but I have omitted names in order to protect teachers' privacy.

Q: I'm a third-year eighth-grade English teacher at a middle school, and people keep telling me to give up on particular students, that I can't save them all. I know this, but I can't give up on Joey. He came to my class two years ago, a tall, skinny kid with spiky hair and an easy smile. He was a fairly good kid in class; the girls loved him but he wasn't a player. Often he would miss my class so that he could stay home to baby-sit while his parents worked. When Joey left middle school, I felt confident that he would continue his education, at the very least getting his GED.

Fast forward to last week. I hadn't seen this kid in two years, and he sauntered into my room during open house. I hugged him and then inquired about school. He dropped his head in shame, then told me a story about how he failed because he stole a car and had a gun. I suspect he is in a gang. When I told him that he had talent and could do anything he wanted with his life, he looked at the girl he was with and said, "I told you someone thought I had talent."

I cried for this kid. Then I sent a letter to his new principal at the high school, enrolled him in a special program, and sent a letter to his guidance counselor. I just found out that he is back in jail, and I don't know what to do. I absolutely refuse to give up on this kid. He has talent—I mean true talent. Please give me some advice (other than you are sorry, but we can't save them all).

—*L. F., Charlotte, North Carolina*

A: I would never tell you that you can't save them all, because I believe we can save young people, if they are still alive. I have had so many students like this boy, and they broke my heart again and again. But going to jail isn't the end of the world. He will keep thinking about your opinion of him. Clearly, you connected. He just has to work out his own perception of himself. This is my theory: kids have a script in their heads for how the movie of their life will play out. Then they meet us, and we see a different script. We try to change the script by telling the kid that he or she has talent and choices in life. But they don't understand because they have always felt powerless and they really believe their script is their destiny. So we can't change the script by trying to rewrite it. But we *can* help them change their perceptions of themselves as people, by telling them how we see them: we see them as intelligent, talented, capable, and so on. This doesn't change their script, but it changes their perception immediately and keeps it changing the more they have contact with us. Even when those students are far away, those new thoughts keep crowding out the old ones until they decide that they can indeed change their scripts. This can take years. I have had many students who believed they would end up in jail (and most of them did), but I encouraged them to use their time in jail to study and learn and think. Many of them got GEDs and good jobs afterward.

Sometimes we can intervene early enough to change a student's perception enough for him to change his script before he goes to jail. If not, we can continue to try to change the perception by calling, writing letters, and so on. If you can get an address, write to this kid every week. See if you can go visit at least once. Whether or not he answers, whether or not you see him, whether or not he ever comes to see you again, your belief in him may be the lifeline that keeps him going. I spoke to a psychiatrist about this once, and he assured me that finding one adult who offers unconditional love and acceptance is enough for many kids. That acceptance will be the lifeline they cling to until they are able to stand on their own feet.

I hope this helps. Never give up. Even when you don't see the flower, if you plant the seed of hope in a child, it will grow. So many people write me letters to tell me about teachers who tried to help them when they were young. They never thanked those teachers, but they write to tell me how much they appreciate what those teachers said and did—and sometimes all the teacher did was say something nice. You have given much more than that to your young person. I'm sure that as long as he is alive, there is hope for him. I'm so glad you are a teacher!

I would like to say something about the people who tell you to stop worrying. They are not heartless people. They simply can't afford to make the kind of emotional investment that you are willing to make. Just as we all have to decide how much of our income we can afford to donate to charity, we have to decide how much emotional energy we can afford to expend trying to save students. Some of us can afford to give more, and some of us can tolerate the loss when our investment shows no return. Just be careful that you don't bankrupt your supply. Find some way to recharge periodically.

Q: I am a first-year teacher of English and speech at an urban high school in Indiana. I am twenty-five years old. I love teaching with all my heart, and I feel that after much soul searching and several unsuccessful jobs, I have found my true calling. However, I have been very stressed out recently over some evaluations that one of my classes filled out. One student, a sometimes hardworking, independent young man, wrote on his evaluation that I should quit my job and find another . . . that I need classes in listening. . . . "if I were to receive a grade, I would be given a U for uncomplete."

I was disturbed by this, mainly because I feel like such things should not bother me or else I shouldn't be a teacher. This incident has forced me to reevaluate my teaching and content-area skills. What advice can you possibly give a first-year teacher experiencing these types of feelings and stress?

—*A. J., New Albany, Indiana*

A: Perhaps it may help to know that I have faced a similar situation and so have many successful teachers. In most cases your teaching isn't the real issue. If 75 percent of your students make the same complaint about your teaching methods, then I would really think about making some changes. If a few kids say something, I consider their comments and decide whether they are just whining or whether I may have done something to merit their criticism. But if you have an isolated example of only one student criticizing your teaching, then that student probably is talking about his own needs.

This boy wants you to listen to him. He can't know whether you listen to anybody else. Perhaps there is somebody in the class who torments him and you don't hear it, so he thinks you don't listen. Perhaps he has some personal problems and he has given you hints (such as refusing to answer when you ask *him* a question— you were supposed to read his mind). Or most likely, he wants to see if he can push your buttons, take away some of your self-confidence, and make you feel a little more the way he feels: scared, uncertain of the future, and insecure.

I know it isn't easy to ignore this boy's remarks. Many teachers (including yours truly) have difficulty handling criticism that is clearly intended as a personal attack. But I have learned to differentiate between students who have a serious concern and students who are making a power play. Your young man sounds like a power-play kind of guy. My suggestion is this: ask him to come in after school; tell him you want to be able to take the time to really listen to his comments. If he won't come, then you will know he was just trying to upset you. If he does come, he still may be playing. Don't begin by asking him to evaluate your teaching; he has already done that. Keep the power in your court. Tell him that you appreciate his comments and that you would like to listen to whatever he has to say. If he says he has nothing to say, then thank him and tell him that in the future you would be glad to schedule a meeting to listen to any concerns he may have but that critiques of your teaching are not appropriate and will not be permitted during class time. Stress that teaching is your job and how you choose to approach your job is up to you, that you are interested in his concerns but that you must also consider the concerns of all the other students.

If your student does have something to say, then listen to his concerns and thank him for sharing his opinions. Tell him you will consider his comments carefully. Don't apologize unless you have honestly done something to offend him. Tell him that if you ever offer him some constructive criticism about his performance as a student, you hope he will treat your comments with the same respect you have given to his. Then, before you conclude your conference, ask your young man something he doesn't expect you to ask, something interesting that may surprise him into actually talking to you. Tell him you've been reading some recent research on education and you would like to hear his opinion about age-based grouping. Does he think classes would be better if kids were grouped by ability instead of age? Or suggest that he check out a Web site that you find particularly thought-provoking.

One way I have successfully avoided the power-player student—after I encountered a few—was to start passing out evaluation sheets that don't evaluate me but evaluate what we have done during a given time period (usually a month). For example, I list grammar, spelling, literature, and videos we have watched and ask students to evaluate each activity or assignment as too hard, too easy, or just right. If students really complain about something required on the curriculum, I say, "I am prepared for you to be angry with me right now because I know that when you are older you won't be angry; you will realize I am truly making the choice that is in your best interest. I want you to be well-educated people so that you can be successful in both your professional lives and your personal lives." Always, always I remind them that I care about their input but that I am in charge of the classroom. I am not in charge of them or their behavior, because they are responsible for that. But I am responsible for making the decisions in my classroom; that's why they pay me so much. (We all laugh here.) Most of them get it.

Here's one more thought. Perhaps your critical young man really likes you and would like to have more attention from you, but he doesn't know how to ask for it in a positive manner. If he wrote you a glowing evaluation, you would just thank him and smile. But now you are thinking about him. Try to think of some role he could play in your classroom that would make him feel important. He could pick up mail from your staff mailbox, if students are allowed to do that. You might ask him to take a note to one of the secretaries for you (you could arrange with her ahead of time to find something important to tell her). If you are planning to show a movie, ask him to set up the VCR and prepare the video so that it is ready to start when you want it and students won't have to wait for opening credits. Explain that roll sheets may seem simple but that they are legal documents and can be used as evidence in court, then ask if he would mind taking roll for you once in a while.

OK, enough. You didn't ask for a novel. Please remember that the reason you care so much about what people say is that you are a caring person; more than anything, that makes you a good teacher. Anybody can be educated, but not everybody can teach. Give yourself the gift of tolerance for your birthday this year: allow yourself to be human and less than perfect.

Q: I heard you speak in Albuquerque once, and you seemed to be totally against any kind of medication for ADHD. I have some kids who really seem to respond to medications. And I even know a few adults who swear by Ritalin. Don't you think maybe you are a little bit close-minded about this?

—*S. M., Albuquerque, New Mexico*

A: Yes, I will admit that I am a bit close-minded on the topic of medicating children, but I also believe there is a huge difference between medicating children, who have no choice, and medicating adults, who are responsible for their own choices and their own health. If adults choose to take a medication that affects their brains, they certainly should have all the information available about possible side effects and documented case histories. Drug companies, newspapers, and magazines don't report the entire story when a company introduces a new drug. For example, on August 19, 2004, the *Philadelphia Business Journal* printed an article about a pharmaceutical corporation's report of preliminary results from three clinical trials of a new once-a-day medication, modafinil, that "significantly improves symptoms of attention deficit hyperactivity disorder in children and adolescents." It quoted the CEO of Cephalon, Inc., as saying, "We expect this product, once approved, to command a substantial presence in this large and growing market that today exceeds several billion dollars." Clearly, money is an important motive in the manufacture of this drug. The article never mentions possible side effects and never refers to sources of further information. A quick visit to the U.S. government's National Library of Medicine and National Institutes of Health Web site (www.nlm.nih.gov/medlineplus/druginfo/medmaster/a602016.html) warns "you should know that modafinil may affect judgment or thinking. Do not drive a car or operate machinery until you know how this medication affects you." Then it lists side effects associated with modafinil, including "headache, upset stomach, nervousness, difficulty falling asleep or staying asleep, dizziness, depression, diarrhea, runny nose, dry mouth, loss of appetite, vomiting, neck pain or stiffness, confusion or forgetfulness." Those are just the regular, everyday possible side effects. Serious side effects, although uncommon, may include "chest pain, irregular heartbeat, rash or hives, fever, sore throat, chills, and other signs of infection." To me this sounds like a potentially dangerous drug, but the *Business Journal* article reports that "studies involved 600 children and adolescents between the ages of 6 and 17." Unless a condition is life-threatening, I can see no valid reason for subjecting young children to clinical drug trials.

All my research on ADHD diagnosis, symptoms, and treatments has convinced me of three things: money is a key ingredient in this mix; the United State uses over 80 percent of the world's supply of drugs intended to treat ADHD; and people don't have enough objective information.

I believe anybody who even considers giving a child medications should visit the Drug Enforcement Administration and National Library of Medicine Web sites and read the information, especially the court testimonies concerning methylphenidate and amphetamine treatments. I devoted an entire chapter in my book *Queen of Education* to this very topic, so I won't go into complete detail here.

Children's bodies and brains are not yet formed, and we don't know the effects of long-term drug use on their development. Look at the number of cases of parents who reported stunted growth, lack of appetite, and depression among their children who are on medications. And some medications cause insomnia, which in itself may exacerbate ADHD symptoms. Also, I have seen too many situations in which school staff members immediately recommend medication for children who have trouble sitting still or concentrating. Worse yet, some parents have been threatened with having their children taken away from them if they do not agree to medicate them.

I do agree with you that a small percentage of children (and adults) truly benefit from medication, but I still believe that medication should be the very last resort. The first resort should be to change the diet to add fruits, vegetables, whole grains, and fiber and to reduce or eliminate caffeine, artificial sweeteners, fried or packaged foods that contain trans fats and hydrogenated oils, and high-fructose corn syrup (which causes severe mood swings and fuzzy thinking). Agave nectar and fructose are natural sweeteners that don't cause dramatic rises and dips in blood sugar. Next, check children's sleep patterns. Children especially need at least eight hours of sleep per night. Sleep deprivation has the exact same symptoms as ADHD. Third, add at least twenty minutes of daily exercise, followed by deep breathing, meditation, or yoga. And finally, investigate the teacher-student personality dynamic. Many students misbehave because they believe (sometimes correctly) that the teacher doesn't like them or know how to teach them.

I firmly believe that if we follow those four steps, most symptoms of hyperactivity will disappear; if not, then I think an extremely cautious approach to medication might be in order. When children report uncomfortable side effects and plead to stop taking medications, however, I believe parents and doctors are ethically and morally obligated to suspend the medication and search for alternative methods to help those children.

Q: I spend more than half of my class time refereeing arguments and fights among students and redirecting their attention to their work. I am so tired of fighting the same battles every day. What can I do?

—S. E., Boston, Massachusetts

A: First, I would announce to your class that you will not tolerate verbal abuse in your classroom. Tell the students that they are in charge of their own behavior but that you are in charge of your classroom. Anybody who wants to stay in the room must follow the rule of treating everybody in the room with respect—including themselves.

Name calling, insults, and rampant disrespect were the reasons that I devised my only classroom rule: treat everybody in this room with respect—no put-downs of other people based on their race, religion, ethnic background, skin color, native language, gender, sexual preference, intelligence, body shape, or body size. (Students are entitled to their opinions and prejudices, but they are not permitted to express those opinions publicly in the form of insults or attacks on other people. You can read more about my discipline approach in Chapter Five.)

In spite of my rule mandating respectful behavior, sometimes one particular group of students seems to include a high percentage of instigators, hotheads, or bullies. When I encounter this situation, I frequently remind them of my rule and post it in very large letters in the classroom. Also I suspend my instruction temporarily for a lesson in psychology. I explain to the students that psychology can help them understand how other people play you or psych you out (or whatever term they will understand).

First, we discuss why people tease each other: some people are trying to make themselves feel better by making other people feel small. Some people are afraid they are stupid themselves, so they try to get smart students in trouble. Some people are bored, and they want to create problems just to make life interesting. Some people are unable to do the work in class but don't want people to laugh at them, so they try to distract the teacher and the other students.

Some people just get a kick out of controlling others' behavior, and this is the motive that kids find most interesting. When kids understand that by becoming angry or responding to verbal insults, they are doing exactly what the other person wants them to do and that they are being manipulated, some kids will stop playing the game. Some students find this a difficult concept to grasp. You may have to restate it in various ways and perhaps stage an example in your room.

Helping your students understand themselves and each other isn't enough. You need to help them learn how to withstand the peer pressure and verbal assault. Teach them what to say and role-play some situations so that they can practice. I teach them power statements; just calling them power statements makes them sound attractive. Word your power statements to suit your students' age level. Some of my favorites include the following:

- You can say what you want, but it isn't important to me.

- I know you want me to get mad, but *I* control my own mind.

- You are not the boss of me. I don't want to fight with anybody.

- You have your opinions, and I have mine. We just don't agree.

- Doing mean things doesn't make you strong.

- We are all human beings. I think we should try to get along.

- You can think whatever you want. I think for myself.

Some children really don't understand why they tease other people; we need to teach these children other ways to get attention from their peers. They usually don't have any real friends because they don't know how to be a friend. We talk about this too in class. I ask students to write in their journals what they think is important in a friendship, what they look for in a friend, how to make friends, and so on. Then we have a class discussion, and we write our thoughts about friendship on the board. Many students have reported that after our discussion on friendship, they feel more confident about being able to make friends.

Of course, you still have to have a discipline policy that works for you. But in my experience, when you face a serious problem in your classroom, it pays to take some time to talk about the cause of the problem and possible cures, instead of simply trying to treat the symptoms.

Q: I'm not a teacher, but after seeing *Dangerous Minds* for the fifteenth time I decided to write to you because I saw that you have very strong opinions on how the schools are teaching our children. I am not sure what to do because I have three children, ages fourteen, ten, and three. My oldest is a freshman, and all they seem to do at school is test. There is no longer that interaction between teacher and student. Instead they give them scan cards; they don't even have books—just math papers. My daughter is finding it difficult in more than one class to keep her grades up. I feel that this is partially due to the lack of teaching being done. It is as though the teachers are just there to observe and not actually teach.

I was wondering if there is anything I could do to get the district to revise its policies and once again teach instead of just observing. I would like to help my daughter and was hoping you might know where I could go to get the instructional material to help her with her math and English. I don't want her to just pass through school. I want her to have learned something she will be able to use. Any information would be greatly appreciated.

—*H. M., Truth or Consequences, New Mexico*

A: I agree with you that testing is out of hand and that we need to return our focus to teaching. First, I would suggest that you call your school district superintendent and request a meeting. Tell him or her exactly what you said in your letter. Ask what he or she can do to help you; don't worry about offending the superintendent. Any good administrator will welcome your input and address your concerns. If he or she makes any promises, such as reviewing the curriculum for your daughter's math class, follow up to find out what, if anything, will be done.

Next, find out who is on your local school board. Get their names and addresses. Send each member a copy of the letter you sent me. Ask them to look into the situation. Offer to meet with them to explain your concerns; if you can find other parents to go with you, better yet. Attend as many school board meetings as you can. Find out when the parent-teacher organization meets at your school. Attend those meetings too. Don't worry about whether anyone will call you a meddling parent. You are just doing your job, and one of your jobs is to make sure that they are doing theirs so that your children are well educated.

School policy takes time to change, however, so in the meantime visit your local public library and ask the reference librarian to help you locate books to help you. I have seen some series that tell what a child should learn in kindergarten, first grade, second grade, and so on. Many books designed for parents who homeschool have curriculum guides or resource sections to help you find additional information. I wouldn't recommend buying any expensive programs of study. You should be able to find sufficient information through the library and other community resources.

If you are within driving distance of a community college or four-year university, call the campus and find out whether community members can use their library. If so, you will find a wealth of information, textbooks, computer programs, instructional videotapes, and so on. Ask the reference librarian for help. Librarians don't mind providing information; that's why they work at libraries. They enjoy helping library patrons find what they need.

In addition to looking at books, workbooks, and instructional videos designed to teach children, you might also look into GED materials. Most communities have free classes. You don't need to attend classes, but you can use the same materials to make sure that your children are on track. GED books cover each basic subject, including math, English, writing, and social studies. Although the sample exercises may be too hard for young children, they are appropriate for teens and will give you a good idea of what your children should know when they finish high school. Because GED materials are designed to teach adults who weren't able to finish high school, they present a good overview of each subject, with special emphasis on basic skills. This can give you a good refresher if your own skills are a little rusty.

One final source of information is the Internet. If you don't have a home computer, check with your local public or college library. Most have computers that you can use for free. If you don't know how to use search engines, ask the librarian for help. To get you started, try going to www.Readinglady.com. This Web site is hosted by a teacher who provides a wonderful series of lessons for teaching reading and English skills to young children. She also provides resources for further information.

Good luck to you, and hug those children. They are fortunate to have a mother who cares so much about them.

Q: What is your opinion of ESL programs? And what do you do when the school puts students who don't speak English in your regular class?

—A. G., El Paso, TX

A: First, as an ESL instructor for adults, I support ESL programs—as long as they are voluntary and challenging. I am not a fan of classes in which students spend all of their time playing games or filling out worksheets, but if students work on the same materials that are being covered in regular classes, I think they can be very helpful. And community-based ESL classes are an excellent resource for adults who need to learn English in order to find employment, earn promotion, negotiate the health care system, and help their children with schoolwork. Even so, I believe that children fare much better overall when they are immersed in a regular classroom, surrounded by English-speaking peers—if their teachers are flexible and capable of connecting with non-native-English speakers. Within a few months in a supportive environment, most children can acquire enough language to keep pace in a regular class, although some may require extra help with writing, because writing skills tend to lag behind speaking and reading. The problem with immersion is that many teachers are confused about how to grade non-English speakers who cannot read, write, or speak at grade level.

"You can't just give them a grade, can you?" one teacher asked me. "But then again, most of my non-English speakers work like the dickens in class. They work twice as hard as the other kids. So I don't want to give them low grades."

My solution falls somewhere in the middle. I make it very clear to my non-English speakers that I expect them to come to class, work very hard, attempt to do every assignment, and ask for help when they need it. I also expect them to listen to National Public Radio newscasts and programs and to watch the news on TV in English so that they can hear proper English spoken. In addition, I provide some books on tape that they can check out to take home and listen as they read the text. They will not understand everything they hear or read, but that isn't important. They will be surrounding themselves with English, and they will absorb it the way babies do. But babies take nine months to a year (sometimes longer) before they are ready to speak. We can't expect students to absorb a new language in just a few weeks. So I allow one entire five-month semester for ESL students to make the transition. During that time they earn a passing grade (C or B, depending on the quality of their work) if they come to class regularly and make an honest effort to complete all the assignments. They do not have to complete every quiz or exam because they work more slowly than other students, but they must work hard during the testing period. They must complete all writing assignments. If they have to write the assignment in their native languages, that's fine. Then they have a week to take the assignment home and translate it into English. It doesn't have to be proper grammar and perfect spelling, but they have to translate the entire composition.

"But I cannot write so much!" they usually complain.

"Yes, you can," I reply. "You may not want to do it, but you can do it if you put your mind to it. I expect you to try."

Newcomers who lack basic skills in their native languages may need another full semester of transition before I begin grading them according to standard criteria, but I expect students who were well educated in their native countries to complete regular assignments during their second semester in my classroom. Although I do not deduct points for ESL students' grammar and spelling errors, I still expect them to be able to do all of their assignments in English. I provide constant encouragement, positive feedback, and motivational pep talks, along with hugs or handshakes, recognition of achievements, and occasional home visits. And in seven years of teaching high school, I only had a few students who were unable to learn enough English to keep pace with the native English speakers (and those students had learning disabilities such as dyslexia or speech impediments). Many of my non-English speakers went on to earn college scholarships after only three or four years in the United States.

Q: How do you make your students realize the importance of education?

—*P. W., Columbus, Ohio*

A: I learned the hard way that I can't *make* students do anything, but I also learned that my own enthusiasm can be an irresistible magnet for students. If I truly believe that something is important, my students tend to at least give me a good listen. I don't discuss the value of education until students know me well enough to believe that I am on their side and that I want them to succeed in their lives (according to their own definitions of success).

Although I don't believe money is the primary measure of success, I believe it is important that students understand that different lifestyles require different amounts of money. We create a hypothetical budget on the board in class to get a general idea of how much it costs to live comfortably but not luxuriously. Then I show them (in writing, so that they can take the figures home and look at them) how much money the "average" person with a high school diploma makes versus the person with no diploma, then how much they average with an associate's degree, with a bachelor's, with postgraduate degrees. (Figures vary depending on the source you use, but most authorities agree that the difference between a high school dropout's lifetime earnings and a high school graduate's lifetime earnings will be roughly $250,000; the difference between the lifetime earnings of a high school dropout and a college graduate will near the million-dollar mark.)

Because their peers or relatives have advised many unenthusiastic students to drop out and just take the GED, I keep one of those bulky books that contain actual GED tests on my desk, so that students can see that the tests aren't easy and that GED classes involve as much work as high school, if not more. Students are invariably surprised to see how much information they will be expected to know as adults, and most change their minds about dropping out.

I don't try to convince students that they will use everything they learn, because they won't. I explain Bloom's taxonomy of cognitive domains (see Chapter Four) to describe the different levels of thinking and why each is important to master. We then look at ways that we use synthesis or evaluation, for example, in different classes. I repeatedly remind my students that I want to help them be successful people in life and in school. I tell them: "The more education you have, the better you learn to think, the more worlds are open to you, the better decisions you can make, and the more options you have in your life. Even if you don't like your job, if you have an education, you can earn a good living at something while you put yourself through school or training to do something else. Without an education, most people work to survive from day to day, and their options shrink with each passing year."

Q: Every time I eat lunch in the staff room, I get depressed after listening to the teachers complain so bitterly about their jobs and their students. Am I destined to become like them?

—*S. T., Lexington, North Carolina*

A: Absolutely not! Unfortunately, it seems that lunchrooms and staff lounges are popular gathering spots for teachers who hate their jobs or who have become so disillusioned that they have forgotten why they became teachers in the first place. My advice to new teachers is to be very wary of joining the lunch or lounge crowd until you have a sense of the atmosphere. Make a quick visit or two during your first week. If moaning and groaning dominate the conversation, make a polite excuse and find another place to take your break or eat lunch. You may find a kindred soul who will join you for a paper bag picnic in one of your classrooms or outdoors on your campus. Some teachers opt to remain in their classrooms and take a working lunch; paperwork is a great excuse when those crabby teachers invite you to join their complaint group. If you connect with your students, you may find stray souls drifting into your classroom to avoid being teased, tormented, or ignored by their peers. Depending on your personality and relationship with your students, you may recruit them to help you with routine tasks or use the time to find out more about their interests and personalities.

Q: I have been given the choice of teaching remedial or advanced classes. You have taught both. Which do you prefer?

—*F. K., Chiselhurt, Great Britain*

A: Remedial kids have so much energy and personality that I enjoy teaching them when I am allowed the freedom to develop lessons that tap into that energy source and help channel it into something positive. To be successful with remedial students, teachers must have administrative support and the authority to accompany their responsibilities. Otherwise, such teaching becomes nearly impossible and can end up making even the most creative and dedicated teachers feel like giving up.

Working with remedial students is very satisfying but can be emotionally draining, so sometimes it's a pleasure to have more scholarly students, although they pose their own challenges. Many of the advanced-level students are adept at creating power struggles—more out of curiosity or boredom than defiance. And if you teach very bright kids, you have to be prepared to meet students who may know more than you do about some aspects of your subject. Instead of feeling insecure, a good teacher has to encourage those superbright students to shine.

I think the trick to successful teaching, regardless of students' skills, is to spend the time to get to know the students' personalities, abilities, goals, and challenges before you solidify your assignments and exams. Of course, you need to consider your own strengths and weaknesses, as well as your personality. If you have the opportunity to observe teachers in remedial and advanced classes before you choose, you may find that one group appeals more to you than the other.

Q: You faced many challenging and potentially dangerous situations in your classroom. How do you handle fear and develop the resolve to deal with the situation?

—K. C., Pittsfield, Pennsylvania

A: Until I know my students, I do not put myself in a position of being alone in a room with anybody, male or female. But I do not fear my students—unless they are heavily involved with drugs and alcohol; then they can be very dangerous, and I can't really contact the student who is hiding behind the substance.

As for gangsters, I am not their enemy and don't prejudge them, so I don't automatically fear them. I explain to my classes that I may not agree with their choices, their politics, or their behavior, but I do not feel superior to them or believe that my values are better. People have reasons for the choices they make. If I do have real gangsters in my classroom, I make clear that my classroom is my turf and that I expect them to respect that, even if they can't respect me personally. During the course of the year, if I have the opportunity to speak to them privately, I encourage them to reconsider the choices they have made.

Many times students join gangs and then have second thoughts, but they don't withdraw because they can't simply cancel their memberships and walk away. And I have seen the physical and emotional damage that gangs do to students who have tried to leave. If I have a student who indicates a desire to change his or her lifestyle, I refer the student to people who have the resources and training to help.

I make sure that students know why I teach: because I want to help them be successful people and not because I enjoy giving orders. I tell them every day that I love them and am working to help them gain knowledge and skills. I make sure they know exactly what is required to earn a passing grade; I provide plenty of feedback with suggestions for improving failing grades and hold them responsible for their own behavior and choices. Nobody ever believes that I "failed" him or her. My students know they have an opportunity to succeed if they choose to take advantage of the opportunity.

A few times students did threaten me physically—but never with a weapon. In those cases I used humor to defuse the situation. For example, once a very large boy said, "You know I could hurt you."

I said, "Yes, you are younger and stronger than I am, but I am older and meaner than you are and I don't fight fair, so I will probably kick your butt, even though

I'm an old lady. But if you really want to beat up an old lady, there isn't much I can do about it except kiss you on the lips if I get a chance."

The boy frowned, surprised by my response to his threat.

While I had his attention, I said, "Listen, before you beat me up, think about this: I'm probably the only person who really likes you. Go look in the mirror. Look how you dress. Look how you act. And you know I love you anyway." He couldn't help making a face, and I laughed, which broke the tension.

He said, "Aw, I was just kidding."

I said, "Yeah, me, too. Besides, you don't want some old lady to kick your butt, do you?"

This method would not work for everybody, but it worked for me. Teachers must be prepared for challenges, so that they are not caught off guard when challenges occur. One of the primary lessons in self-defense classes is to avoid situations where you could be put into danger but to have a plan in mind just in case.

In most instances when somebody challenged me, many other students were standing by, prepared to help me, if necessary. Nevertheless, I keep some heavy-duty pepper spray in my purse, whether it's authorized or not. Fortunately, I have never needed to use either student bodyguards or pepper spray.

I think it's important to note that I have not ever been threatened outside of school and that I have been to some very dangerous neighborhoods.

I believe that aggressive students are like dogs: the ones who bark usually are not the ones who bite. Usually aggression isn't a problem in my classrooms because I spend a lot of time in the first weeks of class discussing my attitudes toward teaching (I start everybody with an A because I want them to begin with something valuable and feel motivated to keep it, rather than feeling that they begin at zero and have to work upward). I don't try to stare students down or demand that they respect me based on my position alone. I explain my belief that all people deserve to be treated with dignity and respect and that I am there to help them be successful people. I work to earn their respect by first respecting them. Many children, especially those who haven't been successful in school, are suspicious when a teacher treats them with true respect. Forging a bond between teacher and student takes time and consistency; and a student's respect, when it eventually comes, is worth the effort and the wait.

Let me take a moment here to discuss respect. I have heard teachers insist that although they respect their students, the students hate them and refuse to cooperate.

My first question is: Do you believe your own values, choices, lifestyle, and judgment are superior to your students'? Can you understand why a young person would choose to join a gang or engage in criminal activity? If you approach students with the idea of fixing them or helping them to see the error of their ways, they sense your attitude and will reject you because they don't want anyone telling them that they are inferior, stupid, or wrong. If you can try to reserve judgment and learn to know your students and understand why they behave as they do, they will also sense this and respond to you. Yes, occasionally you will encounter a classroom that contains incorrigible ringleaders or such incredible peer pressure that students simply will not respond to you no matter what you do; I have faced those situations myself and know how very difficult it is not to take such treatment personally. I have worked hard to accept that I can't fix everything, that I can't undo years of damage in a few months, and that I can't save all the children.

I don't initiate confrontations with kids as I have seen many teachers do (I have been tempted, believe me, but there is no point). During my first year as a teacher, I occasionally allowed students to sucker me into fighting with them, but I soon learned how to resist. Fighting with students is dangerous and unfair. The teacher can always win, but what the teachers wins is not the respect or cooperation of students. If a student challenges me, I ask if he or she would like to step outside and talk, step outside and cool down, or go talk to a counselor. In the event that a student assaults somebody else or threatens to, I call security and explain that the student needs a chance to go somewhere and cool down. If students cooperate with security, they usually end up with a "light sentence." If they fight with security, I know that the kid has a need to fight authority and not me in particular. If students want to return to my class, I insist on an apology, a handshake, and a word-of-honor promise that they will not interfere with my teaching or another student's learning. I don't hold grudges because kids make mistakes, just like anybody else does; it has been my experience that a handshake, a solemn promise, and a second chance are more effective than any amount of threats or punishment.

Q: Do you teach students according to how they react to things, or do you teach the way you planned to teach when you designed your lessons?

—*P. T., Lexington, North Carolina*

A: If there is rampant resistance to a lesson, I explain (usually for the second time) why I want students to perform specific tasks and what I expect them to learn. I ask for their suggestions for alternate ways to learn the objectives. Sometimes students actually come up with better lessons. Usually they agree to do the work once they understand my reasons for assigning it. I explain which level of thinking skills we are going to use for any exercise. I also distribute critique forms periodically, to let students rate different activities as too easy, too hard, boring, interesting, and so on; and I ask for their suggestions. By allowing feedback and criticism, I am able to teach more effectively and avoid the attitude of teacher versus student that often results from a dictatorial teaching style.

Although teachers are under pressure to cover the curriculum, I think we must resist the pressure to teach what students clearly know already or to ignore obvious gaps in basic skills that they should have acquired earlier in their educations. We need to insist that we be allowed to use our intelligence, training, and intuition. If we back up or jump ahead to coincide with student abilities and skills, we end up much farther ahead at the end of the year. Here is an example of what I am talking about.

When I taught in Belmont, California, the math teacher, a distinguished educator and department chair for many years, volunteered to teach in the at-risk program. After the first semester of the program, Mr. A showed up at a team teacher meeting with his grade book, which was filled with Ds and Fs.

"My normal teaching method obviously isn't working," he said. "I thought if I stuck to my standards, the kids would meet them, but they haven't and clearly aren't going to. So I am desperate enough to try something different."

Our group suggested two major changes to Mr. A's standard procedure. First, he would allow the students to see him as a person and not just as a math teacher. He felt uncomfortable at the thought of emerging from behind his barricade of books and lessons, but he agreed to try a small experiment. He brought in one of his floral watercolor paintings.

"Just prop the painting up against the chalkboard in front of the room and wait," we said. "The kids will do the rest."

"The kids didn't believe that I could paint something so pretty," Mr. A reported at the next meeting. They had inspected the painting carefully and were intrigued by their teacher's unsuspected talent. Once they were convinced that the painting was authentic, they bombarded Mr. A with questions about his painting and comments about his teaching methods and classroom policies.

Then Mr. A took his turn. He questioned the students about their obnoxious attitudes and dismal grades in his class. They admitted that they were not rebelling against his strict standards; they were simply lost, hopelessly lost. They didn't even understand the difference between positive and negative numbers. This revelation reinforced the second modification of Mr. A's teaching approach. He abandoned the geometry text temporarily and backed up to where his students were stuck. He taught them the basic skills they had failed to learn or (more likely) had refused to learn.

When they finally believed that he was truly trying to teach them and not to embarrass them, the at-risk students began to work. By the end of the school year, those at-risk geometry students had surpassed Mr. A's advanced placement geometry class, both in content and grades.

Q: When teaching a class with learning disabled students, how do you modify your curriculum to meet their needs? How would you handle learning disabled students' acceptance in the classroom if other students made fun of them?

—*B. G., San Angelo, Texas*

A: I give students with disabilities the same assignments, but I make time to work with them to help them complete the assignments. I may not grade them as severely if they are unable to process certain information or if they lack certain skills. But I don't assume that they can't do something. I do a number of diagnostics and make sure that I know what my students' limitations are. If I have students who are dyslexic, for example, or who cannot think in the abstract, I make two versions of my tests; those students get the version that doesn't require the skills they don't possess. I may allow severely dyslexic students to present oral reports or answer test questions orally. They don't learn less than the other students, but they demonstrate their knowledge in a different way; and they don't feel overwhelmed or humiliated by being asked to perform tasks that are impossible for them to complete.

As for acceptance from other students, I don't tolerate put-downs in my classroom (or outside of it). I explain this on the very first day of class and frequently throughout the year. I hold my students responsible for their behavior and their treatment of each other. If kids laugh at anybody, disabled or not, I stop the class and explain that I don't think it's funny to hurt people's feelings and that I feel ashamed when students degrade others in order to make themselves feel good. I give examples of different insults (you are so weird, what a dummy, hey fatso, and so on) and ask the kids to share other insults they have heard. We discuss how those insults make us feel and why we say them. Often kids are surprised to realize how hurtful their "jokes" are. Then I suggest that we all spend our energy improving our own performance instead of laughing at somebody else.

I know some teachers are thinking, *She never had a class like my kids. They are mean, and they don't care.* I have encountered groups in which no discussion was possible, in which tormenting others was fashionable and the students weren't interested in discussing the subject. In those cases I again explain my rule about respecting other people and remind them that I will not permit people who break the rule to remain in my classroom. First-time offenders stand outside the door until I have a chance to talk to them. Repeat offenders receive more of my attention and their parents' attention and the counselors' attention, until they either stop tormenting others or decide to request a transfer from my classroom. I believe teachers are the first defense against bullies. Our duty and our obligation is to stop bullying because it is a key contributor to student violence.

I don't publicly humiliate the kids who laugh or tease others, but if they persist, I have a private conversation with them in which I insist that they consider why they feel compelled to belittle others. I explain that when they insult other people, I am going to hand them a little blue card, just a blank card. It will be our secret signal that I want the student to remember that I like him or her and that it isn't acceptable to intentionally embarrass other people. Yes, some hard-core kids resist, but when I give them the choice between changing their behavior or changing to a different class, I have never had a student choose to leave my class, where he or she knows that I treat students fairly. Again it comes back to choice and responsibility. I stress that in every possible way.

I truly believe that we have to model the behavior we want our children to exhibit and that we must honestly discuss feelings and interpersonal relationship skills along with our academic studies. Knowledge alone is not enough to enable success in life. Students need to learn to respect and work with people of varying degrees of ability and to see that there are many forms of intelligence.

Q: I sometimes hear teachers complain about overinvolved parents, but I can't even get parents to give me a phone number. I sent notes home with my students asking for contact information, but only a few parents bothered to respond. Some students have even reported that their parents laughed and threw the notes away. How can I convince these parents to care about their children's education?

—S. B., New London, Connecticut

A: You are not the Lone Ranger. So many teachers face apathetic parents, and it breaks their hearts because they can see how much the children want their parents to care about their success in school. After spending weeks and months tracking down elusive parents, I have come to the conclusion that parents have a handful of common reasons for ignoring teachers' requests for information:

1. They are afraid you are going to accuse them of something. They may have already been informed (sometimes directly, often by insinuation) that their drinking, smoking, drug use, or other behavior has contributed to their child's learning disability.

2. Their own school days were not happy ones. Classmates, teachers, or administrators bullied, humiliated, or mistreated them. They still hate school.

3. They are ashamed of their own lack of education and afraid you will judge them for using poor grammar or spelling.

4. English is not their native language, and they don't feel confident about talking to a teacher.

5. They are poverty-stricken, exhausted, depressed, or suffering from abuse.

6. They really are selfish, apathetic people who shouldn't be parents.

You should be able to get the phone numbers from the guidance office because parents have to provide contact information when they enroll their children. Or ask the attendance office for the numbers they call to report student absences. Sometimes the phone numbers that parents provide turn out to be invalid. If so, I ask the child to give me the name and number of anybody older who might be willing to talk to me: a sister, brother, neighbor, aunt, cousin, grandparent. Then I send a note inviting that person to call or visit my classroom. Some families never do make contact, and in those cases I try to find a coach or counselor or somebody to mentor the child. Sometimes bus drivers will develop a good rapport with kids. One bus driver told me that she always asked to see students' report cards and that some kids said she was the only person who ever looked at them. You might also consider holding a parent meeting in their neighborhood at a community center, library, or church. Many parents feel more comfortable on their own turf. When they realize that your goal is not to blame them but to help their children, many of them will change their attitudes and work with you. Don't give up. Just the fact that you make such an effort to contact parents sends an important message to your students, and they are listening.

Q: Did you really kiss one of your students, like you said in *My Posse Don't Do Homework?* If so, why?

—*M. H., Yukon, Oklahoma*

A: I am surprised at the number of people who seem to find that one kiss the most memorable incident in the entire book. Yes, I did kiss a student. It was completely unplanned, and it was very effective. While wearing bright red lipstick, I kissed a sleeping boy loudly and quickly on the cheek. When he woke up, I told him that the lipstick was indelible and would forever after leave an invisible imprint of my lips on his cheek; another teacher came by the following day and "noticed" the imprint, which intrigued the students. There was nothing romantic about that kiss; all my students understood that, including the sleepy boy. It's the people who weren't present who seem to misinterpret the situation. By the way, I never needed to kiss another student. After that day, if somebody fell asleep, the other students would whisper, loudly, "Kiss him, Miss J!" and they would invariably wake up the sleeper.

I have always believed that it's my responsibility to make my classes so interesting that nobody falls asleep. Occasionally I find a sleeper who works at night or stays up late because of social activities, so I developed a very successful anti-sleeping strategy: I carry a little bottle of White-Out correction fluid with me as I walk around the room. When I encounter a sleeping student, I gently paint one of the student's fingernails and keep on walking. A little while later, I pass by and paint another nail, and so on. Just before the dismissal bell, I write on the board, "Five minutes at lunch for every white fingernail." Kids who have been sleeping can't argue because the evidence is on their own hands. They groan and moan, but they don't argue about accepting the consequences. And very few fall asleep more than once.

Q: When is it that you decide that it's not the students who are having a problem learning but you who is having a problem teaching an idea?

—*P. T., Wellington, New Zealand*

A: If more than 25 percent of my students miss a question on a test, do a poor job on an assignment, or tune out during class discussions, then I know I need to question my presentation. I try to remember that there are more visual and kinesthetic learners than auditory learners in any given group, so I need to use different approaches to any new material. Often I ask students who get it if they can help me figure out a way to help those who don't; this helps everybody, including me, because we all learn new ways to communicate information.

One way I work to avoid communication problems in the first place is by modeling the assignments. I try to complete every assignment I give to my classes with them, if possible. When I do the assignment with them, they like to watch and see how I approach a problem, which is a good way to teach them problem-solving skills. If I do an assignment as homework, I can see whether the work is too hard or easy or too short or long.

Q: Being the kind of "middle" student that you describe, I'd like to know how you evaluate and recognize those types of students in your classroom without losing them "through the cracks" since they are not a part of the two extremes. Is there anything that you would suggest to a future teacher on how not to lose them?

—*D. P., Charlotte, North Carolina*

A: I make copies of my roll sheets and keep them at home so that I can include student names on my worksheets and tests, making sure that I get everybody's name at least once. Kids really respond to seeing their own names in print, even if it is just on a vocabulary quiz. I make a tickler file with student birthdays, and on their special day I give them a "magic pencil" that only earns As. Students who have weekend or summer vacation birthdays get their pencils on Friday afternoon or on the last day of school.

To prevent students from being lost in space, I place my desks in a U-shape pattern so that nobody is more than three kids away from me; and I walk around the room constantly and talk to each student. I pat them on the back or shake their hands if they are doing a good job. I encourage them to keep working and ask for their opinions on the assignments.

I use journals to give extra attention to the kids who are shy or quiet. If I find a book at a library sale that I think they might like, I buy it for them.

I ask my silent students to help me collect papers, distribute tests, and so on. If they don't want to, I don't pressure them. I ask them to deliver messages or get things from the office for me. I may assign one to be the official door-answerer during class.

These things may work for you, or perhaps they will inspire you to develop your own strategies for remembering the middle kids. Just being aware that they tend to be ignored will make you less likely to forget about them. If you have an old school photo of yourself, why not tape it someplace near your desk where you will see it and remember how you felt as a child? When your students notice the photo (and they will), you will have the opportunity to begin conversations that may lead to wonderful places.

Q: I read something you wrote about called Little Susie Uterus, but I can't remember where I read it. Could you please provide a reference for me?

—*D. G., El Paso, Texas*

A: The story of Little Susie Uterus was originally published in *Two Parts Textbook, One Part Love,* which is currently out of print. I have incorporated much of the material from that book into this new, improved book. But I had forgotten to include that story, and I thank you for reminding me! The story was inspired by a student who wrote several questions about sex in her journal. Although Darcy had taken sex education classes, she didn't understand her own body, and this story was my response to why people sometimes called their periods "the curse." Here is my response to Darcy's question:

> Menstrual periods are not a horrible, nasty curse. They are the most natural thing in the world, but most of us are embarrassed to talk about them. Men are embarrassed because they don't understand periods, but neither do most women. It's really very simple. Here's how it goes.
>
> Little Susie Uterus has a nice, cozy little apartment inside you. Just down the street from Susie's place, you have hundreds of tiny eggs in storage. Your body doesn't make a new egg every month, as some people believe. Your eggs are already there; that's why you have to wear a lead apron if you have an X-ray at the dentist's office, so that your precious little eggs won't be exposed to X-rays that could harm them.
>
> Every twenty-eight days (or whatever your cycle is), one of your little eggs—let's call her Ms. Egg—comes to visit Susie Uterus. Ms. Egg is lonely. She wants to make a baby. That's her sole purpose in life, but

she doesn't have much time. She only has a few hours, a day or two at the most, to find Mr. Right and make a baby. Susie is a good friend. She is so excited about Ms. Egg and her potential baby that she redecorates her whole apartment: puts up new wallpaper, everything. Then Susie and Ms. Egg sit and wait. Mr. Right isn't the most punctual or polite guy in the world. He's a sperm. He's little and wiggly and pushy and in a terrible hurry. If he shows up on time, Ms. Egg grabs him, hugs him, and they make a baby.

Usually Mr. Right doesn't show up. Ms. Egg gets very upset and leaves in a huff. Susie is disappointed too after all that work. She rips down the wallpaper and tosses it out; that's the tissue that lines the walls of your uterus in case you make a baby. The tissue is your period—old wallpaper, no big deal.

While we're on the subject of little eggs, I'd like to point out that they are your potential future children. Take care of them. Nurture them carefully. Don't eat too much junk food that's loaded with chemicals or artificial sweeteners; and don't drink alcohol, smoke, or take recreational drugs. Those little eggs eat everything you eat, drink everything you drink, smoke everything you smoke, and take every drug you take. If you drink beer, you are giving your little eggs beer. Your body is still developing, and the stronger you make your body, the stronger your eggs will be. Take care of them so that your future children will have the best possible chance to be strong and healthy.

That's the story. And when I gave Darcy her journal with the story in it, she shared it with several friends. Many of them expressed concern that they might already have damaged their eggs by drinking, smoking, and taking drugs. I told them that the body has miraculous recuperative powers and that if they took care of themselves, their chances of having healthy eggs would improve with each day. On Friday afternoons I used to wave good-bye to the girls and say, "Have fun this weekend, but take care of them there eggs." They would blush and giggle, but that one incident turned out to be the most effective antidrug tool I ever used. For the next three years, those girls reported that when their friends tempted them with alcohol and cigarettes, they refused because they didn't want to risk damaging their eggs. And Darcy even wrote me a letter five years after her high school graduation to tell me that she was "still taking care of those little eggs."

Q: I am taking over another teacher's class midterm. Should I expect major behavior problems, or is there a way to avoid that?

—*J. N., Murphys, California*

A: If you take a proactive approach, you may be able to avoid any serious behavior problems. First, I'd ask the students to fill out an evaluation form or write a brief description of their class to date. Ask them to name the best and worst thing they did during the past semester, quarter, or month. Ask what they feel confident about in this subject, what they are struggling with, anything special they would like you to know that will help you teach them. Tell them you'd appreciate their suggestions for activities or special assignments they would like to tackle.

Sometimes students refuse to accept a new teacher because they aren't finished with their previous teacher. Children who don't feel secure in their own lives may resist any change at school, including you. They may refuse to fill out the evaluations or refuse to respond when you call on them. Don't take it personally if this happens. Instead, find out whether the students are rebelling because they loved their previous teacher or because that teacher misused his or her authority by mistreating students, making them feel hopeless, or punishing them with failing grades and impossibly difficult assignments.

If the students clearly loved their previous teacher, you might suggest that they write notes or letters that you can send to the teacher. You might make this an optional assignment, with two or three choices for those students who don't want to write notes. On the other hand, if the students clearly disliked the previous teacher, don't initiate a discussion about that teacher. If students insist on talking about the teacher, then you may choose to let them vent their frustrations by asking them to brainstorm things that the previous teacher did well and areas in which he or she needed improvement. Encourage them to stick to professional issues and not get involved in a personal attack on the teacher. If you get the impression that the previous teacher treated some or all of the students unfairly, I would recommend letting them blow off some steam and then saying, "Fine. Thank you for sharing your feelings. Let's leave the past behind us now and move forward. I'll do my best to be a good teacher, and I expect you to do your best to be good students." Then keep your word. Drop the subject and move on to the next activity.

Ask your principal or department chair for a copy of the previous teacher's lesson plans, curriculum outline, and grade book. You may not get everything, but anything you get will help you assess your students' abilities.

If possible, make a list of students whom the teacher frequently sent to detention or referred to the office; meet with those students privately and tell them you would like to help them solve the problem that has been stopping them from being successful. I would predict that about 50 percent will accept your offer, which will reduce your discipline problems. The other 50 percent will be put on guard, and so will you; you won't expect them to respond to a gentle overture, and they won't expect you to believe that the previous teacher was the cause of the problems.

Review any samples of student assignments and tests so that you won't give them work they have already completed or waste their time teaching skills they have already mastered. Likewise, you won't expect them to do things they are unable to do at present.

Ask the teachers across the hall and the ones whose rooms are next door to yours for advice and suggestions. (Beware the curmudgeons and pessimists; if you do meet them, nod politely and ignore their comments.) Neighboring teachers may be aware of specific discipline problems the previous teacher faced, and they may be willing to offer reciprocal chill-out privileges, so that you can send a disruptive student to each other's classrooms for a short visit occasionally.

If you do nothing else, I would suggest calling all your students' parents during the first two weeks on the job; introduce yourself and offer to answer any questions they may have about your class. This will give you a good idea of which students receive support and encouragement from home and which students are dealing with difficult family situations. Plus, it will send a message to the students that you will be working with their parents to help them succeed in your class.

Q: What became of your students from *My Posse Don't Do Homework,* particularly Raul, Emilio, Gusmaro, and Callie?

—*F. S., Los Angeles, California*

A: I stayed in touch with many of my Academy students for about five years after I left California; then gradually they became involved with their careers and families. Occasionally I receive a card or phone call from them; but I have moved four times since leaving California, and I lose touch with a few more people each time. They are still in my heart, though, and if I close my eyes, I can see every single one of their faces clearly.

In response to your question about specific students, Raul and Gusmaro both began working full-time at the Stanford Linear Accelerator Center in Palo Alto shortly after high school graduation. Raul worked in the warehouse doing data entry, and Gusmaro started as a receptionist but was soon promoted to quality control supervisor.

A few years ago, Gusmaro called me one evening to ask my opinion of his moving his small family to Sunnyvale; he had married his high school sweetheart, and they had a baby girl. Gusmaro told me that his "homeys" accused him of being disloyal for thinking of moving away from East Palo Alto. I asked Gusmaro what his parents thought of the idea of his moving, and he said they supported whatever decision he made. Then I asked him if he wanted his children to grow up in the neighborhood where he grew up.

"This ain't no place to raise kids," he said. He decided to buy the house in Sunnyvale, and a couple of years later, he drove to one of my book signings in his new SUV. He was stopped by the local police while en route to the signing because, in his words, "They didn't think a Mexican kid like me could afford a nice vehicle like that. But I didn't trip. I just showed them my license and my registration and smiled at them because I bet they drive some old beat-up crappy little cars."

Recently Gusmaro accepted an offer to work with a start-up software development company.

Raul enrolled in college but had a hard time attending regularly. If somebody suggested going out to eat or to the gym or to a party, Raul would go. He also found it very difficult to go to work five days in a row. Prior to entering the Academy program as a seventeen-year-old high school sophomore, he had rarely attended school more than three days a week. But Raul never did fit the paradigm. He is a unique character. He is one of the most delightful, lovable, witty rascals I have ever met. He may never be CEO of a corporation, but he won't die from a heart attack caused by stress. He is now working with his family on a ranch near Sacramento. I am convinced that Raul will die a very old man with a host of adventures to savor and a huge grin on his face.

I am especially pleased to report that Emilio didn't really die, as he did in the movie version of my book. Immediately after high school graduation, he was working as a baggage handler at the San Francisco airport, still struggling with the question of establishing his own code of ethics. He came to my classroom the year after he graduated to discuss a problem at work. The baggage handlers were assigned to teams, and apparently some of the teams had been rifling people's luggage and stealing valuables.

"If they can't find anything valuable to steal, sometimes they get mad and trash people's stuff," Emilio told me. "That's not right, is it?"

I agreed that it wasn't right, but Emilio was worried that if he didn't go along with the group, the others would ostracize or physically assault him. He said that a major inspection was imminent because of reports of vandalism and theft among the handlers. I suggested that he approach his supervisor and ask to be moved to a different team for personal reasons.

"Tell him that you don't share all of the attitudes of the people on your team," I suggested. "If the man is aware of what is happening, he will understand why you want to move. Then just keep your mouth shut and see what happens."

A few weeks later, Emilio called me. He had moved to a new team, he said, but he had a problem with his new supervisor, who, in Emilio's words, "kept looking shit" at him.

"Never, ever hit your supervisor," I advised. Because he was a big man with a quick temper, Emilio had always struggled—with not very good results—to avoid physical confrontations. He agreed, however, not to hit his supervisor at work.

A few days later, Emilio called me to report that he was in jail for a few days for assaulting his boss, but not to worry, that he would be out soon and working at a new job that he already had lined up.

"But I thought you weren't going to hit your supervisor," I reminded Emilio.

"You told me never to hit anybody at work," he said. "So when this guy kept talking shit to me, I asked him when he got off work. He said midnight. I said, 'Fine, I'll meet you in the parking lot at five after midnight.' Then I hit him. Ha-ha."

Because he was able to laugh at his predicament, I knew there was some hope that he would be able to gain control of his temper as he grew older. When I first met Emilio, he had lost his sense of humor. It had been overwhelmed by his anger and frustration at a world that left him an orphan at a young age and a target for bullies who used him as a benchmark to demonstrate their own courage as he grew bigger and stronger. During our first discussion about fighting, Emilio had told me he enjoyed smashing people's faces because it meant he had won the battle. When I suggested that perhaps he hadn't won at all if somebody he didn't even know had provoked him into fighting, Emilio's face had darkened into a stormy scowl. By the time he graduated from high school (he graduated from a jail cell because of a fight with a male teacher that the teacher had precipitated), Emilio's innate intelligence and resilience had enabled him to step outside of himself and take a look at the larger picture.

Several years ago we had another discussion about fighting. I told Emilio that if he really wanted to fight and really believed he was tough, he should consider joining the marines. I told him he would find a lot of other men who enjoyed "recreational head bashing" and that he might enjoy being part of an elite fighting force. Emilio did join the marines, and he did quite well after a few run-ins with his drill sergeant.

"I had to explain to him that when you mess with one bean, you mess with the whole pot," Emilio told me with a wicked grin. After four years of active duty, he left the military to get married and start a family. At last report he told me he had two beautiful daughters and a wife who is strong enough to keep him in line.

I'm sorry to say that we all lost touch with Callie. It wouldn't surprise me to learn that Callie was president of a company or working on a doctoral thesis. She did finish community college while working full-time and raising two children. The last time I saw her, she was moving to another town but promised me that as soon as she was settled, she planned to return to college. Callie does not make promises lightly, so I would be very surprised to learn that she didn't follow through.

In mid-2004 I had the good fortune to be invited to give a speech at a conference in California. On short notice I contacted one of my students, Maria del Carmen, who rounded up a dozen Academy students for a small reunion. You will be pleased to hear that they have done very well, far better than anybody (except me, of course) expected. Among the dozen were two software developers, a school secretary, a school nurse, a real estate broker, an investment counselor, an electronics engineer, a nurse's aide, a supervisor at UPS, a video game designer, and two mortgage loan officers.

All of the Academy students had remarkable resilience, talents, and skills. It was my privilege to be given the opportunity and the freedom to uncover and nurture those talents.

Yo! Miss J!

Hundreds of students of all ages have written me letters to ask for advice about parents, siblings, school, and friends. I have changed all of the names in this chapter to protect the writers' privacy, but the letters themselves are real. I hope that teachers will use these letters as a springboard for class discussions about topics of great concern to students, such as bullying. They may also be useful as prompts for journal writing or essays. And most of all, I hope that students who read these letters will realize that they are not alone; everybody has problems, and sometimes it helps just knowing that other people face the same difficulties. I have divided the letters into seven sections: This and That; Friends Till the End?; Brothers and Sisters—Arrgh!; Those Pesky Parents!; Staying Cool in School; The Bully Situation; and A Letter from Me to You.

THIS AND THAT

Q: My grandmother died last year but I can't get over it. I feel so sad and I miss her every day. I just feel like crying. How can I stop feeling so bad?

—Chris, age ten

A: I am so sorry to hear about your grandmother. I know exactly how it feels because I lost both of my grandmothers and then my mother. It hurts so much, and I miss them. But after some time goes by, I don't cry so much and I try to remember things about them. I think of things they did and things they said. I look at their pictures and remember that their human bodies might be gone, but their love is still in my heart and will always be there.

Ask your teacher if he or she could help you find some books about grief. I think Judy Blume wrote some books about kids who had to learn how to handle their feelings when somebody dies. One of those books might be just the one for you. Another thing that might help is if you could write your feelings down in a journal. Write down everything about your grandmother. Paste a picture of her in there if you have one. If you don't, see if somebody has one you could keep. Or put the photo in a frame in your room where you can say "Hi" every day. I have my mother's picture on my desk, and I blow her kisses.

Go ahead and cry and feel bad. It's natural. Someday you will notice that you miss your grandmother but that it doesn't hurt so much. Then you begin to heal. That may take a long time. Nobody can tell you how you should feel, but if you still feel just as sad after six more months, tell your parents and your school counselor. Maybe they will be able to find you somebody to talk to who can help you deal with your grief.

In the meantime I will be thinking of you.

Q: Every time I get a girlfriend she lies to me and then we break up. How can I find a girlfriend who doesn't tell lies?

—Josh, age fifteen

A: Oh, I wish I could help you, but I fell in love with a boy who told lies and I married him. Now I am divorced, so I don't think I am the best person to give advice about love. But I can tell you that everybody gets a broken heart at some time or another. Look at how many songs people write about their broken hearts. You can't escape getting hurt if you are going to love people. But each time you get hurt, you can learn something about yourself and about other people. For example, maybe you will learn some clues that show a person isn't telling the truth. Do an Internet search or go to the library and look up "body language." It's a very interesting topic, and you will learn a lot about people's behavior.

Unfortunately, a lot of people like to play games or tell lies. Sometimes people lie because they want to make a good impression. Or they think if they tell the truth you will get mad at them. But sometimes they are just plain liars.

Don't let other people change your behavior. If other people want to lie, you don't have to do the same. Keep on being an honorable person. Eventually you will find friends, including a girlfriend, who are also honest people. When you find somebody who shares your values, you will have a better chance of being happy. Good luck!

Q: I have a question, but I can't ask my mom or any of my teachers because they always jump to conclusions. Three girls in my school are pregnant, and they all say they just did it once. I want to know why so many girls get pregnant when they only had sex one time.

—Shelley, age sixteen

A: There is a reason: the one time girls can't resist having sex is the very time that their bodies are ready to make a baby. It's biology, not lack of character, that makes girls want to have sex. Your body doesn't know any better. When you start having periods, your body is capable of making a baby; and at certain times of the month, that's exactly what it wants to do. And it doesn't take long to make a baby because those teeny little sperms are faster than lightning.

Your menstrual cycle is supposed to have twenty-eight days, but we all know that isn't usually the case because a lot of factors (sugar, trans fats, caffeine, exercise, medications) affect the hormones that control our periods. Some of us have a period every thirty-two days or every forty-five days or maybe even every twenty-six days. Sometimes we go thirty-one days in one cycle and fifty-three the next. We might have two periods in one month or skip a month altogether. The only thing you can be sure of is that you will ovulate fourteen days before your period starts. When you ovulate, you are fertile. That means you can make a baby. If your periods are irregular, then you won't know exactly which day you ovulate, but you can bet that your hormones know. Hormones are chemicals that tell your body to develop breasts and have periods, and they are strong little chemicals. On the day you ovulate, your hormones take over your brain and say, "Shut up. I'm tired of listening to you. You spoil all my fun." And even if you know in your mind and your heart that you don't want to have sex, your hormones may talk your body into it. Your hormones are the best talkers in the world. "Ooh, baby," they whisper, "just this one time, please, please, please, pretty please." And because hormones do their best talking on the day you ovulate, the day you can't resist is the very day you are most likely to get pregnant.

Sex isn't a bad thing, but too many girls confuse sex with love. They are two very different things. Usually during puberty, boys want to have sex and girls want love. If you think somebody will love you because you have sex with him, ask yourself this: Would you love somebody just because he was willing to have sex with you? A lot of people in this world would have sex with you and never talk to you again. They couldn't possibly love you because they don't even know you.

I recommend that teens wait until they are older to have sex—not because you can't love people but because you are still changing and becoming the person you will be. Remember the games you liked to play five years ago? And the music you loved? Chances are that you have different favorites today. That's natural. And you will continue to change frequently while you are growing up. Give yourself time to develop your talents and skills before you become sexually active. And make sure that you are in a position to support yourself and a baby before you even think about having sex, because no birth control is 100 percent effective.

My advice is to take care of your body by eating nutritious foods and getting exercise so that your hormones will be able to regulate your periods better. (If you have really bad cramps or PMS, read up on evening primrose oil, herbs such as dong quai, and vitamins specifically designed for women.) And don't put yourself in a position in which your hormones can convince you to have sex. Don't go to parties that have no adult supervision. Don't make out in the backseat of a car or behind the bleachers at a football game. Stay where there are lights and lots of other people so that your hormones don't hijack your brain.

Q: I don't know how to figure out what I want to be. Everybody keeps asking me. I think I will be a failure or something because I just don't know.

—Cesar, age fifteen

A: Do you know that there are people who are thirty-five, forty, fifty, or even older who still don't know what they want to do with their lives? They keep searching for something they enjoy so much that it will make them want to jump out of bed in the morning.

One of the best ways to figure out what you want to do is to get a piece of paper and make some lists about yourself. What do you enjoy doing the most? What do you hate to do? Do you like to be around other people, or do you prefer to be alone and private most of the time? Do you enjoy working on things that require a lot of details, such as building and painting a model airplane, or do little details drive you crazy? Would you like to spend your time working in a building, or do you need to be outside, even if it's rainy or cold or hot? Do you like to work with your hands or your brain—or both?

Another good way to assess your talents is to ask other people you trust to describe your talents as they see them. I never thought of becoming a writer until one of my teachers suggested it. She knew I loved to read books and write stories. After her suggestion I started writing more, and I really enjoyed it; today I am a writer, thanks to Mrs. Hodak, my fifth-grade teacher. Maybe your own teachers, relatives, and friends will see something in you that you don't notice—such as artistic talent, musical ability, or special qualities that you take for granted.

Once you have a really good picture of yourself, you can start researching different careers. You would be surprised at all the things there are to do in this world. Many people today are using computers to start their own businesses. I recently met a woman who earns a good living as a pet sitter. She goes to people's homes when they are on vacation and feeds their dogs and cats. Each person pays her $25 to $50 a day, so she can earn as much money as she needs by accepting more customers. A man I know goes to people's houses and cuts down their dead trees and cleans up their yards. This can be dangerous work, so he is highly paid.

Speaking of money, that is something to consider. Some people have to have a lot of money to be happy. Other people would rather have more freedom or privacy than money. Or they value things that money can't buy. You need to think about how much money you need to earn in order to live the kind of life you want. If you want to earn a lot of money, you will need to go to college or else start a very lucrative business of your own. But overall, the more education you have, the more money you will earn in your lifetime. A high school dropout earns about half of what a high school graduate earns during his or her lifetime. And if you go to college, you will earn hundreds of thousands of dollars more over your life-time than somebody who doesn't finish high school.

Your school guidance counselors should have lots of information. You can also ask your school librarian and the librarian at your public library. They have refer-ence books specifically written to help people figure out what they want to do. One book is called *What Color Is Your Parachute?* Another is called *Great Careers for People Who Like to Work with Their Hands.* I'm sure your library will have some-thing interesting.

Think about what you enjoy in life. Then see if you can think of a way to earn a living doing the things you enjoy. If you really want to do something that is rea-sonable, then you can do it. I know I can't jump off a building and fly. But if the thing you want to do is possible, then go ahead and follow your dreams.

Q: I would like to be an author when I grow up. Is it fun writing books? How old were you when you started writing? I'm eleven. Is that too young?

—Rachael, age eleven

A: I really enjoy being an author. When I was ten, I decided that I loved books so much that I wanted to write them when I grew up. And so I did. I read all kinds of books so that I could learn how other people write. I still do. Reading is the best training to be a writer. The more you learn about the world, the better your sto-ries will be.

Being an author is hard work, and you have to work alone most of the time. But the good thing is that I get to work at home, and I can wear my pajamas to work if I want to! And I don't have a boss to look over my shoulder and make me nervous.

Sometimes I wish I worked in a building with other people so that I would have somebody to talk to. But I have a dog who keeps me company. His name is Bog-art, and he is really smart. He laughs at all my jokes. Ha-ha!

Q: Why do kids say such mean things? They make fun of me and it makes me feel really bad.

—Ryan, age eight

A: Sometimes kids say mean things and make fun of people because they don't know any better. They don't realize that they can really hurt people's feelings. Instead of telling on them or getting mad at them, just pretend you didn't hear them if they say mean things to you. Don't let them make you fight or feel bad. If you don't say anything, they will usually go away and leave you alone.

If somebody is really mean to you on purpose and keeps picking on you, then you need to tell your parents or your teacher or your principal. Don't be a tattle-tale all the time, though. Don't tell if somebody says just one mean thing. But do tell if somebody keeps on being mean and won't leave you alone even if you ignore him or her.

Keep on being your nice self. Don't let other people change you. Be friends with nice kids. If mean kids tease you, just say to yourself, *Those mean kids aren't important. They are like little bugs flying around in the air making a lot of noise. Who needs them?* Then, when they say mean things, you can just smile at them and pretend they are bugs. They won't know what you are thinking. It will be your secret. Good luck.

Q: Is it okay to eat waffles on a Tuesday? I just have to know.
—*Big Mama, age ten*

A: Hey Big Mama, are you kidding? Of course, you can't eat waffles on a Tuesday. Waffles is a "w" word. You eat them on weekends and Wednesdays. On Tuesdays you eat toenails and toads. You sure are silly for a big mama!

FRIENDS TILL THE END?

Q: My best friend is getting too nutty. She is just obsessed with one of Harry Potter's friends—and he isn't even a real boy, he's just in a book. She talks about him all the time like he is a real boy. How can I make her stop acting so goofy?
—*Leah, age eleven*

A: It is really normal for girls (or boys or men or women) to get obsessed over somebody—singers, movie stars, even Harry Potter's friend. It won't last forever. But for right now, it's fun for her. Just think about it. If you choose somebody you will never meet to obsess about, then you won't be disappointed because you won't see them in person and see their faults. That's why people love movie stars and celebrities. We don't see their old worn-out underwear or smell their bad morning breath. We see them when they are wonderful and beautiful and exciting.

Instead of trying to get her mind off him, why not ask her why she likes him so much? Let her talk about him all she wants. Then someday when you are in love or obsessed about something, you can talk her ears off. That's what friends are for!

Q: My friends are driving me crazy. They say mean things about each other. I like all my friends. I don't want to stop being friends with anybody.

—*Rosa, age eleven*

A: You are more mature than your friends, and they don't understand that it's possible to share friendship with a lot of people without running out of friendship. Explain to your friends that friendship is not like a bag of cookies. You don't use up your friendship by sharing it; you get more friendship back!

When one of your friends complains about your other friend, try saying something like this: "I know you don't like so-and-so, but I do. I think she [or he] is funny [or smart or kind or interesting]. And I like you because you are . . . [fill in the blank with something good]. My being friends with other people doesn't mean I don't like you as much. I like you very much."

If they don't get it, try this: "Do you think that Santa Claus doesn't like you because he gives gifts to all the other children? Nope, he likes everybody. I don't like everybody, but I do like a lot of people. I'm friendly, and I care about people. Please try to understand that."

If one of your friends decides not to be friends with you if you won't be an only best friend, then try to understand your friend's insecurity. Say, "I'm sorry you feel that way. I still like you, and if you want to be friends later, just let me know. In the meantime I wish you good luck." And then go on with your life and don't talk about your former friends behind their backs. Show them that you really are mature and try to show them a better way to act.

Q: I used to be friends with some girls and now I don't know if they are my friends. Sometimes they act real friendly and then the next day they try to make me fight them. I don't want to fight. I just want my friends back.

—*Alyssa, age fourteen*

A: Friends can come and go, but true friends don't hurt you on purpose. They may not be perfect and they may hurt your feelings accidentally, but they never try to make you get into a physical fight with them. If your friends don't want to be friends with you, then find new friends. It may take a while, but eventually you will find other friends.

I'm glad you won't fight. It's silly and childish to fight in school. When those girls try to fight, just remind yourself that they are like two-year-olds who cry and have tantrums when things don't go their way. Tell them, "I don't want to fight you. I'm sorry you don't want to be friends with me. If you want to be friends later, let me know." Then walk away. Don't talk about them behind their backs or gang up on them with other people. Don't play their childish games. Try to concentrate on your schoolwork, your hobbies, and yourself. Find things you enjoy and focus on those activities so that you won't care so much what some silly kids do.

Also, remember that when you are grown up, you will have the whole world to choose your friends from—not just one school. I have friends all over the world, from age five to age eighty-six. When I was going to school, I didn't want to go along with the crowd, so I only had a few friends. I learned to be a writer, and I taught myself to play the guitar. I was too busy to think about those kids who didn't like me. Then when I grew up, I met a lot of people who liked me just the way I am. You will too. Good luck!

Q: I told my friend I would be in the talent show with her at school but now I don't want to. I want to be in the show with a different friend. This friend says I should just tell my other friend I changed my mind. My mother says I have to decide for myself but I don't know what to do.

—Kaycee, age fifteen

A: Sometimes we have to choose whether to do something with one friend or another, and we don't want to hurt anybody's feelings. But sometimes that just isn't possible. No matter what we do, somebody's feelings get hurt. The best thing you can do is be honest. If you told one friend you would be in the talent show with him or her, then keep your word. Tell your other friend that you are sorry but you promised someone else first. Tell this second friend that if you had promised him or her first, you would keep your word too.

If your second friend gets mad at you because you are keeping your promise, then your second friend will just have to get mad and get over it. If somebody stops being friends with you because you keep your promises, then you don't need that friend.

I think the very best rule for friends is to treat them just the way you would want them to treat you. If you think about the situation and imagine that you were the first friend, then you will know what is the best thing to do. Stick to your principles. Tell the truth. Don't let other people talk you into being unkind or unfair. You are a nice person, or you wouldn't even be worried about this situation. Keep on being nice!

Q: How can I make friends at my new school? I never know what to say and the kids here don't seem very friendly.

—Kyle, age ten

A: Making new friends can be very hard even when you are an adult. I have trouble myself when I am in a new situation. I don't know what to say to people if I don't know them. But I try to think of things to talk about. I ask people questions about themselves to get them talking. I ask them if they have any pets. I ask them if they like sports or movies or music. If I see somebody standing or sitting alone, I go over and say, "Are you trying to get a little quiet time, or would you like some company?" If a sports game is going on, I watch it for a while and then ask somebody else who is sitting near me, "Which team are you rooting for?"

You might ask your teacher to suggest somebody who might like to be friends with you. There are probably other kids in your class who don't have friends, and your teacher might know about it. If not, just keep your eyes open and see who is alone during recess or lunch. Say something nice to that person. Offer them a cookie from your lunch. Be friendly and kind, and people will like you.

If you try to be friends with somebody and they don't want to be friends, don't feel bad. Maybe they already have too many friends. Just say, "OK" and go on by yourself.

Don't spend all your time worrying about having friends. Find some hobbies or interests. Read about trains or cars, for example. Or learn about the work that astronauts or race car drivers do. Learn to build a model car or do jigsaw puzzles. Go to the library and get interesting books. Keep busy and eventually you will find other people who share your interests. Good luck.

P.S. You can count me as your friend. I know it would be long distance, but some of my best friends are long-distance friends.

Q: I have a lot of friends but none of them like each other. They all want to be my best friend. But they don't want me to have any other friends. What can I do?

—Anna, age twelve

A: Maybe it will make you feel better to know that you have a problem that a lot of people have: best friends who are jealous of each other. I have been in this situation myself. It is frustrating and can cause big problems. Here's what I suggest.

Tell each of your friends why you like him or her. Explain that you also have other friends, that each friend is different, but that you like them all in different ways for different reasons. Love or friendship aren't things that you can measure or compare. Each person is different, and each friendship is different. The most important thing to tell your friends is this: remember that love and friendship are not things that have a limit. You don't run out of love just because you love somebody. If you are friends with one person, it doesn't mean you don't have friendship left to offer another person.

If you have a best friend and really do like that person better than your other friends, don't let it become a contest. Explain to your best friend that she is very special and that you value her friendship so much. Don't gossip about your other friends to her, and don't gossip about her to them. Just enjoy them when you are with them. If your best friend gets jealous and angry, remind her that she is your special friend. If she refuses to be friends with you because you have other friends, tell her that she has the right to do what she wants to. Don't fight with her. Just tell her that you still like her and that you respect her decision. Tell her that if she changes her mind later and wants to be friends, you won't be angry or "pay her back." Then keep your word to her and to your other friends. When your best friend realizes that you won't let her manipulate you, she may settle down. Also, she really needs to be reassured that you like her. Tell her you do. Tell her why.

It's hard being more mature than other kids in your class. But you can set the example instead of letting them control your behavior. Good luck!

Q: I used to be really good friends with this other kid but lately it seems like every time we see each other, we start fighting. I don't know what to do.

—Sam, age fourteen

A: Several people wrote about the same problem as you did. Keeping good friendships going can be tricky. First, let's think about why we become friends with people—because we share a common goal or interest. Maybe we are in the same class at school and we both want to pass or be popular or have somebody to talk to. Maybe we like the same music or books or movies or dances. Or maybe we just live in the same neighborhood.

Sometimes friendships last a long time, but sometimes they don't. If you have a long-term friendship, then you are going to have arguments. People can't help doing or saying things that make each other angry or hurt. That is life. The important thing is how you handle the hurt and anger. When a friend becomes angry or upset, think about what this friend says to you. Try to look honestly at what you said or did. If you did or said something you regret, then say you are sorry and ask your friend to forgive you. If you don't regret your behavior, then don't apologize. Try to explain why you did what you did or said what you said. Then tell your friend, "We can disagree and still be friends. Let's discuss this so that we both understand each other's feelings and then we can let go and move on." (If a friend makes you angry or hurts your feelings, do the same thing: be honest.)

If you have a friend who lies to you or who does things that you think are wrong, you need to tell your friend that you are upset. Don't criticize your friend. Just state your feelings. Say, "I feel hurt when you lie to me. It makes me not trust you." Or if your friend shoplifts, for instance, you could say, "I don't feel right about some of the things you do. You have a right to choose your behavior, but I can't be friends with you if you want to steal. Let's just go our separate ways." If your friend changes his or her behavior, fine. If not, then you need to find new friends, because friendship is based on trust and respect.

It would help a lot, I think, if you could talk to one of your parents, an older relative, a neighbor, a teacher, or somebody who will reassure you that you are doing the right thing. Good luck!

Q: My best friend doesn't like me anymore. We used to do everything together but this year she doesn't even want to talk to me. I miss her.

—Danielle, age twelve

A: It hurts when somebody doesn't want to be your friend anymore. But here is something to think about. We can outgrow friendships just like we outgrow our shoes. We like different books and movies and music as we grow up, and sometimes we become different people. When you outgrow a friendship, it can hurt you and your friend. But sometimes growing up hurts. There's no way to avoid pain. It's part of life.

If you think you have outgrown a friendship, then tell your friend, "I think we need to take a little break from being friends and see whether we still have as much in common as we used to." It is very painful to end a friendship, and it's tempting to get drawn into an argument if your friend becomes angry when you try to end it. But try to remain calm and be honest. Just say, "I'm sorry you feel that way, but I have to tell you the truth because I respect you."

If a friend outgrows *you* and wants to move on, then you have to accept that. You can't make somebody like you. If you try to make somebody like you, they will probably not like you because being around you will make them feel bad. The best thing you can do is just back off and hope that they will miss you. Say, "Well, I still like you, and if you want to be friends again later, let me know. I won't be mad or try to pay you back."

Then go on with your life. Make new friends. Find new interests. Be your own best friend, and then you will always have one friend you can always respect—yourself. That may sound silly, but it is true. I had to learn to be my own best friend, and now I really like me. I have fun doing things with me!

Don't talk about your friend behind her back. Just be honest. If somebody says something to you, just say, "I like Sammie, but I don't want to talk about her. It's not polite." Then change the subject. Some people like to gossip, but they don't like people to gossip about them. Strange, isn't it? I don't like to gossip because it doesn't make me feel good about myself.

Here's something interesting: when you are happy, you attract friends. So try to find hobbies and activities that interest you. Enjoy yourself. Then you won't feel lonely, and you will be more likely to attract new friends. It may take some time, but friendship is like a little flower. You plant the seed, and then you have to keep watering it and take care of it before it will grow and blossom. Good luck!

BROTHERS AND SISTERS—ARRGH!

Q: My sister is driving me crazy. She follows me around just to bug me. She imitates everything I do. She makes me so mad that I just pound on the wall and then I get grounded and it's her fault.

—*Patrick, age twelve*

A: I know how you feel. My brother used to drive me crazy, and I would scream and holler. Pounding the wall is a good release for stress, but you could hurt yourself or the wall (or make your parents mad). So why not try this? Write down exactly what you'd like to say and do to your sister on a piece of paper. Say whatever you want. Then rip up the paper into tiny shreds and throw it away. You will throw away your anger along with it. And remember: when you are eighteen, you won't have to live with anybody you don't like. Until then try to find some ways to relieve your tension. Walk, run, ride a bike, get an exercise or yoga video from the library and try it (yoga really helps me calm down).

You didn't say whether your sister was older or younger. But she might do things just to upset you because she enjoys being able to push your buttons. If you can manage to ignore her, she will probably stop, because she does those things for attention. Try saying something like, "No matter how obnoxious you act, I still love you, sister dear." Smile. Blow her a kiss. If she is trying to make you mad, that will drive her crazy!

Q: My brother treats me so bad. How can I make him be nice?

—*Austin, age ten*

A: Lots of kids have problems with brothers and sisters. My older sister used to be really mean to me. There really isn't any way you can make other people be nice. The only person you can control is you. You can't *make* your brother do—or stop doing—anything. But you can change your own behavior and attitude. If your brother teases you, you don't have to get mad. You can pretend you don't notice him. It's very hard, but if you practice, you can do it. If he says means things to you, instead of saying mean things back or crying, you can just say, "That was a mean thing to say." Don't say anything else. Don't threaten to tell on him. Don't scream or hit him.

Brothers and sisters fight for lots of reasons. Sometimes they are angry. Or they feel like nobody loves them. Or they are getting bad grades. Or they just feel mean. So they pick on somebody else to make themselves feel better. Sometimes they try to make you do their chores. If that's the case, you could always just do the chores and get it over with. Just pretend you enjoy doing them. Say, "I don't mind working." Of course, you can't do all of the chores in the house, but one or two chores isn't that much. And if the person is just trying to make you do chores so that you will get mad, you will take the fun out of it for them.

The very best way to make somebody stop picking on you is not to respond to them. Pretend you don't hear them or see them. Pretend you don't really care what they say or do. Pretend you have something better to do. Read a book, go for a walk, pet your dog, or help your parents with some chores. Just ignore the person, and eventually they will stop. It may take a long time, but they will stop if you can ignore them long enough. Good luck!

P.S. If somebody hits you hard enough to hurt, that's different. You need to find an adult and explain the situation. Don't holler, "Billy hit me!" Explain what is going on. Ask the adult to give you some advice to help you out so that the person won't hit you. If that adult can't help you, find another adult. Keep asking until somebody helps.

Q: My older sister is so mean to me and she picks on me all the time. She tries to drive me crazy and I think I am going crazy. Can you help?

—*Ling, age nine*

A: I hear you. My older sister used to be so mean to me—no matter what I did. I tried to be friends with her, but she just wouldn't. When I was young, I didn't understand. It really hurt my feelings and made me mad too.

Now that I am older and have studied some psychology, I understand why my sister seemed to hate me when we were kids. She was trying to be an adult, and my parents wouldn't let her. She thought she was so grown-up, but she was still a child to my parents. So she directed her anger at me because she couldn't do anything about our parents.

When your sister does something that bothers you, don't ask her to stop. She is doing it to bother you, so pretend it doesn't bother you. I know that's hard, but if you can manage to do it long enough, she will stop. She may try something else. The trick is to pretend that you don't care. Of course, you care, but you have to pretend that you don't. Don't scream or cry or hit her. Just ignore her when she is mean. Leave the room if you can. Go for a walk. Read a book. Help your parents with a chore. Do something that takes you away from your sister.

Maybe if you act like you don't care, your sister will stop picking on you. Maybe not. But it's worth a try. You can't make somebody else be nice. You can only control your own attitude and behavior.

Here's something else I learned. When somebody picks on me, I close my eyes and take deep breaths and pretend they don't exist. I imagine I am in a beautiful place where the sun is shining on me. Flowers are blooming; birds are singing; little bunnies are hopping around, and pretty little deer are dancing and laughing.

I guarantee you that if your sister is trying to pick on you and upset you and you close your eyes and meditate and smile, it will drive her crazy because you're supposed to get upset. People hate to be ignored, especially mean big sisters.

THOSE PESKY PARENTS!

Q: My parents are divorced and I live with my mom. I don't like to visit my dad on weekends because he always tells me lies. Every time I catch him, he says he won't lie anymore. Then he lies again. I am just tired of it. I don't want to see him or talk to him but he says I have to because he has joint custody. How can I fix it so I don't have to see him?

—*Kim, age fifteen*

A: When people get divorced, the court considers a lot of factors before making a custody ruling. They have to follow the state and federal laws, and they try to be fair to everybody. I wish the judges would ask the children how they feel before they make a custody arrangement, but that isn't how it works. Because your father is your father, he probably has a legal right to see you. And he must care about you, or he wouldn't bother to see you. So try to remember that he cares, even if he isn't able to show it and can't always be the person you would like him to be.

Fathers and mothers are people too, and they make big mistakes and don't always act right. But because they are the adults, they get to be the boss whether we like it or not. I used to hate it when my father bossed me around, but there was nothing I could do except run away. And that is not a good idea because it just causes more problems instead of fixing the problems you already have.

So you need to sit down and think about how you really feel about your dad. Are you kind of mad at him because he is married to somebody else and has other kids? That would make me feel bad, I think, even though there really isn't anything wrong with getting married again after you are divorced. Or maybe you are mad at him just for getting divorced from your mom. Also think about why he might be untruthful. Does he lie to try to make you like him? Does he lie just to make life easier at the moment? Does he realize he's lying when he does it? You know how some little kids will do something like break a window and then stand there in the broken glass and say they didn't do it because they don't want to get in trouble? Well, sometimes adults act that way too. They say whatever they think will get them out of trouble at the moment. But it comes back to haunt them later. That's why people always tell you not to lie; it just makes life harder.

If you truly and honestly don't want to see your dad, then there are some things you can do. You could talk to your teacher or counselor at school, your pastor at church, your mother or your grandparents or an uncle—whomever you trust to really listen to you. Some adults won't listen, so keep on trying until you find somebody who will listen, somebody you can trust. Ask them for advice about your situation. Maybe nobody will have the answer for you, but sometimes it helps just to talk to somebody who really listens and cares. You might also write a letter to your father and explain why you don't want to visit him for a while and ask him if you could just skip the visits for a few weeks or months. That might hurt his feelings, so think about what you will say if it does hurt his feelings. And remember that sometimes when people's feelings are hurt, they say or do things out of anger and then are sorry later.

I am sorry you have to have this problem. I know how hard it is. I was once married to a man who had kids from his previous marriage, and their mother just made everybody's life miserable. It was awful. I cried every day. But I survived, and so will you. Just be sure that when you grow up, you make sure that you know the person you think about marrying very, very well so that you will have a better chance of not getting divorced.

And in the meantime try writing down your feelings on a piece of paper. Say whatever you want to, no matter how bad or mean it seems. Then tear up the paper into little bits and throw it away so that nobody will ever see. I do that all the time, and it really helps. I just rip up my problems and throw them away. And I feel like I told people what I think about them, even though I didn't really tell them.

Good luck and remember: when you are eighteen, you can live where you want to and spend time with whomever you want. Hang in there. I will be thinking of you.

Q: My parents won't let me play on the computer all the time. They say I need to do something else but I can't think of anything to do. I'm bored.

—*Ricky, age eight*

A: I like playing Scrabble on my computer, so I know how much fun a computer can be. But it isn't healthy to sit in front of a computer all the time, especially when you are young and still growing. You need to move around and get some exercise and be creative and do other things that will stimulate your brain.

Here are some of the things I do to stimulate my brain: I learn a new song to play on the piano or guitar. I read a lot of books and magazines. I make my own greeting cards. I bake easy things like cookies from a cookbook. I go outside and lie down and look at the trees upside down. I get a sheet of paper and try to draw a picture of my dog. I put on some music and dance like crazy all over my room. I go to the library and look at all the art pictures in the big reference books. I ride my bike as fast as I can until I fall down. I try to see how many times I can hit a tennis ball against the wall without missing. I like to make people and animals out of modeling clay and then paint them weird colors, like a blue dog or a pink cat.

Maybe you would enjoy some of those things—or your own things. Have some fun!

Q: I live with my dad and my stepmom. She is really mean. I don't know why. She grounds me for stuff I didn't even do and she always thinks I'm lying. It was better when my dad was here but he's in the military and he's gone right now. Do you know any way I can make my stepmom stop being so mean?

—*Shelli, age twelve*

A: I can tell you from my own experience that it is very hard to be a stepmom. Once I was married to a man who had four children from a previous marriage. I loved those kids, but it took a long time for them to trust me because I didn't always act the way they expected me to. Your stepmother hasn't known you since you were a tiny baby, so she has to learn about you as you go along. Here is my suggestion.

When your stepmother does something that you think is mean, go to your room or go outside and take a walk. Think about what happened and what you said and what she said. Then be very honest and ask yourself, *What would I do if I were her? Would I act the way she did?* If you still think she was mean, then write her a note and tell her how you feel. Don't insult her or call her names. Just say how you felt. Start each sentence with "I feel . . ." This is a technique that therapists teach people so that they can communicate without hurting each other's feelings so much.

For example, if your stepmother grounded you for something you didn't do, you might feel like saying, "You are so mean to me. You are always thinking the worst." Or something like that. But saying those things won't help the problem. If you say, "I feel like you don't trust me and you don't like me when you ground me for something without really knowing whether I did it. I feel really bad because I would like you to trust me because I don't lie to you." See the difference? You say how you feel and what you would like. Then you can talk about the situation and maybe figure out a way to get along better.

Your stepmother probably misses your father just as much as you do. Have you talked about that? It might help you to connect a little bit better. Don't give up if your first effort doesn't pay off. Just wait a while and try again. You seem like a nice person with a big heart. I think if you give your stepmother time to get to know you, she will see how nice you are. Good luck.

Q: My parents are getting divorced and my mom is so crabby. She always blames me for everything. She says I am going to end up in the wrong crowd and get in big trouble but I get good grades and I never get in trouble.

—Tiffany, age fifteen

A: I hope it will help a little bit to know that lots of kids have parents who blame them for things and who tell them they are going to end up with the wrong crowd. It isn't that your mother thinks you are bad; she is afraid for you, but she doesn't know how to express what she feels. So instead, she tries to scare you into being good. I know this because my dad used to accuse me of doing bad things even though I didn't do them and I got good grades in school. It made me very angry, and I was angry for a long time because it wasn't fair. Then I got older and realized that my father just didn't know how to talk to me.

What your mother needs to do is think about what she really feels, but you are the kid, so you can't tell your mother what to do! Whatever you do, don't say, "Well, if my mother thinks I'm going to drink or smoke or whatever, I might as well." That would be a big mistake. Don't let somebody else decide who you are. Decide for yourself. Don't do things that you know are wrong or could hurt you. OK?

I don't know everything, but one thing I have learned from life is that it isn't fair and it never will be. I also learned that other people can think what they want to and that it doesn't have to affect me. I just try to remind myself that they don't really know what I think. Try to make yourself strong by being your own best friend. I mean really be your friend. Write yourself nice notes and tell yourself how much you like you. (Sign them "your secret friend" so that if anybody finds them, they won't know it was you. If anybody does see them and asks who they are from, just say, "I have so many friends; I can't remember.") Smile at yourself in the mirror and say, "I really like you. You are so lovable." You will laugh, but I promise you will feel better.

One more thing to think about: your mother is a person even though she is a mother, and she has lots of problems that she might not even tell you about. Just getting divorced is so hard. I know because I got divorced. Sometimes it seems to be the only way to resolve problems, but it does create more problems because kids end up with stepparents and stepbrothers and stepsisters; and everybody has hurt feelings. So I would suggest this: when your mother yells at you or blames you for something, just try to let the words bounce off you. Then go into your room or take a walk and ask yourself, *What is she really upset about?*

Then after you feel calm, maybe you could write her a note and tell her that you love her and that you are a good kid and wish she wouldn't yell at you or think bad things about you. Don't tell her that she is mean. Just tell her how you feel. Maybe it will help her see things from your point of view. Maybe not, but at least you will know that you tried. Good luck, sweetheart.

Q: My parents are getting a divorce. I feel like my life is over.

—*Shandra, age eight*

A: I am so sorry to hear that your parents are splitting up. No matter how hard people try, it is a difficult situation all around. Kids seem to be stuck in the middle too many times. And you get your feelings hurt. Just remember that it isn't your fault. When adults decide to break up, it is because they are having troubles that they probably can't tell you about. And they shouldn't tell you all their problems. You are the child, and their job is to protect you and take care of you.

People have written books to help kids with problems like yours. I think Judy Blume is a good author. You might ask your teacher to suggest other books. And if you have a brother or sister or a relative or a friend you can talk to, go ahead and talk. Just make sure that the person respects your privacy and will keep your discussion private. It is important to talk about things that bother you or worry you. If you keep everything inside, it will make you feel worse.

Another thing you can do is keep a journal. Just write down your feelings. If you are worried about somebody reading what you wrote, tear it up and throw it away. Just writing it down will help you get it out. You will feel better.

Remember that everybody experiences pain. Sometimes life just hurts so much, but we survive and heal. After a while the pain doesn't hurt so much. We may still be sad, but we go on with our lives. And every problem makes us a little bit stronger.

In the meantime I am sending you a big hug!

Q: Why does my stepdad says mean things to me when my mother can't hear him? If I tell her, he says I am lying. I try to be nice to him but it doesn't work. How can I make him be nicer?

—*Kara, age twelve*

A: I don't know your stepdad, so I don't know why he acts the way he does. But I do know that you can't change your parents. You can't fix them, and you can't make them do anything. That's the bad part about being the kid. You don't have a car or a checking account, so you can't leave home or get a job. You are stuck. So you have to make the best of your situation and try to focus on things that make you happy.

Sometimes I think stepparents feel guilty about getting divorced, so they don't act very nice. And sometimes kids are mad at their parents for getting divorced, so they take out their anger on their stepparents. And sometimes adults just don't act very adult. They act like kids and hurt your feelings. If that happens with your stepfather, don't tell him he is being mean. But you could try writing him a note to say how you feel, not to criticize him. For example, you could write, "Dear Stepdad [put his name here], I would like to get along better with you. Sometimes I feel like you are mad at me or you don't like me. I wish we could think of some way for us to have a better relationship."

Just give him the note and see what happens. If he is a mature grown-up person, he will talk to you about your note and will try to help you figure out a way that you can be friends. If he is not a mature grown-up person, he will not be very nice. He may even say something mean. If that happens, then don't try again. Ask your teacher to help you make an appointment to talk with your school counselor. Talk to your counselor about your situation. Even if the counselor can't change anything, talking to somebody who listens to you and cares about you will make you feel better. If you are too shy to talk to somebody at school, look in the yellow pages under Social Services and see if there is a counseling center you could call for advice. Some places have a teen hotline.

I am sorry you have to be in this situation. It is difficult and can really be painful. But when you are a grown-up yourself, you will probably be a nice, good parent. You will remember how it felt when you were going through this.

In the meantime I would suggest that you read a lot, find some hobbies, try to do things that make you happy. Time passes more quickly when we are busy and happy, so keep yourself busy. Read books, write stories, draw pictures, paint, sing, do housework, mow the lawn, get a book or video from the library and teach yourself to play the piano or tap dance. Focus on things that give you joy instead of spending all your time brooding over things that make you upset or sad.

Don't focus on sad feelings or bad situations. Spend as much time as you can with people who make you feel good. If nobody makes you feel good, then be your own best friend. Write yourself secret notes and say things like, "Hey, I like you. You are cool." And put the note in your book where you will see it at school. If somebody else sees it and asks who it is from, you can say, "I don't know. It must be somebody who likes me a lot." And just smile.

I will be thinking of you and sending you good wishes.

Q: My dad is going crazy. He has too much stress from work. It makes him mad all the time. When he comes home he just yells at everybody. I want to help him but when I try to talk to him, he just yells. How can I help my dad?
—Becka, age eight

A: Your dad must have some troubles or problems that are making him stressed out. You probably don't know all of them, even if you think you do. And that's the way it should be. Your parents are adults, and you are the kid. It is their responsibility to deal with problems and let you be a kid. But that can make your life difficult, I know.

You could try writing your dad a note. Don't criticize him or say he is doing anything wrong. Just tell him how you feel. You could say, "Dear Dad, I feel like you are stressed out and it makes you mad. I wish I could help you feel better."

Maybe your dad will read the note and talk to you about it. If he does, that will be good. If he reads the note and gets mad or if he doesn't talk to you, then just say, "Well, I tried." And try to understand that he may not think it's appropriate to discuss some adult things with you because you are not an adult. He may have problems at work, for example. It isn't your job to take care of your dad and solve his problems. It's his job to take care of you. He is a grown man, so he can figure out how to solve his problems. You can help him the most by just being your own sweet, lovable self.

One thing you can do is try to give your dad some quiet time to calm down when he gets home from work. Don't run up and talk to him as soon as he walks in the door. And turn off the TV before he comes in, so that the house isn't noisy. Let your dad sit down and relax for a few minutes (or talk to your mom privately). Then bring him a big glass of cold water or some iced tea and say, "I thought you might like to have this." Give him a big smile, but don't ask a bunch of questions. You could ask, "Would you like a hug?" If he says, "No," don't be insulted. He just needs some more time alone. But if he says, "Yes," then give him a big hug and say, "I love you, Dad."

P.S. I will tell you a secret about dads: some of them feel very embarrassed about showing emotions. If they feel like crying, for example, because life is making them sad, they may yell so that nobody notices that they feel like crying. (People also cry sometimes because they are so happy.)

Q: My parents are nuts. I can't talk to them about anything. They are so ignorant that it's disgusting.

—Curtis, age thirteen

A: I know parents can be difficult to talk to. And it does seem like they don't know anything or they are nuts. I don't know your parents, but I know we are all ignorant about some subjects. Maybe your parents really are nuts, and maybe they are ignorant. Many parents grew up in a time when they didn't have access to as much information as you have today. They didn't grow up with computers and Internet and TV documentaries about so many different things. And maybe they just don't know how to be good parents. It is hard to be a good parent. There isn't any kind of training; you just have kids and then you have to take care of them. Some parents don't really know what to do. Maybe your grandparents didn't talk to your parents when they were young, so your parents don't know how to talk to you. They are doing the best they know how to do.

Maybe it would help if you could try to imagine your parents as they were when they were children. Do you think they liked school? Did they have a lot of friends? Did they play sports? Were they popular? Did they have happy lives? Or were they very poor? Maybe they had to live under difficult circumstances. If you can see them as people, maybe you will have more patience with them.

I can remember being embarrassed about my parents when I was in high school. They seemed so stupid, and their clothes were just awful. And my father always acted so bossy. I never wanted to be seen in public with them. When I got older, I stopped being ashamed of my parents. I realized that they didn't have the same opportunities that I had to learn things in school.

Maybe you will have to be the person in your family who teaches everybody how to communicate effectively. There are books you can read about interpersonal relationships and how to talk to people. For example, if you try to talk to your parents and they start yelling, don't yell back. Be calm. Don't call them names or slam doors or say you hate them. Try writing them a note that expresses your feelings. Don't criticize them, just tell them how you feel—politely. Treat them the way you would like them to treat you. Maybe your parents will calm down if you stay calm. Maybe not, but it's worth a try. And remember that when you are eighteen, you can go and live where you want and not have to talk to your parents if they don't treat you right.

In the meantime try to remember that parents can't help it if they aren't cool. They aren't supposed to be cool. Young people are cool. Parents are parents. Their main job is to keep you safe and healthy until you grow up.

Q: My parents never let me do anything. I get good grades and everything, but they are still too strict. How can I get them to let me do stuff?

—*Nicole, age fourteen*

A: I know how it feels to have parents who won't let you do anything. I wasn't allowed to do much when I was in school. I couldn't go anywhere in a car without an adult. I couldn't go to parties. I couldn't even go to a dance unless one of my parents was the chaperone. I thought my parents were mean. Now that I'm older, I don't think they were mean, but I still think they were too strict. I also understand that they were so strict because they loved me and wanted to protect me. Maybe that's why your parents won't let you do things. Maybe they just want to protect you because the world can be a dangerous place, even in situations that seem pretty safe.

When you get older, they probably will let you do more things. I know it seems like forever, but you will eventually grow up. It is hard to have patience, I know. I do not have a lot of patience. I used to get so mad at my parents, but it never helped. Getting mad just gives you a stomach ache. Whining and throwing tantrums only make you look like a baby. If you want more freedom, you need to show your parents that you are mature by acting responsible and using good judgment. If you show them that you are trustworthy, they will be more likely to trust you.

Talk to your parents. Ask them what it was like when they were kids. Were they allowed to do things that they won't let you do? Did they think their parents were too strict? Did one of them have a bad experience that makes them worry about you? The more you know about your parents' lives, the better you will be able to understand them. And if you truly try to understand them, you will have more patience and tolerance.

The main thing for you to remember is that when parents don't allow you to do things, they are trying to protect you from being hurt. They don't want you to make the same mistakes they made. (They have forgotten that they used to get mad at their own parents for trying to protect them when they were young!) You are lucky that your parents care enough about you to worry. Some parents let their kids do anything they want to, and many of those kids end up in serious trouble— or even dead. I know it's hard to be patient, but trust me, before you know it you will be out of high school and on your own. After you have spent a few years on your own, you will understand why your parents tried so hard to protect you.

Q: My mom is always calling the school. How can I make her stop?
—*Justin, age nine*

A: I don't know why your mom calls your school, but she must care about you or she wouldn't call. If you think she calls because she doesn't trust you, then be honest. Do you tell her lies? Does she have a reason not to trust you? If you have a good relationship with your mom and she still calls the school, maybe she is just worried about you. Maybe she wants to help you the best she can. Being a parent is not easy.

A lot of kids would be happy to have parents who cared about them. I know that it can be a pain now, but think about how you would feel if your mother didn't care what happened to you. How would you feel if she didn't care if you got bad grades or got hurt? That wouldn't be good.

The best thing to do would be for you to talk to your mother calmly. Ask her why she calls the school. If her reasons are sensible, then don't argue. After you discuss it with her, if you think she calls too much, ask her not to call so much. Tell her how you feel when she calls the school. Do you feel embarrassed? Angry? Ashamed?

You can't tell your mother what to do, but you can show her that you are growing up by having a mature, calm conversation with her. Maybe if you show her that you are responsible, she will treat you like you are more grown-up. But maybe she will keep on calling the school no matter what you say. In that case you will just have to try hard not to give her any reason to call. Do your homework, don't be tardy, don't cut classes or argue with the teachers, be nice to other kids, don't fight or call names, be honest and tell your teacher and your mother when you are struggling to learn something and don't understand the assignments.

STAYING COOL IN SCHOOL

Q: How can I do better in school? I am always the last one to do things and I don't get very good grades.

—Emily, age nine

A: I don't know your situation, so I am not sure what would help you in school. Have you been tested for dyslexia? If you haven't, ask your teacher if he or she can help you get tested. Dyslexia doesn't mean anything is wrong with your brain; it means that you can have some problems reading. But teachers can help you if they know why you have the problems. Also, tell your teacher if reading makes your eyes hurt or gives you a headache. She can give you a colored filter to put over the page and see if that helps you read better.

People are all different, just like trees. Some grow very fast, and some grow slowly. But a tree that grows slowly can grow to be even bigger than a fast growing tree. Don't worry if you take more time than somebody else to learn something. Just go at your own pace. If the teacher goes too fast, ask when she would have time to talk with you. Try to explain exactly what you don't understand. Don't just say, "I don't get it" because that doesn't explain. Do you need more time to do your work, or do you not understand instructions when somebody just tells you? Is it easier for you to remember instructions if the teacher writes them down? Maybe you learn the best when you do something with help a few times and then do it on your own. Try out some different things.

Ask your parents or some adult if they can help you find out if you are a visual learner, meaning that you learn by seeing. Lots of kids learn by seeing, and they have trouble in school when the teachers explain everything out loud. I get lost myself unless I can "see" what I'm supposed to do.

Good luck and remember that you can learn. Look how much you have already learned. You can read and write and do some math. You know the names of all kinds of animals and plants and planets. You can probably make a sandwich, and I'll bet you can tie your shoes. And you typed me a letter, so I know you can type. You have lots of talents.

Q: We read *Dangerous Minds* in my class at school. I like the book but I don't like the language. Why did you put so much swearing in the book? We can't watch the video at school because of the bad language.

—Mirek, age sixteen

A: I apologize to you for the swearing in the book, but I thought it was important to show how my students spoke and the kind of lives they had. I am sorry you couldn't watch the movie in school, but you can rent it at a video store and watch it at home if your parents don't mind. Please remember that there is much more foul language in the movie than there was in my book or my classroom. My students did not go around swearing all the time, but they had permission to write whatever they wanted in their journals so that they could express their feelings instead of getting into fights.

There was a lot of fighting at our school. It was a very violent place, and many students were scared. I wanted to show that in the book because people sometimes don't understand why kids are afraid to go to school. They think the kids are just lazy, but the kids are not lazy. They just want a place where they feel safe to learn. I tried to make my classroom a safe place.

Q: I read your book and I think these American students don't care about school. Many people in the world would love to go to school. I moved to the U.S. from Russia. Many poor children there would be happy to go to school. I work hard in school to make my family proud. What is wrong with those children? Is crazy not to want to learn.

—Anzhelika, age fourteen

A: You are right that many American students don't care about school. They take it for granted that they have the opportunity to learn to read and write. They don't know what it is like to live in other countries where not everybody can go to school. So they don't understand that they are wasting a valuable gift. Maybe when they grow up, they will understand. Maybe if they read your letter, it will make them think.

I am glad that you are working hard in school and that you want to make your family proud. That is important. You are very mature, and I know you are going to be successful. Good luck to you.

Q: We read your book in my ESL class. I like your book but I think my English is very bad so I apologize. Before, I sit in the back of the class because some students laugh at me for not speaking English good. Now I sit in front and I learn more. Maybe you can tell those people not to laugh when somebody is trying to learn. Thank you.

—Carlos, age twelve

A: Your English is very good and thank you for your letter. English is very difficult to learn; it's a crazy language. Spanish is a much easier language to learn. *Estoy aprendiendo hablar y leer español.*

I am very happy that you now sit in the front and learn English. I apologize for those rude people who make you feel embarrassed. Do you know that none of my Spanish-speaking students ever laughed at me for trying to speak Spanish? They helped me. But some Americans are inconsiderate and arrogant. They only speak English, so they don't understand how difficult it is to learn a new language. I apologize for them. Not all Americans are like them.

Remember this: you are bilingual, so you are twice as educated and talented as any person who speaks only one language. When you apply for jobs later on, speaking two languages will be a big plus in your favor.

Don't let the rude people at school bother you. They are not important. Your education is more important. Perhaps one day you will be an ESL teacher who can help students learn English!

Q: Why are some teachers so mean? It seems like some of them really try to be nasty. Don't they remember what it was like to go to school?

—Sara, age sixteen

A: I know exactly what you are talking about. I have had some very mean teachers in my life. They shouldn't be teachers, but they are. Unless they break the law, they are going to continue to be teachers, so you have to learn to deal with them. (Unfortunately, being mean to children isn't illegal.)

Sometimes teachers don't realize they are being mean. They have stress in their lives that you don't know about. They could have rotten kids, sick parents, a nasty husband or wife, kids who take drugs and act terrible. They could have money problems or tax problems or PMS. You can never know what goes on in somebody else's life, even if you think you know them.

You are right; some teachers really have forgotten what it was like to be young. Can you remember what you felt like when you were three years old? Some people can; others can't. The teachers who can't remember what it was like to be a kid just don't get it. And you can't help them get it. So you have to figure out how to help yourself.

Here's the trick I use in a class when the teacher isn't very nice. I figure out what that teacher thinks is important. Is it being on time, being quiet, always raising your hand before talking, staying in your seat, getting homework in on time, finishing class assignments completely, having neat handwriting, having kids who volunteer to read, teaching kids who help other kids, or something else? Every teacher thinks certain things are really important. Watch and listen and you will figure out what yours finds important. Then make sure you do the things that teacher thinks is important. Forget about whether you like or dislike the teacher. Learn the most you can, and just minimize your conversations and conflicts with the teacher.

I wish I could send you a magic carpet to swoop you up and take you away. I bet you wish that too. But the best I can do is send you this letter and promise you that there is life after high school, and it is much much better than life in school. Grown-ups used to tell me to enjoy my school years because they were the best times of my life. Ha! They were not. They were the worst. I like to read and learn, but some of my teachers made my life miserable. And other kids were sometimes mean too. So I learned how to have a secret self that nobody could touch.

For a while I kept a diary, but my brother kept snooping, so I started writing letters to people, telling them exactly what I thought about them and their behavior. I said anything I wanted to say, no matter how mean or nasty it was. I never showed the letters to anybody; I tore them up in tiny pieces and threw them away. But I sure felt better afterward!

Have you ever read any books about yoga and deep breathing and meditating? I used to think it was a little bit nutty, but a couple of years ago I got a videotape from the library about yoga for relaxation and stress release. I did the exercises and the breathing, and it really did help me stop being upset about things. I learned how to breathe deeply and make my mind relax and stop thinking about upsetting things. Maybe you could try that.

Here's another sneaky trick. Sometimes when I had a mean teacher whom I didn't like, I would pretend I really liked that teacher. Instead of ignoring the teacher and being really quiet, I would volunteer to do things for her or him, and I behaved perfectly in class. I smiled when they made jokes and nodded my head when they were explaining things. I made up a problem and asked for their advice so they felt like I thought they were really smart. (Ha-ha.) They thought I really liked them, and they were much nicer to me! They didn't know that I sometimes wished they would trip and fall down right on their stupid noses. Sometimes those mean teachers even started to act nicer to me.

THE BULLY SITUATION

Q: There are two big boys in our class and they hit everybody. They tear our papers and steal our lunch and our money. And if we tell the teacher, they hit us harder. Now they are trying to get my friends to hang around with them. I don't want to hang around with them but I don't want my friends to stop being my friends.

—*Austin, age eleven*

A: There are bullies in every class, and they always think they are cool. But they really aren't. That's why they act like bullies. They know they aren't cool. They know they aren't really tough. If they were really strong people, they wouldn't have to try to make other people afraid of them. They would just know they were cool and go on about their business.

This is something important for you to understand. It's called psychology. People always have reasons for the things they do. Sometimes they don't even know why they act the way they do. At least that's what they say. But if they stopped to think about themselves and how they feel, the bullies would have to admit that they don't feel very good. They may say that they don't care what other people think, but that isn't true. If they really didn't care what other people thought, they wouldn't go around trying to control other people and make everybody notice them.

If your friends want to hang out with the bullies, then make new friends. There are plenty of nice people in the world. You can't make anybody else do anything. What you can do is use your brain. If kids are just talking, you don't have to listen. I know it's hard, but if you can ignore them, the bullies will eventually give up. They are looking for attention. If you refuse to give it to them, they will have to look someplace else for it.

But if somebody really picks on you too much or hits you or steals your things, then you need to tell your parents and your teacher and your school counselors. Write your principal a note to tell him or her what is going on in your classroom. There is no reason for you to keep quiet when somebody is acting violent or physically abusive.

Remember this: there are only a few bullies, and there are a lot of other kids. If you other kids decide you aren't going to tolerate the bullies, then you can stop them—just like in our country. When people do bad things, the rest of the people can join together to make them stop. It doesn't mean you are rats or tattletales. A *tattletale* is somebody who tells on people about little things, such as chewing gum or talking or looking at somebody else's paper. Those are not important things. So when you tell about them, adults don't really listen.

But when people are being cruel and scaring other kids or being really mean to them, then that is important and telling does not make you a tattletale. It makes you an intelligent, responsible person. And it makes you somebody I respect.

You are not the only person in your class who wrote about these bullies. I was very sad to receive so many letters asking me what to do.

Now I have a special letter just for the bullies:

Dear bully,

I think you are acting like a coward and I think it's time for you to grow up and act like a young man or a young woman. You might say that you don't care if nobody likes you, but I don't believe you. I think you do care, and I think you would like to feel proud of yourself. You would like to think that you truly are cool. You can be. All you have to do is stop acting like a jerk.

You don't have to keep doing things. You can decide to be a different person. Just as somebody can decide to stop failing in school or stop smoking or stop drinking or stop whatever isn't good, you can change your behavior. You can be a leader in your class. But you can lead in a good way. You don't have to be the smartest person to be a good leader, but you do have to consider other people's feelings.

Stop acting like a spoiled baby. When you are a little baby, you are selfish; you don't care about anybody else. But when you grow up, you have to start thinking about other people's feelings. If you can't do that, then you are not grown-up. You are stuck in your baby behavior. Definitely not cool.

Do you know that if you decide right now to stop acting like a bully that most of your classmates will forgive you? Yes, they will. They will just accept the new person you decide to be. Maybe a few people will take a little time to trust you. They will want to make sure you really have changed and are not just trying to trick them. But most of your classmates will be cool. Eventually they will appreciate that you are grown-up enough to realize that you weren't acting right. Please think about this.

And please think about something else: I like you, but I don't like your behavior. You are not your behavior. You are a person, and your behavior is something you do. I can dislike your behavior but still like you as a person. I may not like what you do, but I still think you are a valuable human being. I just hope that you will also believe that you are a valuable human being. You have talents and skills. You have good things about you. Why not think about those things and show them to the world, instead of trying to scare everybody into thinking you are fearless?

Use your brain and your heart for a change. You might be surprised what will happen. In the meantime, I'll be thinking of you and wishing you well.

—Miss J

And here is my letter to kids who aren't bullies:

Dear student,

If you are not a bully, then you need to tell the bullies that you do not like their behavior. You don't have to gang up on them and beat them up, but you need to gang up against their behavior. You can decide as a group that you will not accept people being mean and cruel when you are around. When a bully picks on somebody in front of you, you need to join together and say, "Stop acting like a bully. You are not cool. We are not impressed. Grow up."

You need to join together and do this every time you see somebody acting like a bully. If a bully finds you when you are alone and says or does something to you, then you need to tell your teachers and your principal and your counselors and your school nurse. You need to make the adults listen because this is important.

You are not a rat or a tattletale if you tell that somebody is being a bully. A *tattletale* is somebody who tells about little things such as when somebody is chewing gum or looking at somebody else's paper. Those things may not be good, but they are not really important. But when somebody acts mean or cruel, especially if they hurt somebody, then it is your responsibility to tell the adults. You are not being a rat; you are being a responsible, good person. You are being somebody I respect. I always stand up for my principles. If I see somebody being mean, I always say so.

When I hear somebody say something mean about another person, making fun of them for some reason, I say, "That is not nice. You should not be mean to people. It doesn't make you cool or popular. It makes you look weak and ignorant."

Here is something else to think about: What is important to you? What do you want your life to be? What makes you happy or excited?

Focus on the things you want to accomplish in your life. Think about your hobbies and your goals. Think about what is really important to you. Children who act mean to other kids are not important; they are silly children. Don't make them important. Ignore them. If you ignore them long enough, they will eventually stop. They are looking for attention. If you don't give them attention, they will have to look someplace else.

Be strong. Be valiant. Be honorable. Tell the bullies to box it up, cut it out, take a chill pill, and join the human race.

—Miss J

A LETTER FROM ME TO YOU

And now, ladies and gentlemen, ta-da! Here is my letter to every single student in the world (yes, even the bullies):

Dear unique and lovable person,

I want you to know that I did my best to give you really good advice. I don't have all the answers to life's questions, but I do care about you very much. So please care about yourself. Use your brains and your talents. Show other people how intelligent and kind you can be; I really believe that what goes around comes around.

Cherish your friends. If you don't have any friends, be your own best friend until you make friends. The best way to make friends is to be a friend. Help other people when you see they need help. Smile and say hello when you see somebody all alone. Think about other people instead of yourself.

I wish you a good year in school, and I hope that you think about the things I have said. I hope that you will dream big dreams and let your light shine. You have talents, even if you don't know what they are yet. Maybe you aren't the best speller in the class or the fastest runner. But everybody has special talents. Keep looking until you discover yours.

When I was ten years old, one of my teachers told me I could be a writer if I wanted to. So I decided to write books when I grew up. Most people laughed at me and said I would never do it. Some of my friends made fun of me, so I found friends who didn't make fun of me. I found people like my teacher who encouraged me to dream. And some days, when nobody else believed in me, I believed in myself. And now I am an author, and I have a lot of books published.

Your dreams can come true too. Whatever your dreams are, they are valid and important. If somebody else doesn't believe in your dreams, that is not your problem. You can still believe in yourself.

And here's something else to think about. Look at your parents and other grown-ups. Ask them if they see their friends from school now that they are grown-up and working at jobs. Most of them will say that they don't see those people. Or they see one or two people. When you graduate from school, you will probably not see the people in your class anymore. You will be able to choose your friends from the whole world, not from one small class. And if people don't act right, you don't have to be around them. Hang in there. There's life after school, and it can be big fun.

In the meantime take care. I will be thinking of you. So will my dog, Bogart the wonder dog. He says to tell you, "Arf." And he says if he sees any bullies, he is going to bite them in the butt!

—Miss J

Time and Energy Savers

Teaching can steal your time and sap your physical and emotional energy very quickly, so it's important to conserve your precious resources whenever possible. Some of the following tips will save you only a minute or two, but you will be much more effective if you spend those minutes teaching your students instead of plodding through mundane, repetitive chores. And a minute between classes can go a long way toward helping you recharge your mental battery before your next group of eager scholars bursts into your classroom.

LESSON PLANS

Many educational textbooks advise new teachers to make detailed lessons plans, so that you use each minute of class time productively and your classes will progress smoothly through the required curriculum. That concept sounds good on paper. When I first began teaching, I planned each class to the second. I was so nervous that I didn't trust myself to remember what I wanted to cover during a specific time period. I imagined myself facing my students and not being able to think of a single intelligent thing to say. So I planned and outlined and made hourly, weekly, monthly, quarterly, and semester calendars, all filled in neatly and completely, down to the last spelling quiz. I also broke each hour down into five- or twenty-minute blocks of time. I was prepared to walk into the classroom and be the super teacher I knew in my heart I could be. Unfortunately, I hadn't planned time for the daily announcements, calls from the administrative offices, buses delayed by traffic, announcements over the squawking intercom, sick students, or an occasional spider dangling from an overhead light causing momentary chaos. I also hadn't planned—and nobody could—for the variances in student ability and behavior that drastically affect the speed with which a given class will grasp a new concept, master a new skill, or complete a given assignment. Often students would whiz through an exercise in ten minutes when I had expected them to take thirty minutes, leaving me twenty minutes to spare. Or they would labor for an entire class period over what I thought would be a simple fifteen-minute activity.

At first I spent hours revising those detailed lesson plans, but something always seemed to happen to throw my classes off schedule. I finally realized that I was far more likely to lose my mind than create lesson plans that I wouldn't have to change or frequently adjust. Now I make a very rough schedule of what I want to cover during a given school year. After I meet my students and get a feel for their personalities and abilities, I alter the plan to fit their needs. My daily and weekly plans are very general and flexible, with optional activities and exercises that I can add or delete as time allows. With a very cooperative class, I can sometimes reduce my lesson plan to a few simple phrases, such as "Introduce literary elements of fiction; read and discuss examples; if time allows, write responses in journals."

Of course, I include the required curriculum in my plans, but I have found that I teach much more effectively and that my students learn far more (and do better the following year with their next teacher) if I concentrate on teaching them how to think and analyze information, instead of rushing them through materials just so I can say we covered the curriculum. And although I steadfastly refuse to spend any more than the minimum amount of time teaching students to take any standardized tests, they earn higher test scores when we focus on critical thinking skills instead of learning to memorize and regurgitate specific test information.

My advice to new teachers is to make your lesson plans as simple and flexible as possible. If you need to structure each minute during your first few months (or years), do so. But as you develop more experience and confidence, shift your focus from planning to teaching, using your students' performance, instead of the calendar, as a guide. When they fall behind schedule because they need to spend more time on a specific area, they will usually make up that time later on; they work much harder for a teacher who demonstrates that he or she genuinely cares about their education.

INDEPENDENT ASSIGNMENTS

Assigning students to work independently has many advantages. First, you are free to roam the classroom and act as a guide instead of the leader. Second, students learn to take more responsibility for their learning; they enjoy tackling a real challenge; they have the opportunity to practice valuable skills such as setting priorities and managing time; and they can work at their own pace. Third and perhaps most important, by placing more responsibility on your students' shoulders, you demonstrate that you have faith in their intelligence and ability to learn.

I do not mean to imply that you shouldn't teach but rather that you should not try to force-feed information to your students. Instead of telling them what their textbook says, for example, ask them to come up with their own ideas, discuss them, and then compare them to the ideas in their text. If you really want them to learn this material, assign them to work in groups or pairs to create their own criteria, design a visual, and present their ideas to the class. Students may not use the same wording as the textbook. For example, they may say that the people in a novel need to have believable conversations, whereas the text will say characters must engage in realistic dialogue; but students remember new concepts far better when they discover those concepts on their own and then articulate and communicate the concepts to others.

You don't have to create every independent assignment from scratch. Review your textbooks and curriculum materials for content that lends itself to independent assignments. Instead of handing students information, assign them the task of discovering information or developing new skills on their own—with your help when they hit a snag. Depending on your students' maturity and enthusiasm, you may want to provide an outline of the steps needed to complete an assignment or simply state the goal and let students figure out how to reach it.

Note: I have found that students work harder and turn in higher-quality work if I require individual contracts for any major independent project (that is, one that requires a week or longer to complete). Contracts eliminate confusion about deadlines and specific requirements, and they reduce the chances of a student failing to earn credit. Your contract need not be elaborate: the objective, deadline, benchmarks, student signature, and date of signing should be enough. I also schedule an interim check midway between the starting date and the deadline, at which time I check to make sure that nobody is confused or lagging too far behind to finish the project. Your contract doesn't need to be complex, but it does need to make your requirements clear. See the sample contract in Exhibit 10.1.

Don't give up if your students flounder in their first attempt at independent work. If they have problems working without supervision, then they need such assignments more than students who handle them with ease. Provide a timetable for them to check their progress and give them credit in your grade book for completing each step of the assignment, so that they won't worry about failing.

If you misjudge the time or complexity of an assignment, don't panic. Explain the problem to your students and ask them for suggestions. Students are often better judges of their abilities—and much less forgiving of laziness or procrastination—than their teachers are.

For teachers who are unfamiliar with independent assignments, Exhibit 10.2 is a sample project that I have assigned to high school students in grades nine through twelve, in a variety of classes from remedial to advanced. Some classes require more guidance than others, but they all enjoy this exercise and give it a high rating on their course evaluations. (Even younger children could do a more elementary variation.)

INDIVIDUAL PORTFOLIOS

Once your students have learned to manage their time, set priorities, and work independently on short assignments, they are ready for more advanced independent work—individual student portfolios. Some teachers hesitate to use portfolios for any of a number of reasons:

- They fear that if they aren't lecturing or directing, their classrooms will disintegrate into chaos.
- They lack confidence about teaching in a different style; they are comfortable with direct instruction where they do most of the talking.
- They underestimate their students' abilities.
- They have no idea how to design or implement a portfolio project.
- They enjoy the power that comes from having all the answers.
- They don't know how to monitor a long-term independent assignment.

Exhibit 10.1. Project Contract.

Instructions: Fill out, sign, and turn in to the teacher.

I understand that I am responsible for designing and completing my own project. If I choose to work with other people and they do not complete their part, I will still be responsible for completing my project *or* I will fill out a new contract and give it to the teacher.

My project will be (describe in detail):

_____

_____

_____

Check one. Fill in the blank(s) if you are going to work with one or two partners:

❏ I will do my own individual project.

❏ My one project partner is _____

❏ My two project partners are _____
    and _____.

I understand that my rough draft or progress report is due on _____.

I understand that the final project is due on _____.

If I do not turn in my project or I am not prepared to make my presentation on the due date, I will receive a zero for this assignment.

_____   _____
STUDENT SIGNATURE   DATE

- They worry that they won't have enough grades in their grade books.
- They don't feel confident in their ability to grade a portfolio.
- They don't want to have to grade thirty (or 150) big projects all at once.

I urge teachers to give portfolios a try, beginning with a shorter two- or three-day project. I am confident that with a little practice you will find that portfolios help students develop better study habits as well as more self-discipline and internal motivation, enjoy greater pride in their accomplishments, exhibit better morale and behavior, show better retention of information, and demonstrate a much higher level of critical thinking skills. With experienced students, you may be able to design exciting projects that involve several weeks or even months, such as

Exhibit 10.2. Independent Exercise: Short Story Analysis.

Outline: Your group will read the five short stories listed on the board. Three are from our literature textbook; two are from a literary journal (please do not write on the copies because I will collect them for other students to use). Each person must read all the stories. You may read them silently, individually, or aloud in your group. If you read them aloud, take turns reading or let one person read an entire story; it's up to you.

Deadlines: This project must be completed by (date): _____

Be prepared to show the teacher your individual notes and discuss the status of your group's project on (date): _____

Instructions

1. Group task: Read the first story.

2. Individual task: Jot down a few notes about your reaction to the first story in your journal or on note cards. What did you like and dislike about this story? Find a few phrases or sentences in the story that show specifically what you liked or disliked. Copy these phrases or sentences down for future reference. (Don't skip this step because you will need this information later.)

3. Group task: After everybody has made notes about the story, discuss the story in your group. See where you agree and disagree. Of course, you may have similar responses, but don't copy each other's ideas. Use your own brain for your own notes.

4. Group and individual tasks: Repeat steps one to three for each story. Each person should have a set of notes for each of the five stories, so that you can analyze and compare the stories.

5. Group task: Discuss the five stories in your group and decide what makes a good short story. What key elements must a story have in order to be good? List and define these elements. Your group should be able to identify at least three elements, probably four or five. (Don't worry; there are no right or wrong answers to this question.)

6. Group task: Compare and analyze the five stories and rate them, according to your own list of key elements. Which story is best? Rate the stories against each other, using your own system.

7. Group task: Design and create some kind of visual aid* (chart, graph, poster, or illustration) that shows your key elements and your system for rating the stories. Include each story and its rating in your visual aid.

8. Group task: Select one or two people from your group to present your visual aid to the class and briefly explain your group's elements and story evaluations. Choose an alternate to give the presentation in case your presenter is absent on the day your group is scheduled to give your presentation.

9. Individual task: Write a very brief critique of each group member's contribution to your project (please be tactful). Assign each person from one to ten points, with ten being best. Don't forget to include a critique of your own contribution (please be honest).

10. Individual task: Pat yourself on the back for completing a challenging project.

* You may use poster board, paint, a video camera, computer graphics, collages, the white board in our classroom, the overhead projector—whatever you need—for your presentation. You may also read selections from the stories if you choose or dramatize scenes.

designing, writing, and publishing a newspaper or a literary magazine or writing and performing a play.

The first step in designing a major portfolio project is to find a one- or two-week period when students won't be interrupted by a major holiday or vacation such as spring break, because you don't want them to forget about the project or lose their momentum once they get started. Next, select a unit from your curriculum that is likely to be of high interest to your students, one that will allow a variety of different activities and exercises: dinosaurs, poetry, mythology, fables, geometry theorems, insects, pictographs, computer-aided graphics, desktop publishing, child labor laws, the Bill of Rights, and so on. Now think of activities that will involve basic or advanced library research, reading comprehension, writing, art or design, computers, and an oral or written presentation. A well-designed portfolio project will allow for a wide variety of student ability levels and interests; you can establish a minimum requirement and give additional points for additional effort.

If you teach younger children, you might consider giving students one assignment at a time, so that they don't become overwhelmed. As they complete one assignment, you can check it off their list and give them the next one. With other students, I like to provide the entire outline so that they can practice managing their time and setting priorities, because those skills will be so important to them at college or in the workplace.

To make sure that all your students understand a given project, I recommend distributing your instruction sheets and briefly reviewing them with the class as a group. Make sure that everybody fills in the deadline date on the instruction sheet. Then let them get started. Some students will take off on their own, delighted to be freed from having to pace themselves with the group. Others may seem afraid or overwhelmed. Remind these timid souls that they don't have to do the activities in the order listed. They can read through the list until they find something that seems easy and begin there. Let them pair up or form small groups and discuss the project. (Remind them that sharing ideas is fine but that each student must turn in his or her own work. If two students turn in the same work, they each will receive only 50 percent of the grade, because you won't have any way to tell whose ideas are whose.)

Then, although you may be sorely tempted to stand and lecture, sit down at your desk and grade some papers or circulate and observe what students are doing. If you have a reluctant group, you might want to do the portfolio assignment yourself to model for them and show them that you believe it is important enough to spend your own time on it.

If students ask you what a specific instruction says, ask them what they think it says. Correct them if they are way off the mark, but encourage them to think for themselves. Some students become very uncomfortable when they realize that they have to rely on their own judgment, because they have no confidence in the validity of their own ideas. They may need quite a bit of prompting at first, but they will gradually develop more confidence as they complete the activities and have your initials on their papers as visual proof of their progress. Provide abundant praise and encourage students who have done especially well on one task to share their approach with somebody who is struggling with that task, if they are so inclined. Some students love to share; others jealously guard every iota of their work.

Let's take a look at a sample portfolio project (see Exhibit 10.3). This one is quite complex and focuses on higher-level thinking skills such as analysis, synthesis, and evaluation. Based on an eleventh-grade textbook, this project explores the literature and lifestyles of the Native Americans and Puritans.

Exhibit 10.3. Portfolio Project: The American Experience.

Name: _____ Class period: _____

Directions: You must complete each task on the following list, but you may do the tasks in any order you wish. As you complete each task, ask Miss J to initial the appropriate blank on this sheet. This portfolio counts as one-half of your grade for the quarter.

_____ 1. Read "The Historical Setting," pages 2–3 of your text. Be prepared to summarize what you have read orally to Miss Johnson.

_____ 2. Go to the school, college, or public library and find information about Native American tribes in the United States during the 1500s and 1600s. Find something that you think is well written and interesting, because you are going to use this information for other tasks. List your main source below.

Title of publication or Web site _____

Author (editor/designer) _____

Pages consulted (publication only): _____

_____ 3. Complete *at least one* of the following tasks:

a. Write a brief comparison of two different tribes. Describe similarities and differences in their social organizations, customs, housing, clothing, art, and so on.

b. Draw your own illustrations of two different tribes, showing their clothing, customs, housing, art, and so on.

c. Prepare a brief (three- to five-minute) oral presentation on two or more tribes, describing their lifestyles, customs, clothing, art, music, dancing, and so on.

_____ 4. Read the "American Events/World Events" time lines on pages 4 to 7 of your text. Select three entries on the time line (for example, 1609, Galileo builds first telescope) and research more information about these topics in a literature text or at the library. Use at least two different sources. List your sources here:

Title of publication or Web page URL: _____

Author or site sponsor: _____

Title of publication or Web page URL: _____

Author or site sponsor: _____

continued

Exhibit 10.3. Portfolio Project, *continued.*

_____ 5. Using the sources above, write one paragraph summarizing each of the three events you selected for item four.

_____ 6. Create a time line for your own life. Illustrate it with your own drawings, clip art, or pictures cut from magazines.

_____ 7. Write a short essay (one-page minimum) that explains the religious beliefs of the Puritans and compares those beliefs to your own. (For example, do you agree with the ideas of original sin and the Puritan work ethic?)

_____ 8. Read "The Earliest American Literature," pages 9 to 12 of your text. Be prepared to discuss these with Miss J.

_____ 9. List the names of three U.S. states that come from Native American words. Give the meaning of each one's name and the tribal source.

State	*Tribal Origin of Name*	*Meaning of Name*
a. _____	_____	_____
b. _____	_____	_____
c. _____	_____	_____

_____ 10. Read "Upon the Burning of Our House" and write your response to this poem.

_____ 11. Read and write a brief summary in your own words of the following:
   ❏ "Delaware, Navajo" ❏ "The Iroquois Constitution"
   ❏ "The Walam Olum" ❏ "Pima, Chippewa, Sioux"
   ❏ "The Navajo Legend" ❏ "From the Houses of Magic"

_____ 12. Create your own theory of the origin of life. Create pictographs like those in "The Walam Olum" to illustrate your theory.

_____ 13. Write your own legend like "The Navajo Origin Legend" to describe the origin of your own ethnic group(s). Try to use animals, nature, or other symbols to tell your story. You may not have to use words at all.

_____ 14. Choose one of the following:
   a. Write your own Constitution stating the fundamental laws and truths that govern your own life and actions.
   b. Imagine that you are the leader of some people and that you must create a Constitution that will best govern their lives.

_____ 15. Choose at least one of the following tasks (you may do more for more credit):

    a. Write a song or poem to express your feelings about nature.

    b. Write down the lyrics to a favorite song that expresses your feelings about nature and explain why you chose this song.

    c. Make a drawing or painting that expresses your feelings about nature.

    d. Take photos (or clip pictures from magazines) and create a nature display. Write your own captions for the photos.

_____ 16. Place all of these assignments into a portfolio. You may use a folder, binder, or something of your own design. Create a table of contents and design a cover for your project.

_____ 17. Give your portfolio to Miss J on or before (date): _____.

Late work: One day late = minus one letter grade; two days late = minus two letter grades; three days late = maximum grade of D; four days late = no credit.

Optional: Shake Miss J's hand. Feel proud. You are responsible and creative.

GRADING PORTFOLIOS

Portfolios can be a grading nightmare if you don't plan ahead, but with some planning, they can simplify grading. First, review your assignments and see which you can grade individually as students complete them. I usually list the assignments on a cover sheet and have students check with me as they complete each assignment. When I initial the assignment, I quickly review it and include a symbol by my signature that will indicate the student's grade for that activity. For example, I might sign "laj1" to indicate a C, "laj2" for a B, and so on. I use an unusual color of ink for my illegible signature, so I can read it but students can't forge it. Then when it's time to grade the entire portfolio, I just have to average out the numbers I have already assigned in order to give a project grade. Of course, I take into consideration any additional work, corrections, revisions, and overall effort that the student put forth.

I sometimes include individual assignments from the portfolio in my grade book as well. This doesn't mean that students are earning double credit for their work. I look at different aspects of a given assignment. Writing a literary analysis of a poem, for example, could count as an essay graded primarily on content in the portfolio, but I could also grade that essay for grammar and spelling and enter a separate grade in my grade book. I also remind students that they are earning a daily grade for participation. Students who work steadily and make daily progress earn a high grade for participation, whereas students who wander around and bother other people earn a lower grade.

Provide benchmarks to keep your students on track and allow you enough time to grade assignments as they are completed. If your portfolio project covers a two-week period, for example, you might specify that students should complete half the assignments by the end of the first week. Or you might require one assignment per day for each student, in whatever order students choose to complete them. You can eliminate paperwork at the same time as you increase student comprehension if you include some activities in which students must orally summarize, discuss, or explain concepts to you individually.

When students submit final portfolios, you will already have graded most of the individual components and will be able to assign a final grade without having to spend hours reviewing each portfolio. You might consider asking students to evaluate their own portfolios and the amount of effort they expended. Usually students are honest in their evaluations. For those dreamers and fibbers in the bunch, thank them for their input and give them the grades they deserve.

Twenty Years from Now

Twenty (or forty) years from now, you may not remember your students, but they will remember you. They may not remember the lessons you taught them, and they may have forgotten your face, but they will remember quite clearly the way you made them feel about themselves. They'll remember your criticism and your compliments, word for word. I once complimented a bank teller on her beautiful handwriting. She blushed. Thinking she might have misunderstood, I repeated my comment.

The teller looked down at her hands and said, "My second-grade teacher used to hit my knuckles with a ruler because my handwriting was so bad. I loved my teacher and I wanted her to like me, so I sat at my kitchen table every day for months and wrote my letters over and over."

"Well, she must have been pleased to see how beautifully your handwriting turned out," I said.

"I never did meet her standards," the teller said, "but I kept practicing, even after I left her classroom. When I was in the fourth grade, I went back and showed her how nicely I could write."

"Certainly, she praised you for working so hard," I said.

The teller sighed and shuffled through the deposit slips on the counter.

"She didn't remember me." After a moment she forced a smile. "But that was a long time ago, wasn't it?"

Hundreds of people have written to tell me about their teachers. Unlike other memories, time doesn't seem to diminish people's recollections of their experiences with teachers. Although age may allow people to put their childhood experiences in perspective, it doesn't necessarily dull the memory—or the joy or pain, as the following excerpts from readers' letters demonstrate.

One instance really sticks out in my mind. My eighth-grade teacher asked us to write our opinion on a certain subject. I do not remember the subject or how I responded; however, I do remember the teacher practically snickering, the red F for failure and the comment, "This is not the correct answer," written at the top of the first page. When I questioned the grade, reiterating the fact that she wanted my opinion, she just laughed and said she felt I was wrong. . . . I'm forty-two years old now, and I just learned in the past three years that my opinion is valuable and I am worth something.

—*Diane, St. Albans, West Virginia*

I remember my first-grade teacher, a woman whom I can still envision after all these many years, who taught me to read, a habit which has brightened my life for over fifty years since then. I remember a very demanding teacher from whom I took a class in Old English when I worked on my first undergraduate degree. How troublesome he was; how wise he was; what a great gift he gave me in demanding excellence. We have remained friends over the ensuing years. Many teachers stand out like bright stars in my sky.

—*Arthur, Suffield, Connecticut*

My mother and father were divorced when I was about nine or ten, and my mother had only an eighth-grade education. We worked very hard to survive, and I can still remember vividly the stiffness of the shirts I wore made from feed sacks. It was through the help and encouragement of coaches and teachers with the love, compassion, and commitment such as yours that I continued my education. I received an athletic scholarship to college and enlisted as an airman basic in the U.S. Air Force in the middle of my junior year. I then entered the flying training program and graduated with wings and a commission on the same day. I spent twenty years as a fighter pilot and four years in the Pentagon, rising to the rank of colonel. I completed my bachelor's degree under the bootstrap program and my master's degree at night school. I also completed the War College national security management program. I am now vice president and general manager of an aviation company. I am not telling you these things to brag but to let you know that successful lives and careers often begin by warm and loving teachers.

—Bud, Springdale, Arkansas

School was the enemy to me. I was bullied and tormented. I got into a lot of fights and started running with gangs. I am twenty-four now [and a female]. In the first two fights, I was defending myself, but I still got into trouble for it. Then one day I finally snapped and beat the crap out of the school bully. The other kids at school gave me more attention than the school staff did. Then my rep was made, and I did more than live up to it. The vice principal tried to reach out but was convinced by the school board that I was a "danger to other children" after my third fight. If I had had just one teacher who cared, I would have actually gone to high school instead of having to get my GED at seventeen.

Most gangsters I grew up around were just like me. Lonely, feeling there's nothing out there, no place to fit in, and no one who wants to give them a chance or view them as a person. Most kids who were as bad as me don't recover enough to be able to tell the system that they are all backwards and retarded! Most slip into drugs, prison, or worse, then they have kids of their own who never relate to their teachers either.

—Dana, Pleasanton, California

THE GOOD NEWS

Now for the good news. For every negative letter I receive about a teacher, I receive a hundred positive ones, which confirms my belief that there are many more good teachers than bad. Some years ago, while visiting New York City, I had the good luck and pleasure to meet Bill Parkhurst, a broadcast journalist and author. The conversation turned to teachers at one point, and Bill told me the most remarkable thing. As a research project for a true crime novel he was writing, Bill had spent a year working closely with a private detective so that he could write more accurately and realistically about the detective in his book.

"You'll be interested and surprised, I think, to know that the most common reason that people hire private detectives," Bill told me. "It isn't matrimonial surveillance, as many people think. I interviewed over 150 detectives, and every time I walked into an agency, one of the first things I'd hear would be somebody asking for help in locating a former teacher. People want to find their teachers and thank them."

Bill was right. I was interested and surprised to learn that so many people go to so much trouble to track down their teachers. And I was delighted, because I know that for every person who hires a detective, there must be hundreds of other people who are considering the idea, which means that teachers in this country are doing their jobs, educating and inspiring children, despite all the bad press about the failures of our schools.

Of course, there is no way to tell what your students will remember about you, but perhaps you will see something of yourself in these excerpts from three of the many letters I've received in response to *My Posse Don't Do Homework* and *The Girls in the Back of the Class.* The first one is from a man who took his teacher for granted:

Dear Miss LouAnne,

I really don't know where to start. Last night, I read the *Reader's Digest* and I found your story *The Girls in the Back of the Class.* I usually can't read anything longer than a paragraph, but I used my whole lunch hour reading and thinking about that story. I know you don't know me. As you can tell, my English is not that great. I even hate to write. But I felt the need to write to you. Don't ask me why. Maybe it's because you made me cry. I never cry. Only when somebody in my family dies.

After I read that story I went outside. It was a cold and dark night. I work on a loading dock from 9:00 P.M. until 7:00 A.M. I walked and walked where no one could see me and I cried. I cried hard. I had a teacher just like you in high school who did everything she could to help me. She must have said to me, "You can do it" a hundred times a week. She got me to believe in myself so good that I thought I could do anything.

The main reason I wanted to write to you is because I really didn't know how my teacher felt about me. Reading your story gave me some insight—ooh, big word. I know that y'all are two totally different people, but I bet you she felt the same way about her students as you did. As I read, I saw myself in the story a lot of times. I was selfish. I only cared about my feelings. Now I know that she really cared, and I wish I had just one more chance to tell her thanks.

See. There you go again, making me want to cry. But really I wish that I could hug her real tight and tell her thanks for everything. She played a very important role in forming the foundation of my life.

—*Rick, Abilene, Texas*

The second letter is from a young woman who wrote from Germany, where she was attending medical school. Her letter is about a teacher she met when she came to the United States as an exchange student during high school.

Dear LouAnne,

When I came to the U.S. as an exchange student, I was put into English as a second language classes. That day I decided not to like the teacher. This teacher was just as stubborn about keeping me in the ESL program as I was about trying to get out. I finally gave up, not knowing that this would save my life.

I was sure she would hate me for making all this trouble. I expected her to reject me, but instead she kept asking me how I was doing and how things went. For a long time, I was suspicious of her behavior toward me since back then I could not imagine that somebody was truly interested in me and my life. I still remember the day when she offered me to talk to her. She was sitting at her desk and when I was leaving the classroom she called to me. She said that she would always be there if I wanted to talk. I had never heard that before. At that point I had a choice. I could take advantage of her offer or reject it. I figured I had nothing to lose since I would leave the States anyway once the school year was over, so I took the risk and started to open up bit by bit.

In an environment that was filled with respect, understanding, and love, I was able to tell her things I had denied for a long time. By the end of the school year, the teacher I had once decided not to like became the most important person in my life, and she still is today. She was the first person who told me she loved me and cared about me. She always believed in me and my abilities. Though she was on the other side of the world, she helped me get through one of the hardest times in my life. Shortly after I returned to Germany from the U.S., I was diagnosed with cancer. I had a tumor at the ovary. I had surgery followed by chemotherapy, which was hell. What kept me going through this treatment was the knowledge that somewhere out there was somebody who loved me and respected me for the kind of person I am. At times when I was about to give up, she was there in my mind and reminded me of my strength that I have inside of me. . . .

When there is somebody who loves you and cares about you, you can handle almost everything in life.

—Liesl, Dusseldorf, Germany

And the last letter I would like to share came from a young man in India who has written twice to tell me about his wonderful teachers, a college professor and a high school teacher. This is the first letter he wrote, when he was still in high school.

Dear Madam,

I am a sixteen-year-old boy and my name is Jaskirat, but you can call me Anu as I am called at home. The day I read your article I am desperately wanting to contact you. The reasons are many but the main one is that I had a teacher very much like you and I adored her very much, but after teaching us for a few months she went to Canada. I was really shocked, but I could do nothing. I lost her, maybe forever, but her sweet memories shall remain in my heart for all the remaining days of my life. As I went through your article I could see her in you. I began to think what is the magic in the people like her that they make such long-lasting impressions on the minds in such short periods of contact. The day the results of our tenth standard exam were reported, I stood there with tears in my eyes and hoped that she could know that I, an average student for others, had topped in the whole class with 91 percent marks in her subject (general science).

I am writing this letter to you because I wanted to tell her how I felt about her and express my gratitude, but I could not and so I want to tell it to you because I find you just like my good-natured, sweet, loving young madam. I want to be your friend, maybe because my feelings require an outlet which I am not able to express on very many people. I hope you will accept my friendship. I promise that I will not bother you much. With love and affection, Yours faithfully.

—Anu, Modeltown, India

Someday the students you are teaching now will want to thank you for helping them, although you may never know. And it won't be your A students who want to thank you; most of them will have thanked you already. The ones who will wish they could thank you will be those little stinkers who sometimes make you want to give up teaching. Those little stinkers in your classes right now are the kids who need you to love them because quite often nobody else loves them, including themselves.

Yours is the most difficult, frustrating, challenging, emotionally exhausting, uplifting, precious, and important job in the world. On behalf of those kids who won't be able to find you or will be too embarrassed to admit how slow they were to appreciate you, I would like to thank you for being a teacher. Thank you. Thank you. Thank you.

APPENDIX

This Appendix includes a few of my favorite sources of information and inspiration, along with some of my own suggestions for involving community members in your school and raising money for classroom materials and equipment.

Publications

Jones, F. *Tools for Teaching*. Santa Cruz, Calif.: Fred Jones & Associates, 2000.

This is one of my favorites of all the manuals and advice books for teachers because Jones knows his stuff. In his foreword Jones says that this book is "the culmination of all that I have learned about managing classrooms"; and he has done an incredibly thorough and entertaining job. Illustrated by Jones's son, this full-color manual is a keeper. Jones doesn't stop at offering tips for teachers; he goes into the psychology behind each technique and then breaks each technique down into small steps. In addition, his Web site, www.fredjones.com, provides further resources for teachers and administrators. He also provides the full text online of selected chapters from his books on positive classroom discipline and instruction (published by McGraw-Hill). Visual learners will be delighted to learn that Jones also offers tools for teaching in a video format on his Web site.

Coloroso, B. *The Bully, the Bullied, and the Bystander: From Preschool to High School—How Parents and Teachers Can Help Break the Cycle of Violence.* **New York: Harper-Resource, 2004.**

At just over two hundred pages, this book provides a succinct and well-documented look at the bully situation. Coloroso goes beyond providing psychological insight into bully behavior; she also looks at victims and bystanders, whom she believes play an important role in allowing bullies to act or in stopping them. She provides practical suggestions for parents and teachers who want to help bullies or their victims, as well as criteria for evaluating a school's antibullying policies. Coloroso ends her book with a quote from anthropologist Margaret Mead: "Never doubt that a small group of thoughtful, committed citizens can change the world. Indeed, it is the only thing that ever has." Reading this book is a good place for those citizens to begin.

Fay, J., and Funk, D. *Teaching with Love and Logic: Taking Control of the Classroom.* **Golden, Colo.: Love and Logic Press, 1995.**

This is a self-publishing venture by two dedicated educators who turned decades of successful experience applying their own positive discipline methods into a base for their work as consultants. Their focus is on raising the level of student responsibility so that students monitor their own behavior, freeing teachers to teach instead of discipline. This book is especially helpful for beginning teachers who know what they want to say but don't know how to say it. A bit rambling in style, this book is still a worthwhile read because the authors provide a number of scripted conversations between adult and student that any teacher can adapt for use in the classroom. Boxed sidebars throughout the book provide summaries of especially important tips for teachers who struggle with classroom management.

National Assembly of State Arts Agencies. **"Eloquent Evidence: Arts at the Core of Learning," 13 pp. Available from the National Assembly of State Arts Agencies, 1010 Vermont Ave. NW, Suite 920, Washington, D.C. 20005.**

This pamphlet is packed with information supporting the arts in education, including several sources of statistical evidence of the value of incorporating music, art, drama, dance, and creative writing into basic curriculum. One intriguing example is a quote of statistics from the 1995 College Board's profile of SAT and achievement test takers that shows higher SAT scores for students who studied the arts more than four years. Their scores averaged fifty-nine points higher on the verbal exam and forty-four points higher on the math portion than those of their peers who did not study the arts.

Aron, E. *The Highly Sensitive Person.* New York: Broadway Books, 1997.

Teachers tend to be nurturers by nature, and many teachers are highly sensitive. Aron provides suggestions for handling overwhelming stimuli. Even the not-so-sensitive could benefit from some of her suggestions. This book includes suggestions for teachers who work with sensitive children. Teachers who find those suggestions helpful may want to check out Aron's other books.

Haddon, M. *The Curious Incident of the Dog in the Night.* New York: Doubleday, 2003.

This delightful novel can double as a learning text for teachers and a great read for young adults. Teachers who find it hard to empathize with autistic or emotionally distant children may gain some insight that may help them become better teachers. And students will enjoy reading about this fifteen-year-old autistic boy who can do complicated mathematical equations in his head but can't understand even the simplest human emotions. Christopher sets out to solve the mystery of a murdered dog and ends up writing a book about his adventure.

Freed, J., and Parsons, L. *Right-Brained Children in a Left-Brained World: Unlocking the Potential of Your ADD Child.* New York: Fireside, 1998.

This book is among the top ten that I recommend to parents, teachers, and anybody who works with children or adolescents. A former teacher who now works as an educational consultant, Freed devotes his time solely to helping students who have been labeled ADHD. Based on positive results to his methods, Freed maintains that most ADHD children are actually gifted. He discusses diets and medications, but his primary focus is on techniques for working with children.

Web Sites

www.accelerated.org Educators who need proof that it's possible to create a successful school will find inspiration on this Web site. Two idealistic young teachers in inner-city Los Angeles started a charter school in 1994. Every child at The Accelerated School is treated as a gifted child—and they live up to the high expectations. The school's curriculum incorporates culture, fine arts, and physical activities such as yoga, and the combination seems to work. Attendance averages in the high nineties, test scores in reading and math continue to climb, and the school continues to expand into additional sites.

www.borntoexplore.org One of the most comprehensive and competent sites for parents who struggle with the ADHD issue, *Born to Explore! The Other Side of ADD* is hosted by an environmental scientist who homeschools her two children. Scientist Teresa Gallagher provides an array of information in plain English with links to many resources, book reviews, scientific studies, articles, and essays. Visitors can select from an alphabetical list of topics including allergies, hypoglycemia, mercury poisoning, nutritional deficiencies, sleep deficit and disorders, and visual thinkers. The site also links to statements from a variety of professionals who give their views on ADHD and to a discussion board for people who want to share information or ask questions.

www.webbschool.com/rhood/english2/just_walk_on_by.htm This Web site provides the full online text of Brent Staples's brilliant essay, "Just Walk on By: A Black Man Ponders His Power to Alter Public Space," which first appeared in print in *Ms.* magazine in 1986. Born into urban poverty, Staples earned his doctorate in psychology before becoming a respected journalist who serves on the editorial board of the *New York Times.*

This essay is a must for any teacher who has tried to repair the damage to self-esteem and confidence that young brown males suffer when they realize that many people fear them for no reason. Staples's illuminating and inspiring essay may not heal the hurt, but it will show young minority males that they are not alone. It may also help them learn to cope with a widespread and demeaning prejudice that so many Americans seem unable or unwilling to overcome.

www.tvturnoff.org This site promotes an annual day when everyone in the entire country turns off the TV—an excellent idea that is gaining ground and devotees daily. More than thirty thousand school students have participated in this program since its inception in 2001, and the results are impressive and inspiring. The idea inspired the Nickelodeon TV network enough to replace regular broadcasts for three hours one Saturday morning with messages urging kids to go outside and play.

Teachers can receive free information to help them participate in the More Reading Less TV (MRLTV) program, which has shown uniformly positive and long-lasting results. Not only do students who participate in the MRLTV program read better, they read much more often (even former nonreaders). The site also offers facts and figures about how much time Americans spend in front of the tube, along with suggestions for breaking the couch-potato habit.

(Note: if you come up with a blank when you type the URL into the address field of your computer, try doing a search. For some reason the URL will bring up the Web page if you open it from results on a search engine.)

www.adbusters.org This is a great Web site for older students and teachers who are seeking thoroughly thought-provoking articles to spur class discussions, research, and essays. The site's spoof ads for tobacco, fast food, and fashion will definitely appeal to kids who are beginning to realize how advertisers manipulate them. Beware, though, that this site is sponsored by creative folks (this Canadian-based group describes itself as "a global network of artists, activists, writers, pranksters, students, educators, and entrepreneurs who want to advance the new social activist movement of the information age") and they occasionally use four-letter words.

www.bbc.co.uk/learning If you visit only one Web site today, make it this one. Make sure you have a little time to spare because you will want to stay a while. Hosted by the British Broadcasting Corporation, this site literally allows visitors of all ages—preschool to adult—to go to school online. The home page provides a selection of topics ranging from religion and ethics to art and design. The section of free online courses is also worth a look. My favorite section is under the education and teaching subject listing, which brings up several choices including "BBC Schools—Teacher Resources." Teachers have the option of choosing by age group: preschool, ages four to eleven, eleven to sixteen, or sixteen and up. Each age group offers lessons, games, and quizzes, without the annoying commercial pop-up ads that plague American educational games online.

This site clearly is devoted to learning, and exploring all of the associated links and lessons would take months or years. ESL teachers may find that the spelling and reading games for ages four to eleven are perfect for both beginning and advanced ESL students.

www.englishpage.com This is another good resource for language teachers, including ESL. Weekly grammar lessons, vocabulary builders, grammar tutorials, and a host of quizzes and games make this site a winner. The online dictionary is also a valuable resource, especially for low-income students who may not have good dictionaries at home. The highlight of this Web site is the online reading room, which offers a wealth of free reading from newspapers in the United States, United Kingdom, Canada, Australia, New Zealand, South Africa, and India, as well as several popular magazines and full online text of classic novels, from *Alice's Adventures in Wonderland* to *This Side of Paradise.*

www.everydayspelling.com Cross-curricular lessons are the highlight of this Web site from Scott Foresman Publishing. Divided into sections from grade one to grade eight, each section includes a list of twenty-five frequently misspelled words and quizzes that increase in difficulty. Spelling strategies for teachers are also included, but I particularly like the cross-curricular lessons that offer reading comprehension activities in math, social sciences, and health. The colorful graphics are age appropriate and helpful. My students love this Web site and frequently visit it to reread favorite selections and retake the quizzes. Teachers can print out the quizzes or allow students to write down their answers and then check their answers against the online answer key.

www.positivediscipline.com The nonprofit Positive Discipline Association is based on the work of Austrian psychiatrist Alfred Adler, who believed that all human beings are equal and worthy of dignity and respect. This program promotes and encourages the development of life skills and respectful relationships in families, schools, businesses, and community systems. Jane Nelsen and Lynn Lott have built on Adler's work to create a program for families, schools, and children today. Although this Web site heavily promotes the association's books and speakers, it does offer a number of intelligently written and helpful articles for teachers and parents, including "18 Ways to Avoid Power Struggles" and "How Do You Motivate a Teen?" Well worth a look for adults who are seeking successful approaches to discipline.

www.EdibleSchoolyard.org This eye-appealing Web site offers a superb model for any school but especially for science teachers who want to give students an unforgettable hands-on experience. The Edible Schoolyard is a nonprofit program located on the campus of Martin Luther King Junior Middle School in Berkeley, California. The cooking and gardening program began with a collaboration between world-famous chef Alice Waters and the school's former principal, Neil Smith. The school cleared more than an acre of asphalt parking lot, planted a cover crop to enrich the soil, and refurbished the school's abandoned cafeteria kitchen in 1997 to create a kitchen classroom for students.

Today the school's organic garden is integrated into the curriculum. Students are not only skilled gardeners and junior botanists, they are also talented chefs who enjoy the fruits of their own labor. Students attend garden classes where they learn the principles of ecology and respect for all living systems. They plant crops; monitor compost; and harvest their own flowers, fruits, grains, and vegetables.

This Web site offers advice and guidelines to teachers who want to start their own projects, along with a variety of links and resources for more information.

www.thomasarmstrong.com/multiple_intelligences.htm This Web page is one from a number by author Thomas Armstrong, who offers suggestions for teachers who wish to apply Gardner's theory of multiple intelligences in their own approaches to teaching: logical-mathematical (number-reasoning smart), spatial intelligence (picture smart), bodily-kinesthetic intelligence (body smart), musical intelligence (music smart), interpersonal intelligence (people smart), intrapersonal intelligence (self smart), and naturalist intelligence (nature smart).

Armstrong is a prolific author and child advocate who offers the full online text of many of his intelligent and helpful articles.

Raise Money, Get Supplies, Involve the Local Community

Create your own classroom library. Scoop up the fifty-cent books at your local public library and keep an eye out for books at yard sales and flea markets. Ask friends to donate old books, especially children's books. Even older children can use children's books to practice public speaking or as models for writing their own books in your class. One biology teacher told me that she assigns her seniors the task of writing a children's book about the cell and has received quite a number of books that are good enough to submit to publishers for consideration. If you teach science or math, use your classroom library as a reward for students who finish ahead of the class; let them choose something entertaining to read.

Collect magazines. Ask local doctors, dentists, attorneys, and bank executives to donate their used magazines. Many businesses and professionals maintain weekly or monthly subscriptions to magazines that they later discard. They are often quite willing to deliver the magazines so that they don't have to pay a trash or recycling company to collect them.

Rescue convention leftovers. Find the nearest convention or conference center. Ask the management to check with sponsors of events to see if they will authorize the custodians to give you the leftover freebies, instead of throwing them away. One security guard drove his car to my school and unloaded the following items from just one major convention: dozens of T-shirts, sweatshirts, and baseball caps; hundreds of pens and pencils and notebook binders; and enough pads of paper to supply five classes with enough paper for spelling quizzes for an entire school year.

Recycle old videos. Ask the manager of your local video rental stores if you can purchase old videos that the store can't sell at a steep discount. Stores will sometimes offer to give you the videos. Even if they aren't appropriate for your subject matter, you can use them as rewards during awards ceremonies or raffle them off to raise money for school projects.

Sponsor an essay contest. Work out a deal with the local newspaper, radio and TV station, or public library to sponsor an essay contest, with the essay subject "How to Improve Our School." Give the winner of the contest half the prize money and use the rest to buy classroom supplies or equipment. Submit all the essays to your local school board for review and make sure you take pictures of all the entrants for your local newspaper.

Seek out famous alumni. Find famous alumni and ask them to make a speech or sponsor an essay contest at your school. If they don't have time for those projects, ask them to write a letter to students at your school, encouraging them to earn good grades and graduate. Reproduce the letter and give a copy to each student.

Invite an author. Ask an author to visit your school or a local bookstore. If your chosen author charges a fee, ask local businesses to underwrite the cost. Charge a small fee for community members to attend a lecture or workshop with the author. Use the money to sponsor an essay contest, and let the author choose the winner. Or use the money to publish a literary journal of student writing.

Schedule mock interviews. Teach your students how to write a résumé (younger students can write theirs on 4-by-6-inch index cards). Practice answering typical interview questions, and discuss proper dress and behavior. Then hold mock interviews with local businesspeople serving as the interviewers. Give the interviewers a form on which to provide feedback to students (stressing the positive, of course). Invite your local media to film your mock job fair.

Hold a parent-teacher conference at a local venue. Instead of asking parents to travel to your school in the evening when they may not have transportation or energy to make the trip, host a conference at a local community center, public library, recreation center, or church conference room. Provide a light snack and an area for children to play under adult supervision, so that parents who can't afford baby-sitters can attend the meeting. Distribute a handout with phone numbers for parents who have school-related questions or need help. Provide tips to help parents monitor their children's homework and reading progress. If possible, give a quick introduction to using computers for parents who may be computer illiterate, and provide them with local sources of free or low-cost training, such as community college enrichment courses. If you have a large group of parents who are non-English speakers, bring an interpreter. You may find that what you thought was parent apathy was actually fear or lack of confidence.

INDEX

room, 17, 86, 125–126; cowboy's lessons on, 112–114; detention, 129–130; for disruptive students, 16–18, 85–87; emergency disaster plan, 84–87; how to identify bullies/outcasts, 135; humiliation, 26, 111–112; negative credit/extra credit system, 60–61; personalized approach to, 130–131; positive, 108–109, 110, 310; sending students out of class, 87, 122–123, 127–129; for sleeping students, 241; for students criticizing teacher, 221–224; teaching to stop verbal abuse of other students, 226–228, 238–239; warning speeches, 67–68, 125–126. *See also* Classroom management; Misbehavior; Rules

Disruptive students, 16–18, 85–87

Divorced parents, 266–267, 268–272

Documentation, of student misbehavior, 129, 130

Door monitors, 96

Dress, of teachers, 13–14, 68, 133

Drug education, 243–244

E

Edible Schoolyard, 310–311

Education: nonteaching jobs in, 8; teaching students importance of, 231–232, 255–256

"Eloquent Evidence: Arts at the Core of Learning" (National Assembly of State Arts Agencies), 306

Emergency plan: for emergency situations, 54; for student discipline problems, 84–87; for teacher meltdown, 131–135

Emilio (former student), 247–249

ESL programs, 230–231, 278; Web resources on, 187, 309–310

Ethics exercises, as motivator, 181–184

Excellent schoolwork, modeling, 169–170

F

Families, reading as activity in, 190–191. *See also* Parents

Fay, J., 306

Feedback: positive, on improved behavior, 121; progress reports as, 160–163; requesting student, as motivator, 146–147, 148, 149

First day of class, 71–84; discussing rules, 52–53; first activities for students, 72–73, 74–76; gathering student information, 79–80; getting students on your side, 77–79; grab-your-students-by-their-brains activities, 76–77; greeting students at door, 73–74; handling misbehavior, 82–84; learning student names, 79–82; typical scenario, 71–72. *See also* First week of class

First week of class, 84–105; completing power-of-choice exercise, 96–99; discussing Bloom's taxonomy, 102–105; discussing Maslow's hierarchy of needs, 99–102; distributing rules handout, 93–94; distributing student folders, 94–95; giving diagnostic exams or assignments, 92–93; having emergency measures for discipline, 84–87; introducing students to each other, 88–90; selecting student helpers, 95–96; teaching procedures for answering questions, 90–92; thanking students for cooperation, 86–87, 105. *See also* First day of class

Folders: daily lesson, 54; fun lessons, 55–56; makeup work, 56–57; Misbehavior, 59, 85, 130; student, 57–58, 72, 94–95; substitute, 54–55, 132

Freed, J., 307

Friends, 257–263; ending relationships with, 261–263; making new, 260;

Friends, *continued*
obsessions of, 257–258; relationships among, 258–261; teachers as, 12
Fun lessons folder, 55–56; Web sources of material for, 187, 307, 309
Funk, D., 306

G

Gallagher, T., 308
Games, class unwilling to play, 90
Getting to Know You questionnaire, 74–76
The Girls in the Back of the Class (Johnson), 300
Goal setting, teaching, 165–166
Goddard, J., 166
Grades, 27–29; caution on, and child development, 29; computerized system for, 61; deciding policies for, 27–28; distinguishing between students and, 175; for ESL students, 230–231; mentioning, on first day of class, 78; negative/extra credit system for, 60–61; for portfolios, 293; posting sample, for essay question tests, 185–186; preparing system for recording, 60–61; question about improving, 276–277; student letter-writing exercise on, 28–29; talking to teachers about, 158–159. *See also* Progress reports
Grammar, Web site on, 187
Grief, 252
Group work, 176–177
Guardians. *See* Parents
Gusmaro (former student), 247

H

Haddon, M., 307
Hand cleaner, 49
Hierarchy of needs, 99–102, 141, 147
The Highly Sensitive Person (Aron), 307

Humiliation, as discipline technique, 26, 111–112
Humor: as asset in teaching, 2; author's use of, 13; defusing threat of violence with, 234–235; personalizing lessons with, 177

I

In-baskets, 53
Independent assignments: contracts for, 287–288, 289; for quick learners, 174–175; sample, 288, 290–291; for students sent out of class, 128–129; time-saving tips on, 287–288
Index cards: as behavior cards, 124–125; information on student attitudes toward school on, 139–140; recognizing birthdays recorded on, 177, 242; for recording opportunities for praise, 170; student information on, 79–80
Instructions: delivering, first day of class, 73; for future expected behavior, 120–121; for portfolio work, 292. *See also* Reading instruction
Internet. *See* Web sites

J

Jones, F., 305
Journal writing: to deal with feelings, 270; in ethics exercises, 181, 182; extra attention given through, 242; guidelines on, 179–180; modeling, 169; prompts for, 180–181; sex/drug education through, 243–244. *See also* Writing
"Just Walk on By" (Staples), 308

K

Kissing sleeping student, 241

L

Learning disabilities: scotopic sensitivity syndrome and, 195–196; sources of information on, 307; teaching students with, 238–239. *See also* Attention deficit hyperactivity disorder (ADHD)

M

Motivation techniques/tools, *continued*
progress reports as, 160–163; projects
on student-selected topics as, 177–179;
quotations as, 40–42; requesting student feedback as, 146–147, 148, 149;
right-brain and kinesthetic activities
as, 143–146; teaching argument skills
as, 151, 153–157; teaching goal setting
as, 165–166; teaching how to read
transcripts as, 163–165; teaching how
to talk to adults as, 153, 158–160;
teaching problem-solving skills as,
147, 149–151, 152; tests as, 184–186.
See also Rewards

Multiple intelligences, 311
Music, in classroom, 37–38
My Posse Don't Do Homework, 84, 241,
246–249

N
Name cards, 72, 82
Names of students, learning, 79–82
National Assembly of State Arts Agencies,
306
Needs, hierarchy of, 99–102, 141, 147
Nelsen, J., 310
"Night Walker" (Staples), 23
Nonverbal messages. *See* Body language

O
Opinions: asking critical student for,
223; long-range effect of rejecting,
of students, 298; respecting, of reading
materials, 204; thanking students for
giving, 140
Optional agenda, of teachers, 18–20
Outcasts: how to handle, 85; how to
identify, 135

P
Painting classrooms, 39
Paperwork, 53–64, 70; assignments for

rude people, 58–59; daily lesson folders, 54; emergency plan, 54; fun lessons folder, 55–56; grading records,
60–61; makeup work folders, 56–57;
master lesson plans, 62–63; Misbehavior folder, 59, 85, 130; passes, 56, 128;
roll sheets, 56–57; student folders,
57–58, 72, 94–95; substitute folders,
54–55, 132; Welcome to My Class
handouts, 63–64, 93–94

Parents, 266–276; advice to, unhappy with
schools, 228–229; apathetic, 239–240;
divorced, 266–267, 268–272; phone
calls to, 80, 127, 171, 246; reading as
activity of, 190–191; stressed and
angry, 272–273; strict, 274–275;
students' ashamed of, 273–274; tele-
phoning school, 275–276

Parkhurst, B., 299–300
Parsons, L., 307
Passes, 56, 128
Peer support groups, 175–176
Pencils, classroom supply of, 50
Perception. *See* Self-perception
Persona, choice of, 11–13
Personalizing lessons, 177, 242
Philosophy: of discipline, 109–111; of
teaching, 10–11
Phone calls: by parents, 275–276; to
parents, 80, 127, 171, 246; to students,
80, 126
Photos, decorating classroom with, 39,
243
Physical aggression. *See* Violence
Poetry: introducing young children to,
212–213; portfolio project for, 214,
215–217; teaching Shakespeare, 205–
209; using music to introduce, 210–
212
Portfolios: designing, 291; grading,
295–296; instruction techniques for,
292; poetry, 214, 215–217; reasons for

Supplies: classroom storage of, 49–50; suggestions for obtaining, 35–36, 311–312

Support staff, importance of meeting, 69

Swearing, in schools, 277

T

Tattletales, 281, 283

Teacher meltdown, emergency plan for, 131–135

Teacher training: student teaching, 6–7; taking courses on your own, 6, 7–8

Teacher-to-be showers, 35–36

Teachers: adjusting attitude of, 141–143; beginning-of-year preparation of, 65–70; first impressions of, formed by students, 12, 73; good-excellent-super continuum of, 3–5; long-range effect of, on students' self-perception, 26, 31–33, 297–303; mean, 278–280; mistakes by, 158–159, 168–169; questions from, 219–228, 230–249; school photos of, 243; teaching students how to talk to, 153, 158–160; Web site for conversations between, 8

Teachers, new: advice on handling students critical of, 221–224; reasons for failure of, in first year of teaching, 9; reasons for leaving profession, 1; taking over class at midterm, 245–246

Teaching: analyzing problems in, 241–242; argument skills, 151, 153–157; caution on changing style of, 15; how to read transcripts, 163–165; how to set goals, 165–166; how to talk to adults, 153, 158–160; importance of education, 231–232; to increase self-understanding, 99–102, 141, 147; philosophy of, 10–11; problem-solving skills, 147, 149–151, 152; procedures for answering questions, 14–15, 90–92; remedial- vs. advanced-level classes,

233; to think about thinking, 102–105, 232. *See also* Reading instruction

Teaching profession: avoiding teachers disillusioned with, 232–233; deciding whether or not to enter, 1–8; deciding whether or not to leave, 132–135; personal vs. work time in, 3–5; pros and cons of, 1–3

Teaching reading. *See* Reading instruction

Teaching with Love and Logic (Fay and Funk), 306

Teasing. *See* Verbal abuse

Television, Web site on, 308–309

Tests: on classroom rules, 94; diagnostic, during first week of class, 92–93; excessive number of, 228; on first day of class, 81; as motivators, 184–186; preparing students for, 30; reading without, 202; teaching to help students on, 286

Thanking donors of supplies, 36

Thanking parents, 171

Thanking students: for apologizing, 86; for cooperation, 18, 86–87, 105, 125; for doing something kind or admirable, 170–171; for giving feedback, 147; for giving opinions, 140

Thanking teachers, 300–303

Thinking: teaching students to think about, 102–105; time for, before answering questions, 90, 91–92

Time-outs, as discipline technique, 126

Time-saving tips: on independent assignments, 287–288; on lesson plans, 285–287; on portfolios, 288–289, 291–296

Tools for Teaching (Jones), 305

Transcripts, teaching how to read, 163–165

Transfers of students, requesting, as discipline technique, 128

The True Story of the 3 Little Pigs (Scieszka), 28

The Queen of Education

Rules for Making Schools Work

LouAnne Johnson

Cloth ISBN: 0-7879-7470-6

www.josseybass.com

"As a former student of LouAnne's first 'at risk' class, I experienced firsthand her approach to education. The result was nothing less than a miracle. This book has the power to do for the United States education system what it did for our class; turn a flawed reality into an exemplary system of education."

—Dan Mueller, associate producer and designer,
BottleRocket Entertainment Inc.

WANTED: A QUEEN OF EDUCATION

Candidate must be able to take decisive action, cut through red tape, deflate the bureaucratic bloat, wrestle with the diagnostic nightmare of ADHD, and refuse to sell out her students to the corporate fat cats.

Though we have "education presidents" who give lip service to fixing schools, what we really need is a *Queen of Education* who will get the job done. Anyone searching for such a candidate would put LouAnne Johnson's resume on the top of the stack of likely applicants. LouAnne Johnson is the gutsy ex-marine turned teacher who has wrestled with tough kids and even tougher adults. Her life inspired the movie *Dangerous Minds*—which was based on her book *My Posse Don't Do Homework*. Johnson's knack for finding original solutions to intractable problems has made her not only an exemplary teacher but also a popular speaker on the lecture circuit.

In this engaging book, "Queen" LouAnne offers her down-to-earth advice about fixing schools. Johnson makes no secret about the fact that she is fed up with an educational system that is too quick to label and write off children who don't fit the mold. Among her royal rules for fixing the system: no class shall have more than 20 students, all elected representatives must teach in a public school classroom for two weeks, and the testing frenzy must stop this very second! LouAnne is a passionate advocate for schools that are smaller, healthier, more humane, and more attuned to different learning styles. With humor and good sense, she shows how a compassionate teacher or parent can cut through the red tape and make a crucial difference in the life of a child.

Teaching with Fire

Poetry that Sustains the
Courage to Teach

Sam M. Intrator and Megan Scribner, Editors

Cloth   ISBN: 0-7879-6970-2
www.josseybass.com

"In the Confucian tradition it is said that the mark of a golden era is that children are the most important members of the society, and teaching is the most revered profession. Our journey to that ideal may be a long one, but it is books like this that will sustain us—for who are we all at our best save teachers, and who matters more to us than the children?"

—Peter M. Senge, founding chair, SoL
(Society for Organizational Learning)
and author of The Fifth Discipline

Those of us who care about the young and their education must find ways to remember what teaching and learning are really about. We must find ways to keep our hearts alive as we serve our students. Poetry has the power to keep us vital and focused on what really matters in life and in schooling.

Teaching with Fire is a wonderful collection of eighty-eight poems from well-loved poets such as Walt Whitman, Langston Hughes, Billy Collins, Emily Dickinson, and Pablo Neruda. Each of these evocative poems is accompanied by a brief story from a teacher explaining the significance of the poem in his or her life's work. This beautiful book also includes an essay that describes how poetry can be used to grow both personally and professionally.

Teaching with Fire was written in partnership with the Center for Teacher Formation and the Bill & Melinda Gates Foundation. Royalties from this book are used to fund scholarship opportunities for teachers to grow and learn.

Sam M. Intrator is assistant professor of education and child study at Smith College. He is a former high school teacher and administrator and the son of two public school teachers. He is the editor of *Stories of the Courage to Teach* and author of *Tuned In and Fired Up: How Teaching Can Inspire Real Learning in the Classroom.*

Megan Scribner is a freelance writer, editor, and program evaluator who has conducted research on what sustains and empowers the lives of teachers. She is the mother of two children and PTA president of their elementary school in Takoma Park, Maryland.

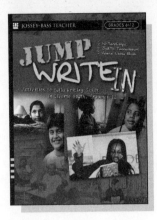

Jump Write In!

Creative Writing Exercises for Diverse Communities, Grades 6–12

WritersCorp, edited by Judith Tannenbaum and Valerie Chow Bush

Paper ISBN: 0-7879-7777-2

www.josseybass.com

Teachers often feel they must choose between using standards-based lessons and offering activities that engage their students' creativity and encourage personal expression. In *Jump Write In,* however, the experienced teachers from WritersCorps offer numerous exercises that build key standards-based writing skills and also reach out in a meaningful way to all students, particularly at-risk youth.

Through poetry, personal narrative, and essays, students from diverse ethnic, educational, and economic backgrounds will improve their writing skills by accessing their personal voices. Perfect for a moment of improvisation or inspiration, these easy-to-use and field-tested activities can transform any lesson into an opportunity to involve a hard-to-reach student through creative writing.

Each chapter includes:

- Dozens of exercises accompanied by teacher notes and suggestions
- Links to standards for each activity
- Examples of student work
- Suggestions for further reading

WritersCorps is an independent program based in San Francisco whose mission is to help children and teens of all ethnic and economic backgrounds improve their literacy and communication skills through creative expression. Founded in 1994 with funding from the National Endowment of the Arts, WritersCorps has helped over 10,000 students. This important achievement was recognized recently when the White House named WritersCorps as one of the two most exemplary programs for at-risk youth. WritersCorps has ties to similar programs in New York City and Washington D.C. and connections to influential education figures, including E.D. Hirsch. The WritersCorp Web site is www.sfartscommission.org/WC.

Partners in Crime

Integrating Language Arts and
Forensic Science, Grades 5–8

E.K. Hein

Paper ISBN: 0-7879-6993-1
www.josseybass.com

"Hein is an innovative and entrepreneurial educator whose cross-curriculum approach paves the way for learning built on creative problem-solving and practical application of knowledge. This model exemplifies what is possible when teachers open the classroom to educational and community collaboration."

—*Patricia M. Roberts, director, Institute for Educational Excellence and Entrepreneurship, College of Education, West Chester University*

Partners in Crime offers middle school teachers an innovative and highly engaging resource for integrating language arts and science strategies that will challenge students while meeting standardized learning goals. With a creative approach of focusing on the practical application of critical thinking, problem solving, and prose nonfiction expression, *Partners in Crime* engages students by asking them to solve a crime using the skills of forensic science while simultaneously teaching them key concepts in language arts. As flexible as it is creative, *Partners in Crime* can be used for a variety of classroom settings whether as a single activity, weekly lesson, full unit, or school and community project.

The activities in *Partners in Crime* can also help build teamwork by tapping into the school community, resources, and technology. Throughout the book, students are encouraged to conduct original research and challenged to draw conclusions based upon their ability to weigh evidence. *Partners in Crime* also contains suggestions for helping both teacher and students make connections with local law enforcement that will provide support for deeper understanding of the exercises. The book is filled with ideas for encouraging students to create written reports, presentations, films, and videos. It also includes activities and guidelines for benchmarking student performance during and after each unit.

"This book is an interdisciplinary masterpiece! Hein's methodology of analytical problem-solving and organized research aligns the writing process and real-world adventures in a way that will intrigue, empower, and motivate middle school writers."

—*Ken Rivenbark, University of North Carolina at Wilmington*

E.K. Hein is a middle school language arts teacher in the suburbs of Philadelphia, Pennsylvania. He has taught language arts and English skills to students for eight years. In 2002 his "Investigating Crime Scenes in Literature" was featured in *The Wall Street Journal* as a model for innovative, engaging curriculum.

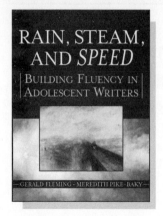

Rain, Steam, and Speed

Building Fluency in Adolescent Writers

Gerald Fleming and Meredith Pike-Baky

Paper   ISBN: 0-7879-7456-0

www.josseybass.com

"With enormous pleasure and pride, the students in *Rain, Steam, and Speed* are writing more, faster, and better than they have ever written before. How to make, or let, that happen with our own students in our own classrooms is what Gerald Fleming and Meredith Pike-Baky have to teach us."

—*William Slaughter, professor and chair, Department of English,*
University of North Florida, Jacksonville

Many books focus on teaching the technical skills and processes of writing, but few works address issues of fluency—how to help students write with ease and facility on a variety of topics. Even when students understand the drafting and revision stages of the writing process, they often stall when confronted with a writing task, feeling they lack ideas or language, or that they have "nothing to say." This book offers a carefully structured approach for helping students overcome writing blocks so they can communicate quickly, confidently, and thoughtfully when the demand arises.

Featuring over 150 writing prompts on provocative topics, the book includes everything a teacher needs to know to inspire and engage students in systematic writing practice, including classroom protocols, grading, assessment, and feedback approaches. Easily implemented in any English/language arts classroom, the program involves about one hour of instruction per week (ideally in half hour segments), taking students through a series of timed writing exercises and enabling them to dramatically improve their thinking and writing facility over time. *Rain, Steam, and Speed:*

- Offers a structured process for improving student writing
- Features over 150 provocative writing exercises
- Includes extensive examples of student work (along with testimonials)
- Benefits all types of students, including English learners
- Strengthens literacy skills for cross-content academic learning
- Adapts to all levels of English/language arts classrooms

Gerald Fleming is an award-winning teacher who has taught in the San Francisco Public Schools for over thirty years. He teaches English, social studies, and journalism, and also teaches curriculum and instruction at the University of San Francisco.

Meredith Pike-Baky is a curriculum and assessment coordinator, a teacher educator, and a teacher consultant with the Bay Area Writing Project.

Listen to Learn

Using American Music to Teach
Language Arts and Social Studies
Grades 5–8   CD INCLUDED

Teri Tibbett

Paper ISBN: 0-7879-7254-1
www.josseybass.com

"Teri Tibbett's book will provide teachers with the knowledge, tools, and confidence they need to make music a part of everyday learning."
>   —*Linda Rosenthal, violinist and professor of music, University of Alaska Southeast*

Listen to Learn, with its companion music CD, offers teachers a dynamic way to use the history of American music to engage their students (grades 5–8) in reading, writing, social studies, geography, music, and multicultural lessons and activities. The book traces the colorful musical traditions of diverse cultures including early Native music, folk, blues, classical, jazz, country, Tejano, salsa, rock, and rap. The CD features authentic music from such American musical greats as Louis Armstrong, Woody Guthrie, Mahalia Jackson, Lead Belly, Lydia Mendoza, and many more.

Listen to Learn features a variety of fascinating activities that encourage students to write about their favorite music, investigate songs as poetry, research the lives of famous musicians, explore family musical traditions, research how instruments make sounds, plot record charts, and much more.

The book is divided into four major sections:

- **Native American Music:** Traditional Native American Singing, Traditional Native American Instruments, Native American Music Regions, and Contemporary Native American Music
- **European American Music:** Colonial Music, Folk Music, Patriotic Music, Early Popular Music, Early Classical Music, and Instruments of the Orchestra
- **African American Music:** Music of the Slaves, Spirituals and Gospel Music, The Blues, Dance Music, and Soul and Funk
- **New American Music:** Modern Popular Music, Contemporary Classical Music, Jazz, Country Music, Latin American Music, Rock Music, and Rap Music

Teri Tibbett is a teacher and musician living in Juneau, Alaska. Since 1976, she has taught music at all grade levels, both as an itinerant music teacher and through her own school, The Juneau School of Creative Arts.